I K A T

Laurence King in association with Alan Marcuson

splendid silks of central asia

IKAT

Published 1997 by Laurence King Publishing
in association with Alan Marcuson
to accompany a touring exhibition of
the Guido Goldman Collection of ikats.

Laurence King Publishing is an imprint of
Calmann & King Ltd
71 Great Russell Street
London WC1B 3BN

The Publishers would like to thank the following people for their work on this project: Felicity Awdry, Annie Carlano, Philip Cooper, Angela Dyer, Mary-Jane Gibson, Sara Hodgkinson, Albert Kampta, Robert Marcuson, Gail Martin, Nicholas Purdon, Vicki Robinson, Jacqueline Rothschild, Mary Scott, John Taylor, Don Tuttle, Mark Vernon-Jones. They would also like to thank Dr Guido Goldman for making his Collection available for this book.

A catalogue record for this book is available from the British Library.

ISBN 1 85699 102 0

Photographs of the Guido Goldman Collection
by Don Tuttle
Edited by Alan Marcuson and John Taylor
Designed by Mark Vernon-Jones
Color origination by The Repro House (London)
in association with Robert Marcuson

Printed in Belgium by Snoeck Ducaju & Zoon

CONTENTS

AUTHORS' ACKNOWLEDGEMENTS

The writing of this book was made possible through the generous assistance of many scholars who helped us to locate publications, provided original research, and patiently allowed us to examine archival materials. In Tashkent, Uzbekistan, we owe many thanks to Dr Sayora Mahkamova, to the indefatigable Irina Boguslovskaya and her director, Mr Innoyatov Kutllugjon Hamdamovich of the State History Museum, and their colleagues Zakhro Alimukhamedova and Farmanova Barno Abdukaiumovna. Dr Umarbekova Daliafruz of the State Museum of Art, Dr Rozia Galievna Mukminova, Karimbek Hassanov of the Navoi Library, Boris Holender and Dr Abdul-Ahat Khodjaev made substantial contributions to our work. In Bokhara we were kindly received by Yusuf Sharipov at the shrine of Bahauddin Naqshband, and by Theodor Vodopshin and Mahsuma Niazova at the Arg Museum. Shahmurad Ruzimaradov of the State Museum of History, Culture and Art in Samarkand, was particularly helpful, as was Dr Timur Shirinov, Director of Archeology, Uzbekistan, and his colleague Hasanov Mutalib. Our research efforts in Uzbekistan could not have succeeded without our peerless organizer, Kamil Khodjaev of

Asian Business Associates, our translator Vosik Shamsiev, and our hospitable host families.

In Moscow and St Petersburg we received assistance from Inna Isidorovna Vishnevskaya of the Oruzhenaya Palata, from Belkis Khalilovna Karmysheva, Tatyana Grigorievna Emel'yanenko, Ol'ga Mikhailovna Bronnikova and most especially from Dr Alexander Nikitin of the Hermitage. Dr Igor Klotchkoff of the Institute of World History in Moscow was our indispensable guide to all.

In England, we owe particular thanks to Dr Ruth Barnes of the Ashmolean Museum, Oxford, to Jennifer Mary Wearden and Claire Woodthorpe Browne of the Victoria and Albert Museum, to Dr Audrey Burton, and to the ever-generous and hospitable Pip Rau. Dr Mikhail Zand of the University of Jerusalem provided us with much needed information and sources, as did Irène Lewitt of the Israel Museum, Jerusalem.

Here in the United States, Dr Elizabeth Barber of Occidental College, Pasadena, and Dr Irene Good of the University of Pennsylvania offered new research and reviewed photographs. Dr Richard N. Frye and Dr John Schoeberlein-Engel of Harvard University allowed us to draw on their many sources and vast expertise. Pierre Apraxine assisted in locating rare photographs. Gail Martin cheerfully devoted many hours to preparing and analyzing textile materials. Many thanks are due our excellent translator, Liv Bliss.

Our friends and associates in Afghanistan introduced us to traditional Central Asia in ways not possible through books alone. Among the many, we wish to recognize our dear friend and mentor, the late Mir Ayaz Elyasi.

Dr Avrom Udovitch of Princeton University, Dr Carol Bier of the Textile Museum, Washington, Dr Robert McChesney of New York University, Mr Robert Pinner and Ms Jennifer Wearden of the Victoria and Albert Museum, London, reviewed the manuscript, and made generous and useful suggestions for its improvement. Their contributions, and those of many other scholars, have greatly enhanced the text; any flaws or omissions are our own.

Final, heartfelt thanks are due to Dr Guido Goldman. His commitment to scholarship and his warm personal support sustained us throughout the project. It has been a pleasure to write this book.

COLLECTOR'S NOTE

My enthusiasm for Central Asian ikats stems from a lifelong love of color. I was privileged to grow up in a home filled with art, primarily a collection of French impressionist paintings that my parents had acquired over a long period of years. While drawn to these canvases, my favorite galleries when visiting museums as a teenager were those filled with German expressionists. I still have a drawer full of postcards stemming from those early museum visits including especially the paintings of Wassily Kandinsky, who became my favorite because his art resonates with such an accomplished and romantic use of color.

I feel there was a direct link between a Kandinsky painting that belonged to a close friend of my parents and my subsequent fascination with Central Asian ikats. The painting in question is an unusual tempera and gouache work from 1908 titled "Morning Hour", which depicts three warriors standing before an exotic mythical city, who are clad in brilliant, multi-colored coats. To this day, I would like to think that these coats were Bukharan *chapans* and that somehow Kandinsky had – during his years in St Petersburg, Moscow or Odessa – seen examples of these splendid Central Asian garments. Whether or not this was

the case, I do believe that there is a strong visual connection between the intensely colorful landscapes and figurative paintings Kandinsky created between 1908 and 1910 in Munich and Murnau, and the vibrant, natural-dyed colors that find such powerful expression in these textiles.

The first ikat that I ever saw was in the window of the Artweave Textile Gallery, New York, in the 1970s. Out of curiosity, I entered the gallery to ascertain what I had seen. There I was met by Gail Martin, the owner, who explained to me how an ikat was made and where in Central Asia this particular piece had been produced. That day I not only acquired my first ikat, but I began a close friendship with Gail. In the course of a delightful partnership spanning more than two decades, Gail became indispensable in helping to build this collection of ikats, of which she soon became the curator.

It was not my intention at the outset to build an important collection. In fact, as I purchased more ikats, I had no well-formed purpose in mind other than the desire to acquire pieces that moved me. It was color and design, and to some degree condition, that determined what I bought. I avoided ikats that were chemically dyed, preferring multi-colored ikats with relatively complex designs, which generally meant those of an earlier period.

Because I approached ikats as though they were "textile paintings", I only bought wall panels, even though the primary production had been for items of clothing. I also remained embarrassingly ignorant of the ethnography of the region and culture that produced these wonderful objects. I was simply moved by a visceral, visual response to them and not until five or six years ago did I begin to educate myself about how, why and where these textiles had been created. As a result of this rather unschooled initial approach, this collection emerged as somewhat unbalanced and less comprehensive than it might have been.

Two events in 1994 significantly affected the contours of the collection. The first was the suggestion by Annie Carlano, the curator of textiles at the Museum of Fine Arts, Boston, to organize a show drawn exclusively from my collection. This inaugural exhibition, to be mounted in the spring of 1997 under the curatorial direction and exquisite taste of Anne Poulet and Julia Bailey, and superbly designed by Michael Davis, is only the second time that an American museum has organized a major show of Central Asian ikats.

It was also in 1994 that Alan Marcuson and Laurence King decided to produce a definitive book on Central Asian ikat and asked whether I might participate. To be able to publish this collection with them under the direction of Alan Marcuson, whose knowledge and taste is so outstanding, was uniquely enticing.

The coming together of these two initiatives catalyzed Gail Martin and me to try to fill some gaps in the collection, in particular by acquiring a number of outstanding velvet coats. But, more importantly, it also led to the commissioning of Kate Fitz Gibbon and Andrew Hale to author a manuscript, which could serve both as a catalogue for the entire collection and, in a separate publication, for the exhibition. Without their exceptional erudition, dedication and the years they had spent researching this topic, the effort to create a comprehensive text would have been inordinately difficult to achieve. Thus, what began as merely a personal adventure to acquire splendid objects, became an effort to inform a much larger audience.

I am grateful to my good friend Professor Avrom Udovitch, who contributed invaluable scholarly guidance. The exceptional photographic skill of Don Tuttle has produced a marvelous pictorial rendering of the collection. The brilliant design of the two books by Mark Vernon-Jones has presented the collection and the historical photographs from General Kaufman's 1871–72 expedition in a superb layout. I also want to thank Robert Marcuson who has played such a valuable role in helping to oversee all of the production details of these beautifully produced books.

Jacqueline Rothschild's masterful competence in launching The American Foundation for Textile Art and co-ordinating all the players has been invaluable to this enterprise. So has the collaboration of Luisa Kreisberg and her talented associates. Annie Carlano and Mimi Leveque have played an invaluable role in preparing the collection for its extensive museum tour. Working with Michael Davis on design issues for the display of the ikats has been fascinating. Finally, I would like to thank Leonard Nelson, who has such extensive museum experience, and who provided so much astute advice throughout this entire process. It has been a privilege to work with such an exceptional group of people and, thereby, to be able to share my enthusiasm for these beautiful ikats with a wider public.

INTRODUCTION

In 1813, Mir Izzatullah, an Indian Muslim, watched the caravans depart from Bukhara for Siberia, Russia and Afghanistan. In dry, clerical style, he described the goods laden on each camel's back. Among the bales of muslin, colored calico and yarn were robes made of a material called *adras*.[1] Izzatullah was not an interested tourist, but a spy in the forbidden Khanates, and his report to British intelligence was the first mention of the *adras* ikat silks that were the most brilliant creations of the artisans of nineteenth-century Central Asia.

The Malay–Indonesian word *ikat* derives from the verb *mengikat*, which means "to bind, tie or wind around". Ikat is an ancient technique, a method of wrapping yarns to form areas of resist, and then dyeing these sections of yarn before the weaving of a cloth begins. Ikat dyeing is well known in many parts of the world – Southeast Asia, Japan, the Yemen and South and Central America all have strong traditions of ikat production. Through wide usage, the word *ikat* has become the generic term for these textiles in the West, regardless of their geographic origin.

Ikat dyeing was practiced in a very simple form for centuries in Central Asia. Then, during a hundred-year-long cultural and economic revival in the oasis kingdoms, the art of ikat dyeing became the most vital, sophisticated and widely distributed textile art in Central Asia. A series of ties and dye baths were used to produce warps of many-colored silk yarns bearing intricate designs, and weaving and finishing techniques were elaborated in order to vary the surface appearance, weight and luster of the rich fabrics. The nineteenth-century textile designers drew inspiration from many sources; in ikat, the decorative traditions of urban embroidery and wall-painting were combined with the dynamic energy of the art of the steppe nomads. In essence, the Central Asian ikats were a commercial art-form that transcended the limitations of the marketplace. Their inventive pattern and explosive color needed no interpreter – ikats traveled across the steppes as booty, as trade goods, and as gifts of robes of honor from proud Khans to the great Tsar.

By the latter part of the century, when ikat production was widespread, the Khanates had become more accessible to strangers. The difficult and dangerous journey to Central Asia was made by intrepid Russian and European travelers, who wrote of the gorgeous costumes of the oasis dwellers and the rich hangings that brought color and beauty to their drab, mud-brick homes.

The first Western collections of ikats were formed during the last third of the nineteenth century, by merchants, adventurers and political emissaries. The steppe kingdoms retained an exotic, medieval character in this period of forced absorption into the Russian empire. In keeping with Central Asian traditions of hospitality, early travelers were presented with textiles and sumptuous robes of honor as they journeyed from oasis to oasis. The ikats collected by Robert Shaw in eastern Central Asia in 1868, now in the Ashmolean Museum at Oxford, the holdings of the Victoria and Albert Museum, acquired in 1883, and the Henri Moser collection from the early 1880s in the Bern Historisches Museum were among the first established public collections. Presentation-pieces given by Central Asian rulers to the Russian tsars in the nineteenth and early twentieth centuries included ikat robes and wall-hangings, and formed a major part of the Central Asian textile collections of the Hermitage, the Museum of Ethnography in St Petersburg, and the Oruzhenaya Palata in Moscow. Many of the ikats now in Central Asian museums were transferred there from Russian institutions in the mid-twentieth century, and their original provenance has been lost in the process.

A hundred years after the first wave of European tourists reached the Central Asian Khanates, the East became a source of fascination to a later generation of seekers. In the 1960s and 1970s, young travelers from Europe and America embraced the exotic cultures of India and Afghanistan, and found treasures, if not enlightenment, in Kabul's dusty bazaars. The Bolshevik Revolution in Central Asia had sent thousands of refugees across the southern border to Afghanistan, and the émigrés carried robes and wall-hangings with them when they fled. The textiles remained within families until necessity and Western demand forced them on to the market. Initially, ikats and embroidered textiles were brought to the West as a complement to the trade in Asian tribal rugs. In comparison to carpets, there were only very limited quantities of antique ikats available in either East or West, and a few knowing collectors quickly dominated the market.

The Guido Goldman Collection is by far the largest and most comprehensive of the several fine private collections in the West. The collection of over two hundred ikat wall-hangings and robes was assembled over a twenty-year period, the first purchases coinciding with the export of large numbers of ikat hangings and robes from Afghanistan in the 1970s and early 1980s. The Goldman ikats were acquired from dealers and private collections in Europe and the United States, in an active pursuit of the finest works available.

The Guido Goldman Collection is almost entirely made up of ikats from the first half of the nineteenth century, the remainder falling into the middle period of production in the third quarter of the century. All the ikats in the Guido Goldman Collection are of exceptional quality, and because the collection consists primarily of larger wall-hangings, the complete patterning of the ikats can be seen and studied. It is an incomparable resource for scholars, most especially for the material of the first half of the nineteenth century, a period insufficiently represented even in Russian and Central Asian museums.

Only a few Western academics, and a single, noted Soviet scholar, Dr Sayora Mahkamova, have given serious attention to the complex ikat weaving tradition in Central Asia. The material that remains from the period before the nineteenth century is so limited that any discussion of the influences on, and antecedents to, the Central Asian *adras* ikats must be sought within the entirety of Central Asia's versatile and extremely lengthy textile tradition. The *adras* ikats were produced within a commercial milieu that involved the work of many distinct specialist-craftsmen, and the role and background of each of these contributors to the craft must be examined separately. Because ikat was widely distributed within Central Asia in the nineteenth century, and eagerly adopted by people of every ethnicity, it is necessary to look to the larger role of textiles in society, and to attempt to define a common aesthetic, in order to explain the immediate popularity of ikat, and the collective Central Asian identity that it came to express.

In the writing of this book we have been heavily indebted to the pioneering work of many other authors. The wide-ranging nature of our subjects required, in many cases, that we rely on scholarly analyses by other authors, far more expert than ourselves, within each particular field of study. The extensive notes appended to this work refer only to those publications which we have drawn from directly in the writing of the text; it is by no means an exhaustive list of the possible sources.

The history of trade along the Silk Route is drawn largely from secondary sources – first from the works of modern archeologists, then from analyses of Roman, Byzantine and Chinese sources and from the critical assessments of Islamic writers and the letters of Cairo-based merchants. Audrey Burton's study of seventeenth- and eighteenth-century trade patterns has illuminated an otherwise dark period in the history of Central Asian textiles. The examination of ikat weaving methods and the social functions of luxury textiles in the nineteenth century are based on the work of a disparate group of writers, though these authors, at least, share a common focus on Central Asia itself. The many works of the Soviet ethnographer O.A. Sukhareva provided us with the basic structure for analysis of this period, and those of Z.L. Amitin-Shapiro and N.O. Tursunov have filled many gaps in our understanding. The writings of Western anthropologists, modern Uzbek historians, and nineteenth-century curiosity seekers and spies from both sides of the Great Game have all contributed pieces to the puzzle.

Our own contribution to the work – beyond that of compiling information – has been in providing a specific point of view, a general perspective on Central Asia. Our years of work in and near Afghanistan have served as a useful counterweight to the writings of scholars who utilize more traditional formulae to explain events and artistic phenomena. We have spent thousands of hours in examining textiles, and in persistent interrogation of the native owners of these fabrics. We cannot claim to have engaged in systematic field work within one of the relevant academic specialties – anthropology, history, or textile study – but we have benefited greatly from the work of many fine scholars whose attention has been entirely devoted to one or another aspect of this extremely complex field of study. The want of earlier exhaustive works on Central Asian ikat – of the corpus of material that exists for the study of art in other fields – guarantees that there will be failings and omissions within our own work. Nonetheless, we are confident that we have provided secure grounds for further inquiry, and a firm basis for the appreciation and understanding of Central Asian ikat.

No more comprehensive source for the study of Central Asian ikats exists than the Guido Goldman Collection. This collection has offered us, and all others privileged to view it, far more than the academic benefits of breadth and sheer quantity of material. In the nineteenth century, when these fabrics were woven, they had a purpose beyond their commercial role as luxury trade goods, and beyond their social functions as presentation robes and ceremonial costumes. The Central Asian ikats were made to give pleasure, to delight and entrance the viewer. They make the same gift to a far wider world today.

1

THE SILK TRADE IN CENTRAL ASIA

This desert, in some places, is twenty days' journey in breadth, and there is neither tree, nor mountain, nor stone therein... We went on towards the east, seeing nothing but heaven and earth...

The Journal of Friar William of Rubruck, 1253–55[1]

The names of Bukhara and Samarkand carry echoes of adventure, of the shouts of camel drivers and the shuffling feet of their beasts, of caravan bells ringing in the morning air. The Central Asian oases are veiled by distance and romance – the temptation is to forgo analysis, to throw away the map, and join the cavalcade.

In the past the road to Central Asia was well marked; the cities of Bukhara and Samarkand were hubs of international commerce and culture, goals as glittering as Wall Street or Broadway. Now, nearly every work on Central Asia begins with a routine explanation of its location, climate and natural resources. The benefits offered by Central Asia's geographic position are not as obvious to the modern observer as they were to the ancient one.

The heart of Asia is rugged and starkly beautiful: a lowland area of desert and oasis-dotted steppe circumscribed by mountains. This enormous, shallow bowl stretches for a thousand miles, from the Urals in the west to the Altai Mountains on the borders of China. Central Asia reaches south to include part of present-day Afghanistan, and north to the plains of Kazakhstan. Its climate is dry, with very hot summers

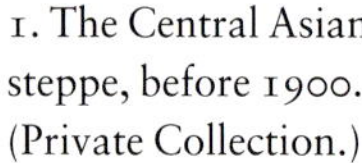

1

1. The Central Asian steppe, before 1900. (Private Collection.)

and freezing winters. The soil is fertile, but only desert shrubs grow where there is no water. The oasis towns are sustained by the Amu and Syr Darya rivers that rise in the eastern mountains. The Tejend (or Hari Rud) and the Murghab rise in Afghanistan to reach into the deserts of Turkmenia. These snow-melt rivers peak in summer in time to irrigate crops, then disappear into the deserts.

Central Asia lay at the center of a natural trade route between China and the Mediterranean Sea. The oasis towns acted as a funnel for goods, people and ideas from the furthest edges of the known world. In turn, Sakas, Parthians, Greeks, Kushans, Sogdians and Turks built wealthy kingdoms from the profits of the trade in luxury goods. From the early centuries AD until the end of the nineteenth century, textiles remained the principal commodity in Central Asian trade, and for much of the same period, the manufacture of textiles in local workshops was Central Asia's chief industry.

There is something to be said for an abbreviated history of Central Asia's long-standing dependence on the textile trade. The endless parade of kingdoms and conquerors on the steppes can be dizzying.

At times it seems that the marchers have passed out of sight – only to reappear after a change of costume. Four thousand years of art and textile history cannot be condensed, but within that lengthy period are episodes which demonstrate the evolution of textile trade and production.

THE DEVELOPMENT OF WEAVING Central Asia was among the earliest areas in the world to domesticate sheep, although the evidence suggests that their initial purpose was to supply meat, dairy products and hides. Spindle whorls appear in sites of the late Djeitun period, around 5500 BC, but only in the mid-third millennium BC is there actual evidence for the use of woven wool textiles.[2] By the middle of the third millennium, many small agricultural settlements had become large towns. Pottery-making, stone-carving and metal-working developed from home-based crafts into the work of skilled professionals in the Bronze Age cities of Namazga and Altin Tepe. The enormous number of spindle whorls excavated indicates that spinning was very extensive, but only a few fragments of plain-woven textiles remain in the archeological record.

Between 3000 and 2000 BC, economic patterns appeared that would continue for thousands of years. Central Asia was actively involved in the supply of luxury goods – most especially of lapis lazuli – to the wealthy kingdoms of Sumeria, Egypt and Mohenjodaro. The "bright blue thread" of the Lapis Route long preceded the Silk Road, and signaled the early reliance of the Central Asian economy on international trade. The route that lapis traveled, through Iran and Iraq to Syria and Egypt, anticipated that of the Silk Road some two thousand years later. Just as the Silk Road carried more than silk, the Lapis Route also carried gold, silver, tin, turquoise, ivory, drugs, dyes and other lightweight luxury goods. This active trade with the West declined dramatically after the dissolution of the Bronze Age culture of the steppe at the beginning of the first millennium BC. A vital commerce was not reestablished until the emergence of the Sogdian states around 500 BC.

SOGDIA AND THE SILK ROAD The daring and intrepid merchants of Sogdia created the Silk Road. It took courage and a degree of foolhardiness to travel without charts through steppeland and desert. The Sogdian merchants piled their camels with the finest wares of each city and set out for the next, ready to confront hostile tribes, to fight off wild beasts, and to hazard death from starvation, thirst or freezing cold. Only the Sogdians were prepared to undertake such great risks to obtain exotic goods. Since the establishment of the Sogdian kingdoms, trade has been the national calling of Central Asia.

Sogdia incorporated the major cities of Bukhara and Samarkand, and occupied roughly the area of modern Uzbekistan. At an early stage of its development, Sogdia was part of the Achaemenid empire of Persia. The Achaemenids installed rulers to head the Sogdian political structure, but the administration of each city remained relatively independent. Although southern Central Asia formed one cultural area, the geography of the region encouraged decentralized government, and rural areas tended to remain under local control. The mutual dependence of nomadic and urban societies in Central Asia is also documented in the alliance between ancient Sogdia and Scythia in the fourth century BC.

A delegation of Sogdians offering the finest products of their region to the "King of Kings" is carved on the wall-reliefs of the Achaemenid

You assign me the region of Sogdiana, rebellious and not merely resolute, but actually impossible to subdue. I am thrown to wild beasts.

Cleitus "the black", offered the job of pacifying Sogdia by Alexander the Great[3]

site of Persepolis. Thus, the first record of the export of textiles from Central Asia is preserved in stone; the Sogdians offer cloth along with vessels, a pair of fat-tailed rams, and an animal skin.[4]

The destruction of the Achaemenid empire by Alexander the Great in 330 BC had dramatic consequences for the Sogdian state. Although he was initially accepted as heir to the Achaemenids, his brutal campaign to impose a centralized, Macedonian-led government in Sogdia led to a popular uprising. An alliance of Scythians and Sogdians against the armies of Alexander made the campaign in Central Asia the most difficult of his career.[5] Initially, the war was disastrous for long-distance Sogdian trade. Many merchants fled to the oasis towns of eastern Turkestan and, eventually, to China. They and their descendants established commercial outposts which would become important in the Roman silk trade with China.[6] The long-term effects of Alexander's invasion further bound Central Asia to the path of commerce, and forced a change in the nature of trade.

A passion for silk was about to overtake the Mediterranean. Silk had been known in China since Shang times (around 1500 BC). The first silk fabrics probably passed into Europe a thousand years later, through the casual relay-race of ancient trade. It is not known whether silk fabrics traveled overland from China via Central Asia or by sea through the Persian Gulf, but it is quite possible that the first Chinese silks that appeared in Europe were handled by Sogdian merchants. The most direct route between China and the Roman world was through Central Asia and Persia. The accomplished traders of ancient Bactria and Sogdia took advantage of their position at its center. By the late second century BC, the scattered exchanges had developed into an organized and regular traffic.[7] Roman trade with Asia was extensive and drew its materials from a wide geographical area. Caravans brought precious stones, furs, dyes, incense, peacocks and eunuchs, spices and drugs, as well as silk. Silk was imported both as dyed thread and as woven cloth which was often unraveled to be rewoven into sheer fabrics that were more to Roman taste. Despite high duties imposed on imports from the East and the banning of silk for men's dress by the Roman Senate in 14 BC, the trade in luxury goods increased.

Although the West sent some goods eastward, the value of the export trade was never equal to that of imported goods, and the Roman empire was being drained of hard cash. The emperor Trajan attempted to solve the problem by invading neighboring Parthia.[8] Although the Romans were unable to defeat the Parthians, they did destabilize the caravan trade to the extent that silk imports into the Roman empire were greatly reduced. The weakened Parthian state was succeeded by the larger and more aggressive Sasanian empire in the early third century AD.

I see garments in which there is nothing to cover either the wearer's body or her shame.

Seneca

The Sasanians sought a monopoly on the East–West luxury trade, and hindered the free dealings of Sogdian merchants. Instability in Northern China at the point of supply of the caravan route, and the establishment of silk trading centers in Southern China were a further blow to Central Asian commerce. Persian ships sailing via Ceylon and India dominated much of the Asian trade to Europe between AD 240 and 440.[9] Yet despite increasing competition from the sea trade, the Sogdian cities prospered.

In the years before the Arab invasion and the coming of Islam, Sogdia was a wealthy and cosmopolitan place. The cities of Central Asia became a place of refuge for diverse communities. Jews, Nestorian Christians, Manicheans, Zoroastrians, Hindus and Buddhists mingled

2

2. Sogdian emissaries bear gifts of cloth and animals. Stone relief. East stairway, Apadana, Persepolis, Iran. Achaemenid period, 6th–5th century BC. (The MacQuitty International Photographic Collection.)

1 WALL-HANGING
probably Samarkand
third quarter 19th century
82" × 54" (208 × 136cm)
5 panels
warp-faced plain weave
Both the dramatic scale and the composition of repeating roundels – common characteristics of 19th-century ikats – are reminiscent of ancient Sogdian fabrics.

The people are addicted to wine, and like to sing and dance in the streets. Their king has a hat of felt, decorated with gold and various jewels. The women have coiled chignons, which they cover with a black kerchief sewed with gold foil.

T'ang Shu, writing of Samarkand around the eighth century AD[10]

freely with members of local cults. Each of these groups had trade connections with the world outside, and Central Asia now derived great benefits from its position between India, Iran, China and the primitive Slavs. Although much of its wealth came from its role as a trans-shipment point for Chinese goods to the West, Central Asia had unique resources which were valuable to the outside world.

Among Central Asia's most desirable goods were horses and precious stones. In addition, the Khotan region of eastern Central Asia was China's sole source for nephrite jade. Not all the commodities traded were exotic; Chinese rhubarb had been an important export for the Central Asian traders since Roman times.[11] Central Asian caravans also brought large quantities of Indian, Persian and locally made cotton fabrics to China.[12]

SILK CULTIVATION IN CENTRAL ASIA Since the first millennium BC, locally woven silk textiles had been made from Chinese thread that passed through Central Asia, but the date of the first native silk production is still unknown.[13] A conservative estimate places the first commercial production within Central Asia around the third or fourth centuries AD, when the Chinese prohibition on the export of silkworms became ineffectual. A sixth-century painted wooden plaque illustrating the legend of the smuggling of silk cocoons into Central Asia was found by Aurel Stein at Dandan-oilik in East Turkestan.[14] Hsuan-tsang, a Buddhist pilgrim traveling in Central Asia, recorded the same story in AD 628. According to the tale, a Chinese princess, given as bride to a nomad ruler, hid cocoons or silkworm eggs in her hair, and brought them to the West. The two sources for this legend, one archeological, the other literary, seem to record an historical event that had become a folk tradition by the sixth century. Legendary tale aside, the reduction in the free flow of silk during the Six Dynasties period in China gave the Central Asians a practical reason to begin their own production.

THE FIRST CENTRAL ASIAN IKATS Hundreds of fabrics have been excavated in Central Asia since the late nineteenth century. The Altaian Mountain sites of Pazyryk and Bashdar yielded a complete pile carpet, several carpet fragments and numerous felts in near perfect condition.[15] Fabrics of Chinese, Iranian and Central Asian manufacture from the great period of the Silk Road, the first century BC to the eighth century AD, were discovered in early twentieth-century excavations at various Central Asian sites. Archeological textiles from these sites included simple twills and tie dye as well as elaborate embroideries and brocades, but no ikat was found.[16] More recent excavations within Soviet Central Asia, at the eighth-century site of Mount Mugh in Tadjikistan, did not yield any ikat. In the face of such negative evidence it is difficult to draw conclusions about the extent of ikat weaving in Central Asia.

There has been a recent find of an ikat fragment, about four to five inches square (10–12cm), with a woodgrain-like pattern in silvery gray and beige from the fourth- to ninth-century site of Astana in Xinjiang Province, China.[17] This as yet unpublished fragment appears to be the only ikat from an archeological site anywhere in Central Asia.

The only other surviving examples of what may be ancient Central Asian ikat were found not in Central Asia, but Japan. A small panel of all-silk warp ikat was preserved for centuries in the Horiyu-ji Temple repository in Nara. It is known that it was imported, probably via

3

My family sent me off to be married on the other side of heaven.

They sent me a long way to a strange land, to the king of Wu-sun.

A domed lodging is my dwelling place, with walls made of felt;

meat is my food, with fermented milk as the sauce.

Lament of a Chinese princess, first century BC[18]

4

3. Wooden plaque depicting the legend of how silkworms were smuggled from China. 6th century AD. (The Stein Collection, British Museum, London.)
4. Silk-warp ikat fragment, probably of Central Asian origin. Horiyu-ji, Nara, Japan. Asuka Period, AD 552–644. 7"×12" (18×30cm). (National Museum, Tokyo.)

2 WALL-HANGING
probably Samarkand
third quarter 19th century
83" × 69" (211 × 175cm)
6 panels
warp-faced plain weave
The widely produced, early twentieth-century ikats with large roundels are related to this early wall-hanging. This motif may also be loosely based on suzani designs.

China, during the Asuka period (AD 552–644). Although the panel lacks any provenance beyond its unquestioned age, this fragment has generally been regarded as the earliest known ikat from Central Asia.[19] Its identification as Central Asian has largely been based on the elimination of any other possible source of origin, and on parallels in design and technique with modern Central Asian ikat materials. The ancient fragment has rich, vibrant colors and a bold abstract design; it was a highly valued object that was used as the centerpiece of a banner, and carefully preserved for a thousand years.[20] A group of smaller fragments that reached Japan close to the same period are very different in design; the scale of the pattern is smaller and the colors are sober and restrained. These fragments resemble later Central Asian ikats in their reliance on an animated line and in the play on negative and positive space within their composition. Given the wide variety of motifs and styles within the ancient Central Asian weaving tradition, it is certainly possible that these fragments are from Central Asia.

Ikat fabric appears at about the same time in mural paintings in the fifth to seventh-century Vakataka period shrines in the Ajanta Caves in

5

5. Detail of Sogdian mural depicting the "Amazon cycle", 7th–8th century AD. Pendjikent XXI:1. (from *Sogdian Painting, The Pictorial Epic in Oriental Art*. Guitty Azarpay. University of California Press, 1981.)

India. The Ajanta ikats in no way resemble the ikat from the Nara repository; the Indian style is more closely related in color and design to the later ikats of the Yemen. The Indian material is made up of simple patterns – stripes, arrowheads and jagged lines – and appears to have been woven in generous widths. The murals from Ajanta also depict a number of foreigners, some with Central Asian features, in their native dress, but none of these foreigners wears ikat.[21]

A group of seven fragments of warp-ikat fabrics has been excavated at Nahal 'Omer in the 'Arava Valley, Israel. These cotton ikat fragments date between AD 650 and 810, and are the earliest documented appearance of the ikat technique yet published.[22] The Nahal 'Omer ikats resemble those depicted in the Ajanta Cave paintings, but are also similar in pattern and construction to the cotton ikats of Yemeni origin discovered by Alfred Buhler in Egypt, which bear inscriptions dating them to AD 862–64.[23]

Several authors have nominated Central Asia as the area responsible for the origin and transfer of the ikat dyeing method. It seems more likely that the ikat technique evolved independently in a number of areas. Phyllis Ackerman has suggested Central Asia as the point of origin for the technique based on the use of the Turkic word *alacha* for ikat in both India and Iran, as well as on a noted fondness for striped textiles among the Central Asians themselves. However, the word *alacha* refers not only to ikat but to striped fabrics made in a variety of techniques.[24] Carl Schuster has attempted to show the diffusion of the ikat technique from Central Asia through India and on to Indonesia in the form of a specific design that occurs on one of the ikats in the Horiyu-ji Temple. He has suggested that Central Asian influence on textile design can be demonstrated by tracing the route of a "genealogical pattern".[25]

The question remains as to why so little ikat has been found in Central Asia from the ancient period. It is possible that archeologists have simply been unlucky; that the fabrics are there, buried under sand dunes, waiting to be discovered. If the archeological evidence is typical of the material goods available at various periods, then it is unlikely that there was major production of ikat in Central Asia either at this time, or at any other in Central Asia's early history. Until the nineteenth century, ikat weaving appears to have remained a relatively minor element within a far larger tradition. The importance of the silk textile trade in Central Asia is best demonstrated through the extensive, long-term production of other types of antique fabrics. The commercial and social motivations that made weaving the most vital industry of the nineteenth century are present even in the early years of trade along the Silk Road.

ZANDANIJI Wall-paintings from the houses of ancient Samarkand (Afrasiab) and Pendjikent of the fifth to ninth centuries are a rich source for the study of Central Asian textiles and costume. Textiles are important elements in the composition of these sensuous renderings of epic tales, but none of the frescoes so far discovered depicts anything resembling ikat. Although local Sogdian artisans produced complex and luxurious fabrics in this period, many of the textiles in the paintings have designs that more closely resemble the iconography of Sasanian textiles from Iran[26] and the patterns of Chinese multicolored silks.[27]

These wall-paintings as well as numerous archeological remains identify the most popular luxury fabrics in Central Asia during the late Sasanian and early Islamic periods. *Zandaniji* was by far the best known of these fabrics. The name of the cloth originally derived from a village a few miles from Bukhara called Zandane.[28] Although Zandane may have been the place of origin for the cloth, production soon became widespread. *Zandaniji* silks are the earliest identifiable Central Asian fabrics to have survived in any quantity; over 200 pieces have been found distributed between the Far East and Western Europe.

The term *zandaniji* has been applied to different types of material at different times. Until about the ninth century, the term was applied to a multicolored silk twill with geometric designs or pairs of animals arranged within repeating roundels. Between the roundels were smaller rosette designs. A series of patterned borders framed the rectangular field of large medallions and smaller interstitial designs. The weaving of a border may suggest that *zandaniji* was used for wall-hangings as well as for clothing.

TRADE WITH CHINA AND BYZANTIUM The first wave of Turkic tribes arrived on the western steppe in the sixth century AD. The new rulers were of nomadic background, yet were dependent upon

3 WALL-HANGING
Samarkand or Bukhara
mid-19th century
91" × 58" (231 × 147cm)
5 panels
warp-faced plain weave
A familiar floral pattern is given theatrical scale and enormous vitality.

international trade, urban craft production and agriculture. The Turks sought to secure a direct trade relationship with Byzantium, bypassing their mutual enemy, Sasanian Iran.[29] Although the Byzantines had recently established their own silk industry, their local production was insufficient to supply the needs of both the court and the Church.

In order to meet the demands of the Byzantines and other clients, the Turks needed a regular supply of Chinese silk. For centuries, the Chinese had eased tensions along their northern and western borders by the granting of gifts of silk and silver, and the arranged marriages of Chinese princesses. A stable and quiescent steppe was maintained under rulers who were in part empowered by Chinese riches.[30] In return, all goods entering China were regarded as tribute, as homage to Chinese cultural and political superiority. Tribute-bearing envoys received rich gifts, and merchants occasionally took advantage of the system to represent themselves as ambassadors. The rhetoric of the tribute system was so important to the Chinese that they went along with this petty deception. The value of the gifts was dictated by political considerations, not economic parity, and often far exceeded that of the tribute.[31]

6

6. Miniature on paper in "Siyah Kalam" style. Iran or Central Asia. 15th century. A procession scene which contains elements of Persian, Chinese and Mongol artistic styles. (Topkapı Saray Library, Istanbul.)

These uncertain arrangements were not acceptable to the Turks in their new role as middlemen between China and Byzantium. In the late sixth century AD the Turks began to state exactly what gifts they expected in return for their tribute. The Chinese were forced to agree to the Turks' demands,[32] and a regular trade was established that brought Chinese silks to the West. Sogdian textiles traveled the Silk Road along with the Chinese materials. From Byzantium, the Central Asian *zandaniji* silks were passed on to Europe, where a number were preserved, many of them in reliquaries in which the cloth was used to wrap the bones of saints, a sign of the esteem in which *zandaniji* was held.[33]

THE ISLAMIC PERIOD AND WORLD TRADE Two events in the first half of the seventh century were to have profound effects on Central Asia. The first, the emergence of the Chinese T'ang Dynasty in AD 618, opened inward-looking China to foreign trade and ideas as never before. The novel and exotic materials of Central Asia fascinated the T'ang court, and trade prospered.

The second event, the rise of Islam, was to have a far greater impact on life in Central Asia. The Arab conquests, which swept through northern Africa and Asia after the death of the prophet Muhammad in

AD 632, united the worlds of the Mediterranean and Indian Ocean. By the beginning of the ninth century the Islamic world extended from Spain to India, and the cities of Islamic Africa and Asia became avid consumers of luxury goods, especially of textiles.[34] Ideally placed between T'ang China and the West, Central Asia was one of the cultural and commercial centers of Islam, and an integral part of a vast Islamic trading zone.

Textile production was the major industry of the Islamic world. Textiles were seen as a basic industrial commodity, as fine art, and as a measure of status and accumulated wealth. The reasons for the cultural concentration on textiles were complex. In part, they derived from the former nomadic background of many early Islamic leaders. The material culture of both the Bedouin Arabs and the Central Asian Turks had always been textile-based. The nature of Islamic ideals had still greater impact on the forms taken by art in the Muslim world, and on the choice of textiles as an appropriate medium for artistic expression. Early Islam promoted a simple, ascetic lifestyle. Its goal was a pious, egalitarian society. Lavish displays of wealth were frowned upon; the use of gold and silver utensils was discouraged. Art objects made of precious metals were associated with the pagan Sasanian and Christian worlds. In a sense, Islam defined itself by rejecting ostentation.

Early Islamic art made use of humble materials: plain brick, stucco and tile in architecture; ceramic, copper and glass for vessels; cotton and linen for textiles. Some religious authorities held that it was improper for Muslim men to wear pure silk, so it was often woven in a blend with cotton, linen or wool: modest materials made valuable by the work of man. Islam moved quickly away from its early purity and idealism. Nevertheless, the association of the luxurious and precious with spiritual impurity remained, and the textile trade benefited by the essentially utilitarian nature of cloth.

Within Islamic society fabric had uses and significance not found in any other. Textiles were used to pay taxes and tribute. Weavings often decorated the walls of mosques, and carpets covered the floors. The austere architecture of early Islam was designed to be enlivened with textiles. Clothes were an important item of prestige, and defined status and identity in Islamic society. Twenty-five dinars, enough to support a family for a year, was not an uncommon price for a fine robe in the eleventh century.[35] Gifts of robes of honor, *khilat*, by the Caliph or his governors were a customary reward for the favored of the courts. The vast quantities of textiles used by the courts were supplied by *tiraz*, state-controlled factories,[36] or by scattered independent workshops. An order for 2000 *tiraz* garments from Iraq for delivery in Bukhara in the late tenth century was typical and probably constituted only a fraction of the requirements of the Bukharan court.[37]

Fabrics were the ideal trade-goods of the early and medieval Islamic period. They were universally in demand and their qualities of material and workmanship were easily understood. Textiles were easy to transport: they were lightweight and unbreakable. Under these circumstances weaving of all types could be expected to flourish. Although there were important regional styles, the entire Islamic world shared many of the same tastes in textiles.

Fabrics and current fashions are described in many of the surviving works of the great Muslim geographers and historians of the tenth to fourteenth centuries. Although specific fabrics are often listed, in most cases it is impossible to match the names with actual textiles from the period, and apparent geographical references in the literature are not

They make there stuffs called Widhari, woven of cotton on cotton, and made with an astonishing art; they are made raw and without being cut. There is not a prince, minister or cadi in the whole of Khurasan who does not wear one over his clothes. The beauty of these stuffs is evident and their splendor is famous...In short, it is impossible to find anything better, whether as regards beauty, whether as regards solidity.

Idrisi, *Geographie*, mid-twelfth century[38]

4 WALL-HANGING
mid-19th century
83" × 62" (211 × 157cm)
4 panels
warp-faced plain weave
An almost three-dimensional effect is created when a familiar rosette is given geometric form, and then superimposed on to a complex, striped surface.

reliable. Well-known types of cloth were copied all over the Islamic world, but often retained the name of their place of origin. The early sources do make clear the great variety of fabrics produced, and the appreciation for them throughout the Islamic world. Writers took pleasure in ranking the finest fabrics produced in various regions, but although many Central Asian textiles are mentioned by name in the early sources, only three fabrics, *zandaniji, mulham* and *kirbas,* can be identified with certainty. Islamic texts provide clear definitions of the fabrics *mulham* and *kirbas*, and *zandaniji* textiles have been discovered which contain inscriptions identifying them by name.[39]

The important Central Asian centers for textile manufacture were Bukhara, Samarkand and Merv. *Mulham* cloth, made of silk and cotton, was associated with Merv although it was also copied outside Central Asia.[40] The cotton muslin fabric called *kirbas* was produced and sold in Bukhara, Samarkand, Merv and in Iran. The antique *kirbas* was probably identical to the cotton ground cloth of the nineteenth-century embroidered *suzani* of the Bukharan Emirate.[41]

Narshakhi's tenth-century *History of Bukhara* states that *zandaniji* was exported to Iran, Iraq and India, and was a preferred fabric for royal robes. By Narshakhi's time, the term *zandaniji* referred to a fabric made of cotton rather than silk, which was woven in patterned and unpatterned varieties. It is not known to what extent Islamic cotton *zandaniji* resembled the earlier silk textile, or why the base material changed, as many other fine-quality silk fabrics continued to be made at this time. The name *zandanaji* continued in use for various types of export fabrics from Central Asia. The thirteenth-century writer Djuwaini mentions *zandaniji* among the fabrics that a traveling merchant unwisely attempted to sell at inflated prices to Chengiz Khan. The Mongol ruler ordered the merchant to be severely punished for insulting his understanding of the textile market. The trader's companions had the wisdom to insist that they had brought their goods as a present to the Khan, and harmony was restored.[42] The episode makes clear the extent to which textiles functioned as a basic commodity even at the furthest reaches of the Islamic trading zone.

Having donned barchin,

be thoughtless and weak.

Makhmud Kashgari, *Divanu Iugat at Turk*, 1072–74[45]

Narshakhi also mentions a workshop that had produced a unique fabric which was exported to Egypt, Syria and Byzantium, and worn by "kings, amirs, chieftains and functionaries".[43] A single door-hanging from the workshop was sufficient to pay the yearly land tax for all of Bukhara. According to Narshakhi, the workshop had produced prayer rugs, carpets, robes and cushions. Narshakhi also refers to a town near Bukhara called Tawais where a very large, ten-day-long annual fair was held that sold nothing but defective weavings. The output of the Bukharan workshops must have been tremendous, since quality goods were undoubtedly made in greater numbers than flawed fabrics.

MEDIEVAL ISLAMIC IKAT The fifteenth-century *Chronicles* of Mujir-ed-din describe an event that took place many centuries earlier, the inauguration of the Dome of the Rock mosque in Jerusalem. In the *Chronicles*, the mosque servants are described as wearing striped *'asb* (the Arabic term for ikat) from Merv and Herat.[44] The account relied upon earlier written records, since lost, and may have been adapted to reflect a later Arab familiarity with Central Asian silk production. This reference may be sufficient evidence to suggest that Central Asian ikat existed, but hardly enough to speculate on the extent of its production. Among the thousands of words written about textiles during the Islamic period, no author yet discovered has ventured to remark specifically on the manufacture or appearance of Central Asian ikat.

Sayora Mahkamova has suggested that there may be a philological relationship between the *esri iishig* of Makhmud Kashgari's eleventh-century dictionary, and the verb *esrila*. Makhmud Kashgari glossed *esri* as "dappled, variegated" and its cognate *esri iishig* as "variegated thread", meaning a thread comprising two yarns of different colors or multicolored yarns. Mahkamova's interpretation of *esrila*, the verb derived from *esri* – "to lay a design, to make something resemble a tiger skin" – led her to the conclusion that the ikat technique was practiced in Central Asia in the eleventh century.[46] Richard N. Frye has countered Mahkamova's suggestion by pointing out the likely application of Makhmud Kashgari's usage of *esri iishig* to the multicolored twisted rope used by both early Turkic tribesmen and modern Turkomans to tie down and magically to protect their animals and possessions.[47]

By far the best known ikat production of the early Islamic period is that of the Yemen. Within the Islamic world, the Yemen has the longest tradition of ikat manufacture, dating back at least to the seventh century AD. Yemeni *'asb*, ikat-dyed fabric, has been defined as "a particular sort of the garment called *burud* of the fabric of El-Yemen: a *burd* of which the yarn is put together and bound, then dyed, and then woven..."[48] Early Islamic writers often imply the uniqueness of the Yemeni ikat production. Educated Muslims of the medieval period knew a great deal about fabrics made throughout the Islamic world. Both the material evidence and the early writings that remain emphasize the obscurity of Central Asian ikat before the nineteenth century.

He also said: "After us the descendants of our clan will wear gold embroidered garments, eat rich and sweet food, ride fine horses, and embrace beautiful women, but they will not say that they owe all this to their fathers and elder brothers, and they will forget us and those great times."

V.A. Riasonovsky, "The Yasa of Chengiz Khan"[52]

Though culturally and geographically distant from Central Asia, a glance at the Yemeni production may be seen to illustrate the status of ikat fabric in the Islamic world in general. During the pre-Islamic period the Tubba kings of Yemen were said to have covered the Kaaba, later the holiest shrine of Islam, with Yemeni ikat. The *Kitab al-Aghani* states that *'asb* cloth was available at a fair in during the late sixth century.[49] Many Yemeni ikats from the early Islamic period have survived, some with painted or embroidered inscriptions which indicate the date and place of manufacture.[50] They are woven in cotton with relatively simple patterns and a narrow range of colors. The tradition of Yemeni ikat weaving is both lengthy and conservative; ikats very similar to those made in the early Islamic period continued to be woven well into the twentieth century.[51]

THE ILKHANID AND TIMURID PERIODS Chengiz Khan's invasion of Central Asia (and much of the rest of the Muslim world) in the early thirteenth century began a new and traumatic chapter in the history of the region. The Mongol armies were powerful and ruthless; they flattened cities, slaughtered the inhabitants and looted their possessions. Artisans were considered booty and were often spared, then shipped off to the courts of Mongol princes. Although the descendants of Chengiz' in Central Asia eventually converted to Islam and created stable, prosperous states, many cities never recovered from the initial Mongol onslaught. Traditions and skills had been built up over generations. Once destroyed, they could not be brought back overnight.

In the fourteenth century, the empire of Timur Leng (Tamerlane) succeeded to the Mongol Ilkhanids. Under Timur and his descendants, Central Asia began a renaissance in architecture and painting, but it was a renaissance based largely on traditions from outside Central Asia. The destruction of the cultural centers of Merv, Bukhara and Samarkand, the dispersal of artisans during the Mongol period and the

5 WALL-HANGING
Bukhara
first half 19th century
63" × 33" (160 × 85cm)
3 panels
warp-faced plain weave
The spandrels are reminiscent of the cloud-like designs on oriental ceramics, which were widely imported into Central Asia. They also bear a resemblance to minor design elements of the carpets from eastern Turkestan.

6 WALL-HANGING
first half 19th century
84" × 22" (213 × 57cm)
2 panels
warp-faced plain weave

importation of craftsmen from outside Central Asia tended to shuffle the stylistic deck, and makes the attribution of artifacts from the thirteenth to the sixteenth centuries extremely difficult.

Very few identifiably Central Asian textiles survive from this period. Much of what is known about the character of weaving comes from contemporary literary sources and from the rich tradition of book illustration. It is not known whether the miniature paintings accurately represent the range of textiles made at the time. The painters may have been selective in their choice of subjects, preferring to show only the most luxurious and exotic fabrics and not the more common, local stuffs.

Timur's imperial ambitions led him to conquer a vast region of the Eastern Islamic world, and then, to make his capital, Samarkand, a cultural center in which all the arts of the empire were practiced. The importation of craftsmen created an eclectic style in the textile arts of the court.[53] Chinese, Persian and Near Eastern influences are all present in works of the period: dragons and lotuses are found combined with palmettes and Islamic inscriptions. The hybrid style was the work of the designers of the *kitabkhana*, literally, bookhouse or library. This court institution was responsible for the design of tents, carpets and textiles as well as for the creation of books. The *kitabkhana* artists were primarily painters, and textile design reflected book illustration rather than any specific weaving tradition. The artists' chief aim was to create the impression of a sophisticated, cosmopolitan world. There is no indication that they were concerned with the symbolism or origin of the designs. Variety and exoticism were prized.

Chinese-style *zatuni* and *kimkha* cloth, and Egyptian-style *sinizi* and *dabiqi* were all reportedly woven in Samarkand.[54] Monochrome and two-toned fabrics were popular, as were gold and silver brocades. In the fifteenth- and sixteenth-century Central Asian fabrics, the early heraldic style was replaced by small, almost dainty, designs and motifs. The material seems detached from the rigorous aesthetic of the pre-Mongol period. Central Asian vitality, boldness and invention have been replaced by a cold standardization that reflects the centralized control of the *kitabkhana*. Though elegant and precise, the fabrics have a slightly decadent quality that hints at the impending decline of the weaving arts.[55]

> *And in that plain they had pitched for him many tents of different sort of which one had the upper and lower border woven in gold and was adorned within and without with the finest feathers: another was all woven of silk and decorated with various figures and flowers of diverse hues interwoven...*
>
> Ahmed Ibn Arabshah, describing the nuptial celebrations arranged by Timur for his grandson Ulugh Beg in 1405[58]

THE SEVENTEENTH AND EIGHTEENTH CENTURIES Local wars and political instability eroded the trade-based economy of Central Asia at the close of the sixteenth century. The economic stagnation of the seventeenth and eighteenth centuries also resulted in part from the discovery of the sea passage around the Cape of Good Hope in 1498. The co-existent, and often complementary, overland routes fell into disuse as political tensions rose along Central Asia's border with Iran.[56] The emergence of Bengal as a major silk producer was another blow to the Central Asian textile industries. By the late seventeenth century, Bengal's silk trade was larger than that of Iran or China.[57] Deprived of the markets of the Mediterranean, Central Asian traders turned their attention northward, toward Muscovy and Siberia. Bukharan traders became the mainstay and support of the early Russian colonists of Siberia, carrying food, medicines, dry goods and horses at great risk across the steppe. Bukharan merchants traveled far beyond Central Asia to organize caravans from China, Turkey and India.

7 WALL-HANGING
Bukhara
first half 19th century
68" × 45" (172 × 113cm)
4 panels
warp-faced plain weave

The primary sources of information on the textile trade at this time are the Muscovite and Siberian customs records, the official exchanges between the Khanates and the Tsar, and the reports of the few Western travelers to visit Central Asia. One of the earliest European visitors was Anthony Jenkinson, who spent two months of 1558 in Bukhara as an agent of the Muscovy Company.[60] Although from Jenkinson's account he was not impressed by the quality of the material found in the bazaar, Russian records show that there were substantial commercial activities centered in Bukhara during the seventeenth century.

FABRICS IN THE TEXTILE TRADE Fabric, furs, precious stones and rhubarb were the essentials of the caravan trade. The customs records list names that have been used in Russia for Central Asian textiles over several centuries: *kirbas, kamka* (related to *kimkha*) and *zenden.*[61] Caftans, Bukharan sashes and other items of finished clothing were popular in Muscovy, where an Asian style of dress was still in vogue. A ruler of Khwarazm (the region situated just northeast of the Caspian, now part of present-day Turkmenistan) bartered three horses and three *azyam'* satin or damask robes for a Muscovite slave.[62] Carpets also traveled the caravan route; a valuable Bukharan rug "with a green fringe" was sent by Shah Abbas of Persia to the Russian Tsar in 1590.[63] The trade in luxury goods often took place directly between rulers. Stripped of diplomatic niceties, these embassies were really trading missions.

... the bazaars, or marketplaces, have been stately buildings, but are now the greatest part of them in ruins...

The English merchant George Thompson on Bukhara, in 1740[59]

A selection of fabrics, many from these official exchanges and dating from the fifteenth to the seventeenth centuries, is preserved in the Oruzhenaya Palata in Moscow. The Oruzhenaya velvets include materials from at least ten countries, among them a seventeenth-century ikat saddle-cover from Iran, but none of the velvets appears to be from Central Asia.[64] The residual use of Persian and Bukharan terms for fabrics from the Oruzhenaya Palata that were not of Central Asian origin may demonstrate the status of Central Asian cloth in previous centuries.[65] Sayora Mahkamova has suggested a parallel between the Russian *obyar* and the Central Asian *'abr*, which means both "cloud" and "ikat".[66] The term *obyar* (probably from the Persian *abdar*, "watered") was applied in the Oruzhenaya records to both Eastern and Western fabrics with different technical structures.[67]

If there is any evidence of a continuing ikat weaving tradition in Central Asia prior to the nineteenth-century production, then that evidence is most likely to be found in the references to *dara'i* and *alacha*. Russian records of the seventeenth and eighteenth centuries indicate that *dorogi*, from the Persian *dara'i*, was a valuable material, brought by the Bukharan caravans in small quantities for a limited, luxury market. In some instances *dara'i* or *dorogi* may have been ikat.[68] *Dara'i* was made in Turkey and Iran as well as in Bukhara. Bukharan *dara'i* is described as a silk or cotton/silk mix woven in stripes – sometimes with a checked or floral pattern.[69]

The name *alacha* was very widespread, and applied to cloth from Persia, India, Bukhara and Khiva. Bukharan *alacha* was described by a Russian envoy in 1669 as a "strong fabric with mottled appearance made of different colored threads and a mixture of fibers".[70] *Alacha* was woven either in cotton or in a cotton/silk blend, and was always striped. Early nineteenth-century Central Asian part-silk *alacha* sometimes included sections of ikat-dyed warp, but this fabric was replaced by a similar cloth called *bekasam* in the mid-nineteenth century, when the term *alacha* was used to refer to a striped cloth of pure cotton. An *alacha*

from Kashan in Persia was called *abri*, *abrej* or *abrash* in seventeenth-century Russian documents, and included sections of ikat-dyed warp.[71] Although the ikat technique was sometimes used to apply pattern to sections of the warp, none of these early fabrics resembles the brilliantly patterned *adras* ikat silks of the nineteenth century. The majority of the textiles traded from Central Asia were utility fabrics, not luxury goods.[72] In an eighteenth-century account, Bukhara and Khiva are described as exporters of coarse printed cloth of "the poorest quality".[73]

Central Asian commerce reached its nadir in the eighteenth century. Bukhara, once an important center of international trade, was cut off from its neighbors. Religious and political conflicts limited travel through Iran and Russia both for Central Asian merchants and for Muslim travelers on pilgrimage to Mecca.[74] China also attempted to reduce the number of Central Asian caravans entering its borders.

Constant internal warfare made Central Asia dangerous and unstable. The few European travelers who were brave enough to enter the Khanates have left a bleak picture of the time. The envoy Florio Beneveni was sent by Peter the Great in 1718 to investigate the possibility of trade with Bukhara. He found the Khanate in a state of turmoil; travelers were harassed by gangs of thieves on the roads and Bukhara's impotent ruler lived in fear of powerful Uzbek tribal leaders. Beneveni found no products from Iran or India, and only a "modest turnover" of English and Russian goods.[75] The English merchant George Thompson visited Khiva and Bukhara in 1746.[76] He was frightened by the slave-trading nomads of the deserts and found the bazaars of Bukhara and Khiva disappointing and their products plebeian. A near total breakdown of public security outside the walls of the towns made the transportation of merchandise very difficult. Only the Persian trade was worthy of note. Iran supplied velvets, silk and woolen cloth, and indigo and cochineal dyes to the Khanates.[77]

The vicissitudes of the seventeenth and eighteenth centuries left Central Asia an impoverished backwater of the Islamic world. No great empire would emerge during the nineteenth century, but instead a number of tiny kingdoms with barely the strength to hold their borders. Lacking strong commercial and cultural ties with either the Far East or the West, Central Asia would look inward, and discover an entirely new art founded on ancient traditions. The weaving arts held pride of place in traditional Islamic society. To the conservative elite of nineteenth-century Central Asia, textiles would appear the ideal medium for a popular art. The entrepreneurial character of the inhabitants of the Khanates allowed the development of a textile tradition sustained by popular demand, and only indirectly supported by the wealth of the court.

Central Asia's geographic position on the edge of the steppes placed her in constant contact with both nomadic tribes and the urbanized, sedentary society of Iran. The arts were enriched by each wave of immigrants, revived after every conquest. Throughout history Central Asia had depended upon trade, a trade based on the production and transmission of textiles.

The scant archeological and literary remains make it impossible to trace with any accuracy the history of ikat weaving on the Central Asian steppes. Its appearance was sporadic, its level of production never sufficient to prompt early Islamic sources, otherwise so rich in detail, to comment. The many centuries of trade in textiles provided the framework and support for the re-invention of ikat, the last of the great urban arts of Central Asia.

8 WALL-HANGING
mid-19th century
82" × 52" (209 × 131cm)
4.5 panels
warp-faced plain weave
The surrounding element of the repeating palmette has grown into a peacock's tail or crown.

THE CULTURAL BACKGROUND

It was a most curious army, men in every kind of uniform, some on foot, some on horses, camels or donkeys, often several on one animal, and as they were on the march, of course keeping no order... They had with them a band...and displayed many banners, one of them, I remember, being a red teapot on a white ground. Eugene Schuyler describing a Central Asian militia, *Turkestan*, 1877[1]

Though this saline clay, upon which hardly any wild plants can thrive, is the highest degree unfruitful, yet Bucharia is a large and beautiful garden, where all the fruits of France and Spain come to perfection.

Dr Eversmann and P.L. Jakovlew, on Bukhara in 1820[2]

THE ESTABLISHMENT OF THE KHANATES At the turn of the fifteenth century Timur Leng, known in the West as Tamerlane, ruled in Central Asia. In Timur's time Bukhara and Samarkand were great centers of culture and intellectual activity. The cities' libraries were among the world's richest. Astronomy and mathematics were honored sciences. Artists and architects vied with colleagues from throughout the Muslim world to paint the most exquisite miniatures and construct the grandest edifices yet built. Merchants, travelers and adventurers were drawn to the oases from around the world.

When Timur died in 1405, his successors made their capitals elsewhere, and the glow of Central Asia began to fade. The far reaches of Timur's empire, which stretched from Kashmir to the plains of Anatolia, were relinquished to his former vassals. After the death of his son, Shah Rukh, even the center became vulnerable. The far smaller Shaibanid kingdom supplanted the later Timurids in 1500, taking both Bukhara and Samarkand. The Shaibanids were succeeded in turn by the Janids a century later. Although the Shaibanids and the Janids were nominally rulers of southern Central Asia and northern Afghanistan,

7

7. The Bibi Khanum *medresse*, Samarkand. Photo: N.P. Petrovski. Third quarter 19th century. (Private Collection.)

the independent Khanates of Khiva and Kokand were established during their reign. The last Janid ruler was deposed by his vizier, who established the Mangit dynasty in Bukhara in 1785.

In the two centuries preceding the establishment of the Emirate of Bukhara by the Mangits, matters had gone from bad to worse. The toughest blows to Central Asian trade had come from far outside the region's borders. The discovery of silver in the Americas radically altered the economic balance within the Old World. The Islamic kingdoms, which had held the greater part of the world's precious metals, found their currencies devalued on the international market. The wealth of Spain and Portugal enriched the coffers of much of Western Europe, and the East in turn grew poor. The seventeenth and eighteenth centuries saw a much diminished and often disrupted trade across the deserts. The roads grew less and less reliable as bands of marauding Turkomans attacked caravans with impunity. The influence of feudal lords grew greater as the oasis kingdoms shrank. The bazaars were empty, students abandoned the religious schools, and the great domed mosques cracked and were left unrepaired.

In the late eighteenth and early nineteenth centuries, the inheritors of the fractured Central Asian states took steps to centralize and consolidate their rule. With the end of the Janids, a period of relative stability began between the oasis kingdoms of Bukhara, Khiva and Kokand. Khiva touched on the Aral Sea, its southern and western boundaries dissolving into the Turkoman steppe. Kokand was the easternmost of the Khanates, with the Kazakh steppe to the north, China across the mountains to the east, and the fertile Ferghana Valley at its center. The Emirate of Bukhara reached north to the Kara Qum desert, but its cities lay between the Amu and the Syr Darya rivers, at the southern center of the oases, and included Samarkand, Karshi, Hissar and Shakhrisabs.

While the borders of these states remained in flux throughout the nineteenth century, general areas of influence were recognized; the same troublesome areas were disputed again and again. Local commerce with the adjoining countries of Iran, Afghanistan and China became somewhat more secure. Despite Russia's sporadic wars with the Kirgiz and Kazakh of the northern steppe, Bukharan caravans continued to make the journey to Orenburg and the Urals, and to Siberia.

Political and economic organization within the oasis towns began to reflect their new position as peripheral states within the Islamic world. The little kingdoms looked inward, to an intensive agriculture, rather than outward to international trade. In the nineteenth century, the most precious commodity within the Khanates was land. Agricultural land was the source of the greatest revenue and in short supply, as throughout the century greater numbers of Uzbeks abandoned nomadism.

The same Turkomans who disrupted the caravan trade brought large numbers of Persian slaves across the deserts to work the fields.[3] Skilled workers among the captives remained in the towns, and helped to stimulate production within the craft industries. The busy oasis towns attracted artisans from the borders of the steppe, and local industry revived.

The most economically active of the Central Asian kingdoms was Bukhara, the stronghold of the Mangit dynasty. In the early decades of their rule, many crafts – pottery, metal-smithing, leather-working and weaving – regained their strength. The Bukharan Emirs regarded their capital as eminent among the cities of Central Asia. More than any others they encouraged the traditional arts, and most fiercely resisted change. Bukhara became the center of Central Asian silk-weaving in the early part of the nineteenth century, when the art of ikat weaving reached its highest development.

Bukhara was a local market center for the hinterlands, and the major supplier of wholesale goods to the entire Emirate. It was also the entrepot for goods from all over Central Asia intended for foreign destinations, and the most cosmopolitan of the Central Asian kingdoms. The wealth that the nineteenth-century economic boom brought to the Emirate made a flowering of the arts possible. But the court that it supported, the luxury goods that the artisans made, the books and poetry that were written, all looked back to an idealized age of Islam. There was no desire to seek out new industry, to mechanize, modernize, or explore new ideas. The world was kept at bay.

THE OASIS CITY OF BUKHARA The barren deserts that surrounded the oases isolated the Khanates from the world beyond. Reaching the Khanates from anywhere outside Central Asia was very difficult. There was no set route, no safest road, but many possible ones, all dangerous. The Qizil Qum desert to the north, and the Kara Qum to the south supported sparse vegetation only briefly, in the spring, and much of the available water was salt or sulfurous. The leader of each caravan that crossed the desert to reach the oases had to decide whether to hazard a journey on the route with the best wells but the most robbers, or to take the chance of dying of thirst on a path less likely to be frequented. It could take months to gather sufficient numbers of merchants to form a caravan, and mercenaries had to be engaged to protect the travelers and their goods. Jewish traders faced additional risks, as many refused to travel on Saturdays, and had to hire special guards to protect them if they lagged behind, or bribe the chief of the cavalcade to call a halt. Even poor pilgrims, who owned nothing of value, risked their lives. The desert raiders made impromptu and sometimes arbitrary decisions between those who qualified as true Muslims, merely to be stripped of their goods and left without transport in the desert, and those who, as heretics or Shi'ite Muslims, were to be dragged off and sold in the Bukhara slave markets.

Even for those who reached Bukhara with trade goods intact, there was no certain welcome. The collection of customs duties and taxes was farmed out by the Emir, the city's ruler. Levies were not set at fixed amounts; the duties varied according to the day and the officer in charge. Still, the sight of the city and the prospect of refuge was probably sufficient to cheer travelers. By the time they approached the oasis, they found a real road beneath their feet. There was pasture on the hills around the city, and goats and sheep grazed on the fringes of the Arab nomad camps. Canals brought water great distances to soak green fields of cotton, wheat and barley.

Close to the city, walled orchards surrounded the town, providing food and serving as parks and pleasure gardens for well-to-do urban families. Travelers arriving from the open steppe stumbled through a maze of tiny paths around these gardens and open watercourses to reach the gates of the city. Bukhara's enormous and irregular walls of stone and brick were pierced with gates at the mouths of the caravan roads. The narrow streets within could barely accommodate those who tried to enter. Horsemen, camels and carts pushed in toward the market squares. Peddlers and farmers jostled with sheep and goats, trying to keep out of the muddy ditches that ran down the middle of each road. The main streets passed through many of Bukhara's two hundred neighborhoods on their way to the city center. In the nineteenth century, each of these tiny enclaves had a distinctive ethnic makeup, a special craft or a history by which it was defined.

The city of Bukhara had a very diverse population, a complex mix of peoples, languages and religions. Each neighborhood tended to be dominated by one of the many ethnic groups that made up Bukharan society. The two largest of these groups, in linguistic terms, were the Uzbek and the Tadjik. The dominant political group, the Uzbek, formed the court and military elite of the city. Poor Uzbeks worked as farmers, artisans and laborers throughout the Emirate. A number of smaller Uzbek clans were pastoralists, and raised horses, sheep and goats outside the oases. Within the city itself, Uzbeks were widely distributed throughout the crafts, working as potters, metal-smiths, leather-workers and weavers. According to a Russian orientalist of the early nineteenth century, there were at least ninety-seven divisions of the Uzbek, of which twenty-eight lived in the Emirate of Bukhara.[4] Even highly urbanized Uzbeks retained a clan or tribal identity which defined certain shared privileges as well as communal obligations. The Uzbek are

9 WALL-HANGING
Bukhara
first quarter 19th century
47" × 31" (119 × 78cm)
3 panels
warp-faced plain weave
The mottled blue and green background and the saturated color are characteristic of some of the earliest Bukharan ikats.

10 WALL-HANGING
Bukhara
first half 19th century
83" × 48" (211 × 123cm)
5 panels
warp-faced plain weave
A complex interlacing of smaller designs characterizes a group of early Bukharan ikats with saturated mottled blue and green background colours.

not a race, but a politically related congregation of many small Turkic groups that became a major force in western Central Asia around the sixteenth century. While these clans felt a degree of kinship, and shared a history and culture, they did not recognize loyalties beyond the immediate, blood-related, clan group and its temporary allies.

The most ancient inhabitants of the oases were the Tadjiks. In the nineteenth century they were accounted the most numerous group within the city of Bukhara.The Tadjik made up the class of shopkeepers and small traders, clerks and the official bureaucracy. Among the artisans were many Tadjik silk-weavers. Confusion about the ethnic background of many town-dwellers arises from the several names given to Tadjik-speaking residents of Bukhara. Families who had been in the area for hundreds of years are called Old Bukharans in much of early Soviet ethnology. Recent immigrants from small Tadjik farming villages were identified as simply Tadjik. In much of nineteenth-century travel literature, the term *Sart* was applied to anyone who lived in an urban environment and spoke Tadjik. This group included many former Uzbek speakers, as well as families of mixed Uzbek and Tadjik ethnic background.

Nineteenth-century Western travelers collected numerous unflattering remarks and sayings current among each group in respect of the other. According to these stories, the Uzbek held the view that the Tadjik were altogether too clever in money matters, dishonest and deceitful, cowardly and base. The Tadjik view was said to be that the Uzbek were a bunch of bumbling, oafish louts, lazy and belligerent, and needing Tadjik assistance to get anything done. These accounts are sweeping generalizations, of course, and highly suspect, especially in light of the frequent intermarriage between the two groups. Hundreds of years of fluid alliance gave both the Uzbek and Tadjik a very mixed racial background, and a varied appearance. Some Uzbek had purely Mongoloid faces and no beard, others were large-eyed and ruddy-faced, with full beards and luxuriant hair. The Tadjik were taller and fairer than most Uzbeks, and slightly more Iranian in appearance.

A large number of Arabs lived within the borders of the Emirate. Primarily pastoralists, these nomadic and semi-nomadic herders supplied meat, milk and hides to the oases. According to nineteenth-century travelers and early Russian writers, the nomads were not literate, but retained some knowledge of spoken Arabic centuries after all contact had been lost with their homeland. The Central Asian Arabs were tall, dark, handsome, and had a reputation for scrupulous honesty.

The Turkoman, who inhabited the desert and steppe outside the boundaries of the oases, had a less savory reputation. Nomadic pastoralists throughout most of the nineteenth century, they retained strong tribal and clan identities, and valued their independence more than any other inhabitants of the Emirate. Aside from raising large flocks of sheep, the Turkomans made their living by kidnapping Persians for the slave trade, robbing caravans, serving as mercenaries for the oasis rulers, and breeding extremely hardy horses, which they trained to serve them as indispensable tools in the pursuit of their other occupations.

Kazakh and Kirgiz nomads, also of Turkic background, were primarily pastoralists, and made long-range migrations through the mountains and across the northern steppes. They also supplied meat and other animal products to Bukhara, and acted as escort to caravans on the journey to Russia and Siberia, but unlike the Turkoman, neither group came into close cultural contact with the southern oasis towns.

Other ethnic groups included the Persian-speaking *Irani*. The term *Irani* had a pejorative sense because it referred to persons who were slaves or the descendants of slaves, as well as to voluntary immigrants from Iran who were members of the minority Shi'a sect.[6] There were also immigrants from Merv, many of whom were artisans, among the Irani. Initially, most Irani worked in agriculture. By the end of the nineteenth century the Irani were found in large numbers in the silk industry, particularly as weavers of delicate all-silk fabrics.[7] Many also served in the military, presumably because their loyalty was to the individual person of the Emir, and not to a larger clan. In the 1840s, the major part of the Emir's personal army was made up of Irani, both freedmen and immigrants from Merv.

The Jews and the Chala Muslims formed special categories within society. The Jewish community in Bukhara dated back at least to the fourteenth century, but its size and vigor varied according to the disposition of each succeeding ruler, and the degree to which neighboring Jewish communities in Iran and Afghanistan were persecuted. A harsh and intolerant ruler in Bukhara would encourage emigration to Herat or Kabul. After a massacre in Meshed, the Meshedi community that survived might move to Bukhara. The Chala were nominally Muslim, former Jews who had been forced to convert to Islam, sometimes becoming true Muslims, but more often continuing to practice the Jewish religion in secret.

In Bukhara, Jews managed the market in dyestuffs, importing dyes and medicine from outside the Emirate, and acting as wholesale distributors to other cities in Central Asia. In the latter part of the nineteenth century, Jews also became major wholesalers in cloth, exporting silks to Russia, and importing factory-made cottons in return. By the second half of the nineteenth century there was also a sizable Jewish population in Samarkand, and smaller communities could be found in many of the towns of the Khanates. Jews worked in traditional occupations: as traders, money-lenders and dyers.

Throughout most of the nineteenth century, while each ethnic group in Bukhara maintained a separate character, there was a general recognition of the useful contributions of each group to the community as a whole. People's identity remained fixed, but cultural borrowings – shared festivals, costumes, music and art – were common. In the Soviet period, ethnically based terms became politically unpopular, and a practical encumbrance. If one lived in Uzbekistan, one ought to be an Uzbek, in Tadjikistan, a Tadjik. Ethnic, linguistic and religious differences disappeared, at least officially, in a merging of the "Great Soviet People".

The neighborhood got its name from a holy relic... a large stone that had supposedly been pulled from the cistern. It was believed to "unloose the tongue" and cure speech defects. So children being sent off to school were brought here to lick the stone... adults came to lick the stone before appearing in court.

O.A. Sukhareva, on the Bukharan neighborhood of Hauzi Lesak[5]

THE MARKETS AND PUBLIC ENTERTAINMENTS Aside from the dominant ethnic group in a neighborhood, the craft practiced along its main street often gave each neighborhood a special character. The borders of a neighborhood were defined by the high back walls of its houses, and the street was its center. The inner city was a warren of tightly packed one- and two-story residences with courtyards in front and sealed walls behind. In the less secure times of the seventeenth and eighteenth centuries, the neighborhood could be closed off by shutting the entrance to the main street.

In the nineteenth century, the neighborhoods had an active commercial life. In many, the main street was lined with small shuttered shopfronts with a mud-brick ledge or wooden counter extending from the interior. There were no sidewalks, so the customer stood in the

11 WALL-HANGING
Bukhara
mid- to third quarter 19th century
85" × 70" (216 × 178cm)
6 panels
warp-faced plain weave
The repeating diamond shapes are closely related to those in a group of tent-bags woven by the Ersari Turkomans.

street or sat on the shop's ledge to inspect the merchandise. Many goods were made to order, sometimes while the customer waited. Most workshops were very small, only five to ten feet square. The articles that were produced in a neighborhood were often sold there; each local bazaar supplied a particular commodity. Prices were not fixed, and the best bargain was got by inquiring up and down the street for the cheapest wares.

Shoppers also headed for the city center to find the goods brought from outside the Emirate. Here were neighborhoods named after caravanserais: Kofar Rabot, caravanserai of the camphor traders, or Char Caravanserai, four caravanserais, where Afghan merchants as well as traders from Iran and Merv congregated. Caravanserais were also the residences of Indian money-lenders, non-Muslims who could offer commercial and personal loans at interest. For the money-lenders, in perpetual fear of angry and insolvent debtors, they were safe havens. For the traders, the caravanserais served as emporia for cotton cloth, dyestuffs and drugs. Other neighborhoods housed open-air markets to which nomads brought livestock, hides and animal products from the

8

8. Corridor of the Shah i Zindah complex, leading to the *mazar* of Hazret Shah-a Kusam ibn Abbas. Samarkand. Photo: N.P. Petrovski. 19th century. (Private Collection.)

steppe. In Alokabandon, Kirgiz women made felts in the heart of the marketplace, beating and rolling the wool in rush mats.

Many nineteenth-century Western travelers were fascinated by the slave markets, and the authorities were equally consumed by a desire to conceal them. When European visitors did managed to locate the caravanserais of the slave dealers they found only a few pitiful children and bedraggled old men, as the healthy men and women were quickly bought up on arrival. Most slaves were captured in raids on isolated villages and fields near the Persian border, and dragged across the desert to the Khanates where they raised the equivalent of five pounds sterling a head.[8] A few slaves were Russians, soldiers captured in battle by the Kazakhs, or traders detained by hostile tribes. The oasis officials recognized that slave trading was a sore point in their relations with neighboring countries, and either denied the existence of the market, or excused slavery as a fate less onerous than being held by the Turkoman.

The bazaars were the center of social life for urban men. In the heart of Bukhara, near the Arg, the citadel of the Emir, were located a dozen or more enormous and finely decorated fifteenth and sixteenth-century buildings housing mosques and *medresses*, religious schools. Large markets were also close by. There were *hauzes*, manmade pools that held the local water supply, in the plazas in front of the mosques. The pools were surrounded by tea houses, which held perpetually bubbling samovars. Customers brought their own tea in little bags hung on their belts, and were supplied with hot water and a teapot.

Entertainments were few in nineteenth-century Bukhara. It was common for the members of a craft guild to make a tea house their meeting place. The men conversed, smoked tobacco from hookahs passed from hand to hand, and drank copious amounts of *chai*. Patrons often pooled their funds to hire dancing boys, youths with long hair who dressed in the brilliant silks worn by women. A tambour or clapped hands provided rhythm for the dance, and the boys stamped, gestured and spun in a parody of feminine motion.

In the bazaars, crowds gathered to watch troops of players and acrobats. Performances began with beating drums and blasts on ten-foot-long horns. Playlets and farce were followed by stunts and comic wrestling matches. The actors wore robes of rags and tinsel, the clowns giant dunce caps and donkey's ears. Gathered at the many shrines in Bukhara were mendicants and pilgrims, singing with their begging bowls in hand. And wandering everywhere, for no one dared stop a man touched by God, were dervishes, who muttered prayers and threatened passers-by with their wooden staffs.

The cost of the harem, as far as dress, board and other necessaries are concerned, is very small. The ladies make not only their own clothes, but even the garments of the emir, who is known to be a strict economist, and to exercise severe control over everything.

The traveler Arminius Vambery on the harem of the Bukharan Emir, 1865 [10]

THE PALACE OF THE BUKHARAN EMIR The Arg of the Emir loomed over the center of the town, above the noise and bustle of the streets. It was built on an eminence that overlooked the holy shrine of Chashma Ayub, Job's Well. Behind its fortifications, the Arg was an undistinguished collection of buildings: administrative offices, reception rooms, storehouses, a mosque and a private residence for the Emir and his family.

Of the five Bukharan Emirs who ruled between 1800 and 1920, only the first three held actual power. The greatest pomp and ceremony were found in the courts of the last, and least powerful, of the Bukharan rulers. Life at the Arg was not particularly luxurious in the early part of the nineteenth century. Politics and administration occupied the first Emirs of the Mangit dynasty. Several early Emirs did serious work in theological studies, and their patronage made Bukhara once again eminent in religious scholarship. Within the relatively opulent setting of the court, these early Emirs affected a simple dress and ascetic lifestyle in keeping with their scholarly interests, although they did share in the general preoccupation with fine horses, and played with ordinary Uzbeks at *buzkashi*, a traditional Central Asian game. Certainly, no one was better mounted than the Emir in this violent precursor to polo, a game in which participants instead of using a mallet and ball would bend down at full gallop to grab hold of a decapitated goat.[9]

The Emirs ate and drank much the same food as their subjects, and slept on the same kind of bed. Cuckoo clocks, Chinese porcelains and Belgian carpets decorated the most intimate apartments, and sometimes champagne was served under the guise of lemonade, but in essence the surroundings of the court were not very different from that of a well-to-do merchant's home. In the latter part of the nineteenth century, the most striking aspects of Central Asian court life were its costumes, and the sumptuous textiles that decorated the walls and floors. Even in the refined setting of the court, many activities took place on the floor. Meals were served on cloths laid directly upon carpets, and bolsters and pillows served as chairs for guests. Curtains were hung at the interior doors, and cloth panels made temporary walls to screen and divide indoor rooms. In one of the largest open spaces, the Emir held public audience on a silk-canopied, carpeted dais.

Much of the decor of the palaces was in the form of wall-paintings. Plaster moldings were applied to walls and ceilings, and the rooms were painted in bright geometric and floral patterns. Each large wall was divided into many smaller rectangles, and the wall-paintings echoed the shape, and sometimes the pattern, of the textile hangings.

The textile items most valued by the Emir and his court are of limited interest today. The rarest and most prestigious fabrics were those imported from Europe and Turkey, and a common French velvet was held in greater esteem than the hand-finished products of the Khanates. Likewise, the heavy, gold-embroidered cloth worn by the highest ranking officials had greater intrinsic value, but less artistic merit than the ikat silks worn by the middle rank. A court factory made the gold-embroidered cloth for the use of the Emir and his officials. This gold work was the only kind of embroidery done by men in the early part of the nineteenth century, for women's hands were thought to tarnish the gold.[12] Large panel pieces were made to decorate the walls and cover the limited furnishings of the reception rooms, and robes were decorated with garlands and borders of embroidery work. A vast store of elaborately decorated clothing and saddlecloths from the court factory was kept at the Arg, to be presented as gifts to visitors and given in recognition of services performed for the court.

Not all the Emir's guests lived in luxury. Another hill, close by, held the most notorious of Central Asia's dungeons, and the infamous Black Pit.[13] Punishment was harsh: blinding and the severing of limbs were common penalties for even minor crimes. At times the prisoner was paraded through the streets below, before the executioner came suddenly up from behind, and slit his throat.

The Emirate had no standing army, only generals and officers drawn from members of the court. On special occasions, dire emergencies, or when the Emir desired to make a good impression, weapons were distributed to the general population. The lack of a standing army made the rulers reliant on the sometimes fugitive loyalties of their outside administrators. The feudal aristocracy and village chiefs supplied troops when needed, and the Turkoman raiders temporarily became legitimate mercenaries. Special taxes were imposed on the population to pay for campaigns, so that the strongest and most determined Emirs earned the harshest reputation among their subjects.

We Turkomans do not mind who governs those countries of Bukhara and Khiva; whether Behadur Khan, or England, or Russia; if we only get khelats [robes of honor] *and tillahs, i.e. ducats.*

Rev. Joseph Wolff, quoting the Turkoman chiefs at Merv, 1843–45[11]

THE COLLAPSE OF THE KHANATES The blossoming of the arts within Central Asia could not be sustained under pressure from the forces outside it. It was not only that handmade crafts were supplanted by cheaper imports, or that modern notions of commerce, industry or education were undermining traditional concerns. The Khanates themselves were soon to disappear.

Nineteenth-century Central Asia coveted obscurity, but was denied it. Together with Afghanistan, the oasis kingdoms became the unwilling focus of the Great Game played out between Russia and the British empire. The tacit acknowledgement of each other's sphere of interest, and of the need for buffer states, was never seriously questioned by either Britain or Russia. The Game in Central Asia was primarily about minor issues of strategic advantage. The Russians had the more practical aims. Russia's textile industry was enormously important,

12 WALL-HANGING
third quarter 19th century
77" × 54" (197 × 138cm)
5 panels
warp-faced plain weave
This simple, colorful ikat with roundels floating on a striped pattern is a rare, early version of a type related to the Samarkand style.

and was threatened by the distance from her sources of supply in Egypt and the United States. Soon after mid-century, Russian administrators were spurred to action by influential manufacturers, who needed a secure supply of cotton from Central Asia. In addition, the Khanates were not just a new market for Russian finished goods, they were the only market which Russia could hope to control.

Russian frontier posts were established in a chain across the Kazakh and Kirgiz steppe-lands to the north by the middle of the nineteenth century. After several decisive defeats, all that was left of the Kokand Khanate in 1865 was its center, the Ferghana Valley. The most capable of the Russian commanders moved swiftly to consolidate their gains. They refused to relinquish territory and established administrative networks, often without waiting for official consent to arrive from St Petersburg. The building of railroads and post roads followed immediately, and military expansion continued under the guise of the defense of Russia's commercial interests.

Organized resistance to Russian occupation came far too late. Internal rivalries and continual strife between the various factions within Central Asia prevented the Khans from any real understanding of the political or economic bases for foreign interest. The Khanates were not nation states, but petty kingdoms, constantly engaged in minor wars. Instead of joining forces to push back the Russians, Central Asia's rulers at first regarded Russian incursions against their neighbors as opportunities for their own expansion. Periodic uprisings led by Kazakh, Kirgiz and Turkoman nomads were passionate, hard fought, and in the end, disastrous failures. Unlike their fluid alliances with the Central Asian states, once the tribes submitted to Russia, it was very difficult for them to back out.

In 1873, the Russians justified entry into Khiva: the Khivan Khan remained on the throne, but without the power to govern. By 1875 the Kokand Khanate to the east had completely collapsed. Although the Emirate of Bukhara remained theoretically intact, by the end of the 1870s Russia controlled all her foreign and many of her domestic affairs through treaty arrangements. Thoughtful decisions on administrative boundaries by the Russians broke up traditional ethnic and political alignments and severely weakened resistance movements.

The period just after the collapse of the Tsarist government offered a brief opportunity for independence for Central Asia. In the cities, the Islamic hierarchy, entrepreneurs, White Russians and students argued Central Asia's future. In the smaller communities and on the steppe, a merging of Enver Pasha's pan-Turkists and Muslim traditionalists into renegade military bands had some success up to the 1930s, especially in the most fractious and disputed areas. But nomad horse breeders and urban intellectuals had little in common, and disunity made them easy prey for the Bolshevik central authorities.

The interests of the Soviets lay in converting the former Khanates into contributors and suppliers to the national economy. Agricultural development was focused entirely on cotton production. Forced collectivization dealt a heavy blow to pastoralism, which disappeared entirely in many areas. The many Central Asian identities were to be subsumed within the national consciousness of the Soviet people. Traditional customs remained within family life, but education and upward mobility within Soviet society depended upon assimilation into the dominant Russian culture. The medieval life of the Khanates, preserved by distance, ignorance and, at times, by a dogged rejection of the modern world, was at an end.

9

9. The Khan of Kokand, Seyid Mohammad Khudayar Khan, wearing an ikat robe. *Turkestanskii al'bom*, 1871–72. (Archives of the State Museum of History, Tashkent.)

13 WALL-HANGING
Bukhara
first half 19th century
78" × 58" (198 × 147cm)
5 panels
warp-faced plain weave
This exceptionally detailed, striped design was created by dividing the patterned warp yarns twice along the vertical axis before placing them on the loom. It is likely that the two sets of warps were tied and dyed at the same time, as their colors are identical.

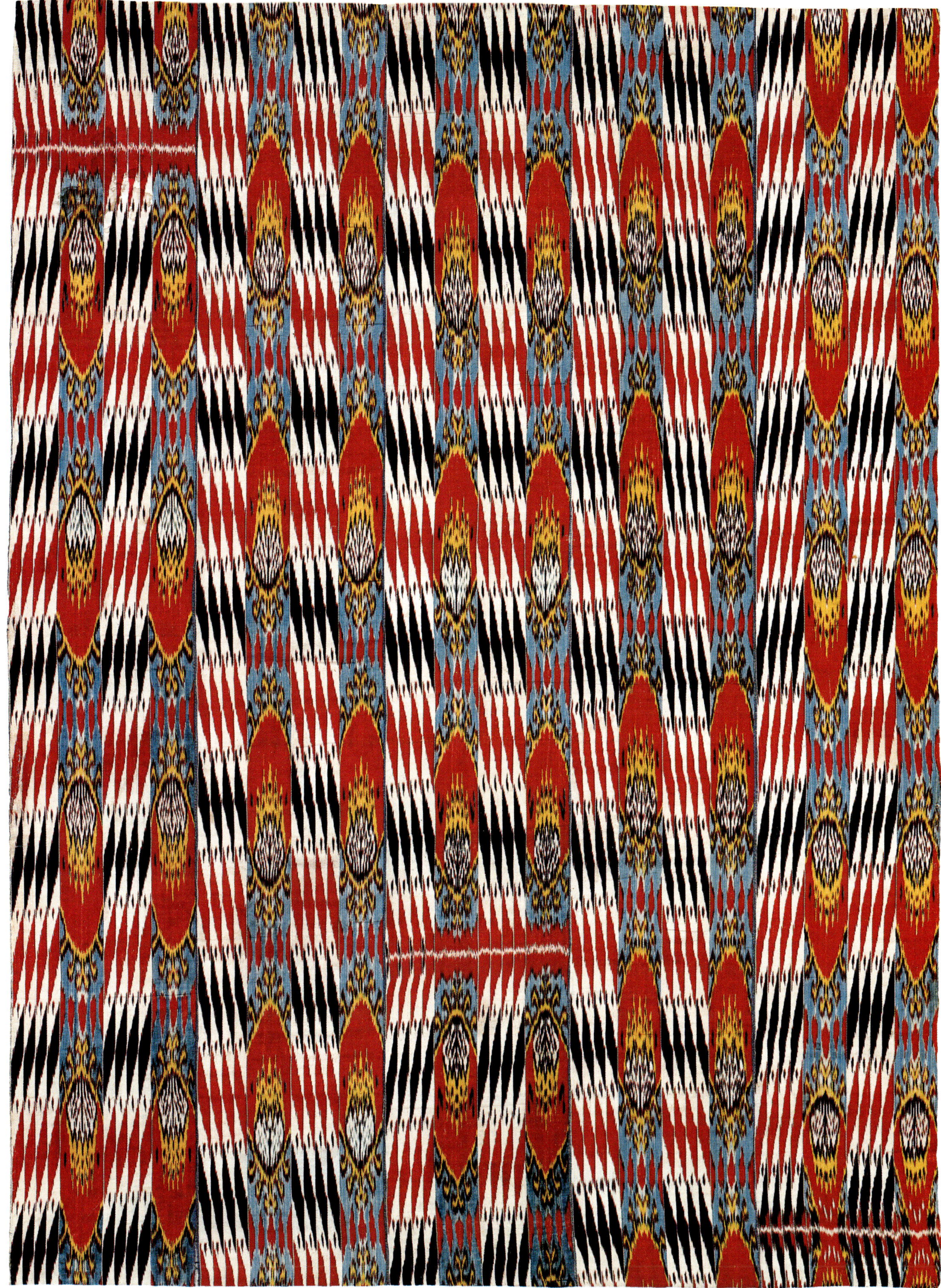

3

WEAVERS' WORKSHOPS & GUILDS

Two looms on which silk is woven, friend! The bride winds the yellow threads. Her mother-in-law grumbles ceaselessly; I am wasting away at the loom… Measure by measure the cloth is woven. Sweat drips from my brow. Tell me… Did my lover forget me? *Tara gosgusi* (Song of the Weaver), Turkmenistan[1]

Paradoxically, one of the more obscure periods in the history of Central Asia is a time close to our own, the late eighteenth and early nineteenth centuries. Detailed information about the silk-weaving industry in Central Asia is available only for the latter part of the nineteenth century. It is not surprising, therefore, that no one knows exactly how, or why, or even where the weaving of *adras* silk ikat began. Most of the evidence suggests that *adras* weaving began only in the first quarter of the nineteenth century, and that the city of Bukhara was the initial site for the development of ikat weaving as a high art.

The population of Bukhara comprehended the ethnic diversity of the whole of southern Central Asia. Every linguistic and tribal group in the Khanates, indigenous or migrant, was well represented. Every kind of textile craftsman could be found there: silk reelers, warpers, weavers and most especially dyers, skilled in the application of the entire range of available natural colors. All the raw materials necessary for the production of ikats – silk, fine cotton and natural dyestuffs – were readily available. There was a court and an upper class eager and willing to wear the most exotic and gorgeous fabrics that could be found, and Bukhara's vital economy ensured that there was plenty of money to pay for them.

10

10. Robe seller. Most clothing was sewn at home by urban dwellers, but robes were also made in standard sizes and sold off the rack in the bazaar. *Turkestanskii al'bom,* 1871–72. (Navoi Library, Tashkent.)

No other major city in Central Asia could claim all these advantages at this time. In the early part of the nineteenth century Samarkand had not yet recovered from the economic decay and isolation of the previous century; only during the latter part of the nineteenth century would it become an important commercial center and active silk producer. The city of Marghilan, in the Ferghana Valley, lay far to the east of Bukhara. This rich agricultural area of the Kokand Khanate was to become the center of commercial silk-weaving by the turn of the twentieth century, but writers in the early nineteenth century did not consider it a serious rival to the Bukharan silk industry. The Ferghana Valley silk-weaving boom came about much later, as a result of efforts to promote and organize the industry by Russian and Central Asian entrepreneurs following the Russian conquest. In addition, Ferghana's weaving labor force at the turn of the century was largely made up of freedmen and the descendants of slaves who had worked in the valley's fields until emancipation in the 1870s.

By virtue of its economic strength, the availability of skilled craftsmen and its inhabitants' decided taste for rich and colorful fabrics, Bukhara must have been the original setting for the renaissance of silk-weaving in the Khanates. One theory accounting for Bukhara's pre-eminence in weaving is mentioned by several nineteenth-century Western travelers. There are said to have been many silk-weavers among the skilled craftsmen forced to emigrate from Merv to Bukhara in 1785 after that city was captured by the first ruler of the Mangit dynasty. This movement of craftsmen certainly accelerated production in many branches of silk-weaving, but it is not known if the ikat technique was practiced in Merv. In fact, Merv craftsmen were only one of many groups of skilled workers who came from all over Central Asia to the Khanate of Bukhara in the late eighteenth and early nineteenth centuries. It seems most likely that it was the very mixture of nationalities, skills and tastes that gave birth to the sumptuous and glittering ikat silks.

THE GUILD STRUCTURE Because Bukhara was the last of the Khanates to fall under Russian control, many craft institutions within the city remained unaffected by outside influences for some time after Western travelers and orientalists began to arrive in Central Asia. As a result, there is substantial evidence from the third quarter of the nineteenth century to illuminate the traditional structure of the guilds and other weavers' organizations.

The weavers' guild performed several functions in all the larger cities of Central Asia. Its officers set the various rules that defined the relationships between masters and hired workers, and in instances of conflict, acted to enforce statutes or to mediate between parties. The guild maintained dormitories for out-of-town or undomiciled weavers and assisted them in finding work. It oversaw the marketing of goods produced by its members, and set prices for wholesale and retail trade. A final, and extremely important part, of the guild officers' duties was to ensure the success of the craftsmen's efforts by supervising the rites and rituals due to the craft's holy patron.

In the sixteenth century, a neighborhood essentially constituted a trading district. The local guild organization and the neighborhood were fairly equivalent. By the nineteenth century, arrangements were much looser. The fact that a neighborhood was named after a craft no longer meant that the craft was the only one practiced in that neighborhood. Especially in the more developed trades, occupations had spilled over neighborhood boundaries. In Bukhara there were 51 neighborhoods occupied by weavers of a variety of textiles, 32 neighborhoods of shoemakers, 30 of jewelry makers, and 15 where blacksmiths congregated.[2] As occupations became scattered, the most enduring elements of the guild/neighborhood relationship were the communal responsibilities for defense, for maintaining the neighborhood infrastructure of streets and watercourses, and for the care of *waqf*[3] property. If a guild dormitory, a *takiya*, was located in a certain neighborhood, the residents of the dormitory were expected to join in family and neighborhood festivals.

No records remain of guild organizations made up specifically of craftsmen who made ikat. With the exception of the craftsmen who marked and tied the warps for ikat dyeing, the skills required for weaving ikat would have been the same as those needed to make other types of silk fabric. It seems most likely that ikat-making craftsmen were allied with the guilds of artisans in closely related weaving occupations. In towns with fewer craftsmen, a range of specialists within the same field would make up a guild. In late nineteenth-century Khodjent and its surrounding villages, most of the textile craftsmen were joined together in only two guilds, based on the craftsman's place of residence.[5] In Bukhara, the weavers' guild was so large that it was divided into four smaller sections for administrative purposes, and other types of textile craftsmen had their own, separate guild organizations.

Guild officers were elected at a meeting of all the craftsmen. The *Baba* represented the interests of the apprentices and the live-in hired workers. He often lived in the guild dormitory, and worked on his own loom there.[6] With his consent, the workers could mount a boycott against an unfair master, and the *Baba* would himself place a lock on the master's door. The *Baba* could also protect any live-in weavers from having to work for a bad master. The *Kaivoni* was the female equivalent of the *Baba*. In some instances she worked with the wives and families of guild members. Other early nineteenth-century craft associations were composed solely of women. The female cotton spinners formed a guild-like organization, maintained holy rites that were practiced during the craft process, and participated in communal festivals. Later, especially in Marghilan, the home weavers of silk fabrics included many women, and the *Kaivoni* of the weavers' guild would have represented their interests. There is little data on the guild-like organizations for women, and in comparison to the guilds for male artisans, their activities were very limited. The *Aksakal* acted as the guild's representative between the weavers and the wholesale purchasers in the marketplace, checking market prices and the quality of the goods for sale. The *Aksakal* is not mentioned in the accounts of guild structure until the latter part of the nineteenth century, when the cult aspects of the guild functions diminished, and the weavers' market position was threatened by imports.

If [the teacher] *should be asked what the winders ought to say when the thread is applied to the reel, he should answer: "They should think of the way to Paradise and should recite the verse 'Direct us to the right road.'" When the pupil regulates the fire he should remember that fire is of hell, which burns people and even stones.*

Eugene Schuyler, from the *risola* (guild rules) of the silk reelers, *Turkestan*, 1877[4]

THE SACRED ASPECTS OF THE CRAFT The *Golib*, who was chosen from among the literate members of the corporation, had the *risola*, the guild rules, in his charge. The *risola* was a sacred history of the origins and development of the craft. It began with the miraculous genesis of the art, and continued with many exhortations to the craftsman to recall an event of religious significance at each stage of the craft process. *Risolas* for metal-craft workers are known from the sixteenth century; the oldest *risolas* of the textile trades that remain belonged to the woodblock printers of cotton textiles, and date to the late eighteenth century.[7] These sacred texts were preserved in writing, but many of the documents used in the latter part of the nineteenth century were not of great antiquity. The *risolas* were often revised, and were adapted to changing circumstances or technical innovations.[8]

The *risolas* of all the crafts are full of miracles, the implication being that the making of an object is itself a sacred activity. Craftsmen were expected to look with awe upon the process of creation, and see the hand of God in every step. Indeed, in some cases the craftsman was required to recite so many verses that his work would have become impossible, had he followed all the promptings of the *risola*.

Actions that would damage the craft were prohibited by the guilds. A closely observed proscription was that no cocoons were unreeled for twenty days in May, during the time the new silkworms were being fed. Lighting a fire under the kettle where the cocoons were heated for unreeling would burn the legs of the silkworms still being bred. Spinners did not spin on Wednesday, the day of holy Bahauddin Naqshband, the Sufi saint "who turns away misfortune", or the afternoon of Thursday, nor on Friday until after the evening prayer, when the spinners prepared

14 WALL-HANGING
probably Bukhara
mid-19th century
77" × 50" (196 × 127cm)
5 panels
warp-faced plain weave
The warp yarns of this ikat appear to have been separated three times before being placed on the loom. Dividing them only once would have produced a single line of repeating red oval shapes; dividing them twice, a double row of red circles. The third division resulted in an elongated striped pattern with four smaller circles across each fabric width.

15 WALL-HANGING
second half 19th century
85" × 64" (216 × 163cm)
4 panels
warp-faced plain weave

all the things they needed for Saturday's work; this was called "tying up Saturday's legs".[9] The spinners needed to begin the work properly, or things would go badly for them in the following week.

All the expertise that a craftsman had was considered a gift from the holy patron. The implements of the trade were also considered holy – burning them was a major sin. A spinner would keep her tools for a very long time, even if she abandoned the trade. The spinning-wheel was laid on its side when not in use, to prevent impish spirits from turning the wheel. The ritual handling of other tools protected the workshop from harm. After a disastrous – or a particularly profitable – week, the workshop master would slaughter a ram, and prepare a dedicatory feast to honor the patron saint. If anything went wrong in the workshop during the week, especially if a tool broke, two candles were lit in the bread oven, and verses were read from the Koran, dedicating the prayers to the protector's spirit.

There were many tales outside the official guild texts that gave a magical context to the evolution of a craft. While not often mentioned in the written *risola*, the Devil, a wily and innovative sprite, was a common feature of oral tales of the crafts. Particularly complicated and technical professions required his assistance. The Soviet ethnographer O.A. Sukhareva refers to a small fee paid to the Devil by the craftsman, but gives no indication of the form or manner of payment.[10] Sufi saints, often clever and unpredictable fellows, also have roles related to technical innovations in the craft histories.

Very ancient holy patrons are credited with the basic inventions of weaving in the oral histories. The founder of all weaving was Shishi Nabi, who sprang from the seed of Adam without the assistance of Eve. The patron Hazrati Burkh, the Drunken Holy Man, is linked to animal-hair weaving in Bukhara, where his image is connected with the totem cult of the mountain goat.[11] Burkh is a much duller and more religious fellow in Khodjent, where his prayers entice angels disguised as doves to help him work faster. The Soviet ethnographer N.O. Tursunov has identified many patrons of specific branches of the textile crafts in Khodjent – the Archangel Michael (silk and muslin weavers), the prophet Job (silk weavers), the Bukharan Sufi saint Bahauddin Naqshband (warp binders), the saint Ali (loom reed binders), the "holy man" Jesus (fabric glazers), and finally, Eve and Bibi Fatima [the prophet Muhammad's daughter Fatima] (spinners).[12]

In the written texts, a biblical, more steady sort of prophet often has the role of originator of the craft. In the *risola* of the silk-weavers, the worms that first spun silk are the same ones that infested and tortured Job. In a tale still current in Bukhara, the silkworms are also responsible for his death.

The Prophet Job was walking in the country in winter, and passed a leafless mulberry tree full of starving silkworms. Job did not want to leave the silkworms to die, but the nearest settlement was far away, the worms were very weak, and he had no way to carry them. So Job lay down beneath the tree and the silkworms climbed on to his body and drank his blood. Then Job walked, with the worms still hanging to him, to the nearest village. When the people saw the worms on his body, they were afraid to come near to assist him, thinking that he had a great sore. So Job walked alone to a mulberry tree in full leaf, and the worms climbed from his body on to the tree, and there Job died.
Interview with Yusuf Sharipov, a student of religion at the shrine of Bahauddin Naqshband in Bokhara, 1995

16 WALL-HANGING
probably Samarkand
mid-19th century
89" × 66" (227 × 169cm)
6 panels
warp-faced plain weave
Red and pink are often juxtaposed in the vibrant early ikats from the Samarkand area.

The *Golib* arranged guild festivals, ritual offerings and other sacramental matters to do with the guild's holy patron. At the end of the nineteenth century the position of the *Golib* was absorbed into the functions of the guild's other officers. The cult activities were no longer as important as the regulatory functions of the guild: the last weavers' guild festival in Samarkand was held at the end of the nineteenth century, whereas other guilds continued to have many cult activities up to the Revolution. Certain trades preserved cult rituals well into the 1950s. It was felt that the establishment of a new craft or profession required the creation of a sacred history and sacramental rites. The rites usually included a gift to the teacher from the former student and the presentation to the new master of a tool representing his trade. A common mechanic's wrench became the sacred symbol of initiation into the profession of motor-car drivers after the Revolution.[13] Without a holy patron and a protocol for doing a job properly, it was not possible for any kind of work to go well.

THE ROLES OF MASTER, WORKER AND APPRENTICE

Weaving workshops tended to be very small in the early part of the nineteenth century; many consisted of only a master and one or two apprentices. A large number of weavers worked independently, often in their own homes. Towards the latter part of the century there was a movement away from cottage work to artels headed by a master craftsman, an *ustad*.[14]

In nineteenth-century Samarkand the masters still worked in the actual production of fabrics, in some cases dyeing the yarn, warping the loom, laying out traditional patterns, and even creating new designs. Gradually, the masters took on more administrative functions, obtaining raw materials for their workers and acting primarily as supervisors. By the end of the century, merchant entrepreneurs who did no weaving themselves became more important than traditional masters, especially in the areas of greater Russian influence.

While twentieth-century reports from Marghilan reflect a significant number of women weavers, particularly among the home workers, almost all nineteenth-century urban ikat weavers were men.[15] Weavers almost always wove only a single type of cloth. When more than one type of fabric was woven by a single weaver, it was an indication that one of the fabrics was a recent introduction.[16]

The actual weavers had a humble role, and certainly received little compensation for their efforts. In the late nineteenth and early twentieth centuries it became common for an artel to have twenty or more craftsmen, called *halfa*. The *halfa* were hired weavers, who received room and board in the house of the master, and were paid on a piecework basis. When a craftsman was given employment in a workshop he usually received a lump sum from the owner. This was considered a debt, to be paid off by the hired hand's work, and the worker was given only a small sum each week for his personal needs. The workshop owner also paid for special expenses, for a wedding, a feast, a funeral or a wake. The artels kept their best workers by offering a bonus, paid in cash or in prepared warps, every six months.

Workers who misbehaved, gambled, got drunk or who did not complete their work either left the trade or entered into a special agreement that began with a ceremony called *maynibazar*, "staying away from the bazaar". A physical boundary was set beyond which the worker might not go, generally the mosque and the graveyard: the worker had permission to pray, and permission to die if he wanted to. If the worker

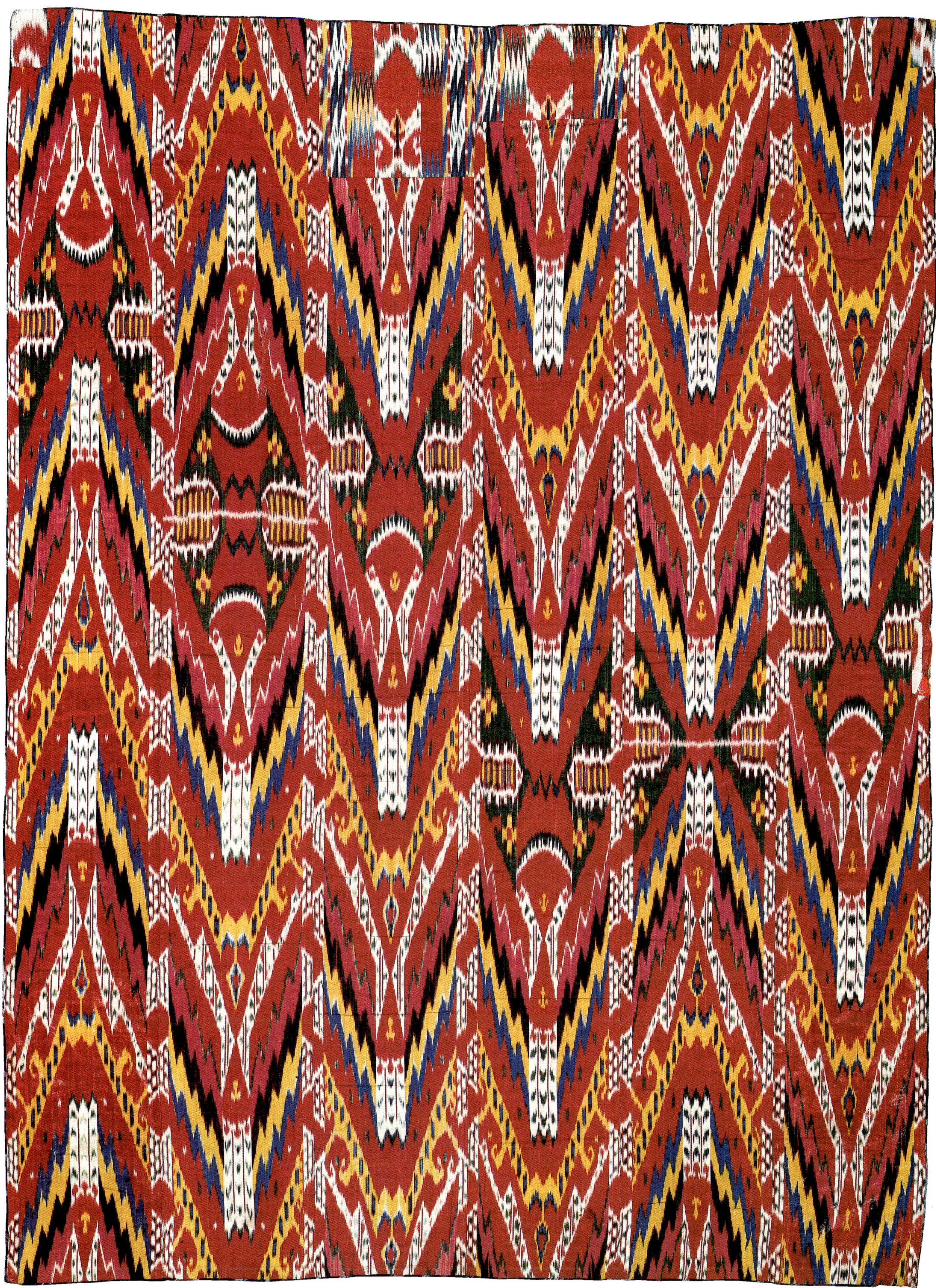

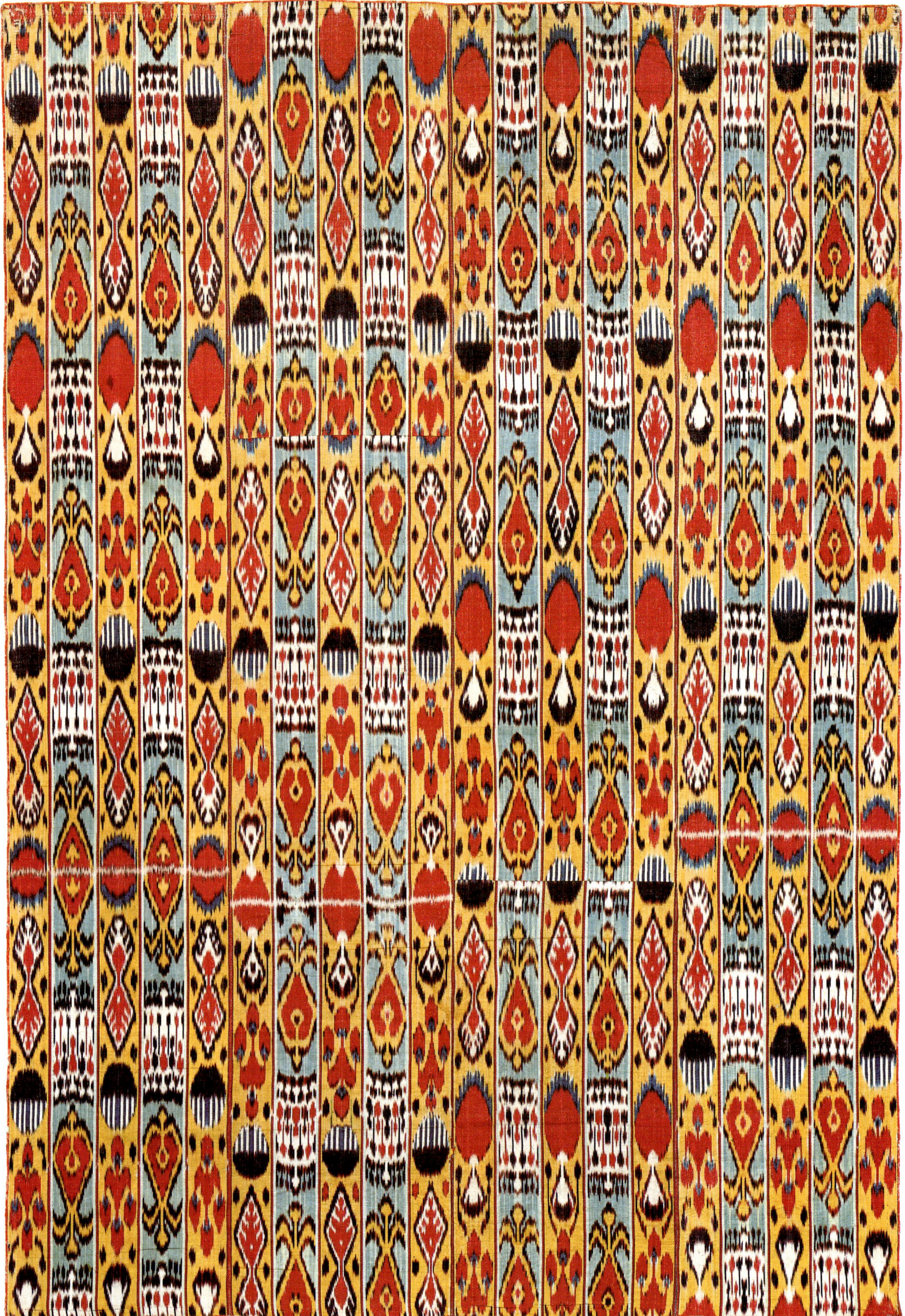

17 WALL-HANGING
mid-19th century
88" × 62" (225 × 158cm)
4 panels
warp-faced plain weave
Sections of the dyed warp have been split and arranged in stripes separated by solid lines of color.

was caught in the bazaar he could be punished: in the early twentieth century that could involve doubling his debt. If he successfully completed this period, his debt would be paid off. Respected officials gathered at the workshop and announced that the punishment was over and that the debt had been met. The hired hand would then be allowed to go off with his friends to the bazaar, hopefully a wiser man. Any worker who tried to escape from his debt would be tried by the guild, and expelled.

Some hired hands did not accept a lump sum at the beginning of work, and were free to come and go as they pleased.[17] Hired hands left workshops because of poor living conditions and bad treatment. Workshops with large numbers of workers built dormitories for them near the master's house, in which conditions varied greatly. Despite the low pay, most weavers preferred to work in larger workshops, where employment was guaranteed all year round.

The patriarchal protection of the master and the guild did not extend to independent weavers, called *harchibaft*, who worked in their own homes and on their own equipment. Independent weavers had no

11

11. Making a silk warp. Silk threads for the warp were wound on a giant wheel. A vertical frame held bobbins of silk thread, and the threads were drawn from the bobbins in a split pattern, forming the shed of the loom. Photo: S.M. Dudin, c. 1900. (Archives of the State Museum of History, Tashkent.)

guarantee of work or consistent pay. Individual craftsmen were often obliged to purchase their raw materials from workshop owners, and in many cases gradually fell into debt. By the close of the nineteenth century, most of these home weavers were attached to a larger workshop. They received prepared warps and weft threads from the workshop owner, and brought their finished materials back to him each week.

Boys from fourteen to twenty years of age could gain entry into the weaver's craft through apprenticeship. The relationship between apprentices and masters was codified within a written agreement.[18] Depending upon the nature of the craft, the apprenticeship lasted one to three years, and in some instances up to ten years were required. Apprentices were fed and housed, but were paid very little, and it was always in the interest of the student to shorten, and the master to delay, the apprenticeship stage. By the end of the nineteenth century, few young men were willing to commit themselves for such a lengthy period of time.

When the apprentice became skilled at some elements of the craft he earned a minimal salary, and when he could weave a standard warp into fabric within 40–50 days he was paid half the salary of a hired hand. After this he could, at least in theory, be initiated into the craft. In order to receive initiation he was required to give a feast, inviting all the officials of the guild and other respected members of the craft. The expenses of putting on the feast often delayed the initiation of apprentices for years. At the feast, the master tied his girdle around the pupil's waist, saying "God is great! From henceforth you are a craftsman!"[19]

18 WALL-HANGING
Bukhara
first half 19th century
80" × 69" (204 × 175cm)
6 panels
warp-faced plain weave
Mixed among the pomegranates descending from stalks are pairs of water jugs, *aftaba* – a flourish to show the designer's skill.

WEAVING AREAS OF BUKHARA Central Asian silk-weavers came from a variety of ethnic backgrounds, but in nineteenth-century Bukhara, at least, there was a preponderance of weavers who considered themselves Tadjik or Farsi, especially among those making all-silk fabrics. Uzbek weavers specialized in half-silk fabrics. According to O.A. Sukhareva, Irani immigrants in Bukhara were found among the weavers of all kinds of silks, including velvets, and the production of plain weave all-silk ikat, and other all-silk fabrics within Samarkand was entirely in the hands of the Irani population.[20] Jews are noted only as weavers of a diaphanous silk fabric called *khalili*.[21]

The town of Bukhara was made up of quarters, sections comprising many individual neighborhoods. The Djuibar quarter was traditionally a weaving center. The quarter only came into being in the late sixteenth century, and was one of the most recent sections of the inner town of Bukhara. In one of the twenty neighborhoods there, all-silk ikat and silk velvet were made by descendants of migrants from Merv, who came to Bukhara between the sixteenth and the eighteenth centuries. Tadjik-speaking Old Bukharans living in another Djuibar neighborhood wove both pure silk and cotton-wefted ikat fabrics. In another was an *abr-bandi*, ikat-tying workshop. Still another had workshops specializing in dyeing in which both Jewish and non-Jewish dyers worked.[22]

The ethnic diversity of the workers involved in the crafts was striking, but in no way remarkable for the Bukharan textile trades at that time. Another typical example of the mixed ethnic background of workers in a single, and relatively simple, textile craft was found in Karkhana, a much older neighborhood than Djuibar, and also a weaving and dyeing center. In Karkhana, Uzbeks made batik designs on finished fabrics, using silk kerchiefs made by Jews. The batiked fabrics were then taken to Tadjik workshops for dyeing in red and yellow colors. Tie-dyed cotton fabrics were taken to Jewish workshops for dyeing in indigo. *Chit* making, cotton stamping with woodblocks, was also practiced by both Tadjik and Uzbek workers.

According to legend, there was a factory, a *karkhana*, located deep underground near a neighborhood mosque, where invisible spirits wove silk fabrics. If a person stood very quietly in the right place he could hear the treadles clacking and the shuttles being passed through the shed. The grave of Yusuf Hamadani, the teacher of 'Abd al-Khaliq Ghijduvani, the founder of the Sufi order of Khwajagan, was located at the main mosque in the Karkhana quarter. Both Sufi holy men were patrons of various branches of the weaving trade. Weavers came to worship at the mosque and brought flat cakes, fried in oil or butter, as offerings.

DYEING AREAS OF BUKHARA In Central Asia, the expression "to go to the Jew" meant to have an article dyed blue. Nineteenth-century Western travelers often presumed that all dyeing was done by Jews, but this was not the case.[23] Non-Jewish neighborhoods in

19 WALL-HANGING
Bukhara
mid-19th century
86" × 57" (220 × 145cm)
5.5 panels
warp-faced plain weave
The warps have been divided twice, then one of the two half sections has been separated and moved more than a foot, as is shown by the distance between the white tie lines that cross, in each instance, only half the finished fabric.

Bukhara had strong associations with ritual aspects of the dyer's trade, and there was an Islamic bias in much of the folklore surrounding the craft, as in the legend of Sheikh Rangrez, who magically altered the color of threads dipped into clear water. Jewish dyeing establishments were also sometimes located in the same neighborhoods as those of Tadjik hot dyers. Poii Astona (holy threshold) was a Tadjik-dominated neighborhood in which there was a closed bazaar selling dyes, and indigo dye workshops operated by Jews. Caravanserais in the neighborhood were dye trading centers and other dye workshops were located there, as well as a big market in cochineal and *buzgunch*, a black dye and tanning agent. In addition to the Jewish traders, Afghan merchants brought aniline dyes here from India.[24] The business of dyeing was messy and foul smelling, and the Bukharan city authorities tried to concentrate nuisance occupations in the same neighborhoods.

PRODUCTION AND DISTRIBUTION There was a very effective distribution of both silk and cotton fabrics in the early nineteenth century which continued under the Russian Protectorate administration of the late nineteenth and early twentieth centuries. Within the Khanates, all dry goods cost more outside their local manufacturing area, but less than comparable goods that came from outside Central Asia. Finished fabrics came from small traders in each local bazaar. Local wholesalers brought their goods by caravan from the major cities.

In the first half of the nineteenth century, the largest wholesale suppliers of silk fabrics were found in Bukhara. Toward the close of the century Marghilan, in the Ferghana Valley, surpassed Bukhara in silk production. Both of these silk-weaving centers made goods to fit the tastes of their local customers and for general distribution throughout the Khanates.They also organized small-scale production of cloth in special weaves or specific colors for the Kirgiz and other nomad clients.

With the exception of fabrics made in the Ferghana Valley for Chinese Turkestan, goods intended for export often traveled first to Bukhara from other cities of the Khanates. The big brokers had their emporia in Bukhara, and caravans consisting of several thousand camels were organized here. Bukharan merchants were the most enterprising in Central Asia, and took these caravans across the desert and steppe to Afghanistan, India, European Russia and Siberia.[25]

From the middle of the nineteenth century until its close, the wholesale trade in cottons imported from Russia, and the export trade in silks, were said to have been mostly in the hands of the Bukharan Jews. Unfortunately, there is very little economic data of any kind available for Bukhara from this period, and Jewish merchants often screened their activities by working behind groups of smaller entrepreneurs. After the establishment of the Russians in Central Asia there are far better records for the areas under their control. The export of silk cocoons increased dramatically at the end of the nineteenth century, although most silk was still consumed in local weaving enterprises. In 1899, 353 tons (320,909 kg) of cocoons were exported, primarily to Russia; in 1909 exports had increased to 1,583 tons (1,439,090 kg).

It appears that most of the ikat and other Central Asian fabrics that were exported in the nineteenth century left in the form of finished garments. Between 1840 and 1850, 190,000 robes of all kinds were exported from Turkestan to Russia and Siberia.[26] Other exports included *adiol*, padded coverlets popular in Russia, and *pardah*, wall-hangings, which were extensively used in the oases, but not popular outside Central Asia.

In previous trade relations with countries outside her borders, Central Asia had been a net exporter of finished silk and cotton goods; by the end of the nineteenth century raw cotton and cocoons dominated the export market. This move from the production of finished goods to the export of raw materials had taken place almost a century before in other parts of the Islamic world. The delay granted Central Asian artisans several decades of production free from the competition of factory-made fabrics, and in this respect the nineteenth-century art of silk-weaving and dyeing benefited from isolation.

20 WALL-HANGING
mid-19th century
88" × 58" (224 × 147cm)
5 panels
warp-faced plain weave
Unlike many striped ikats, the warp yarns of this wall-hanging have been divided only once. The striped pattern was created in the initial binding process.

LATER IKAT PRODUCTION The hand-loomed fabrics of Central Asia came under increasing commercial pressure from imports after the turn of the century, and the weaving of many half-silk fabrics was abandoned by the time of the Russian Revolution. The heavily ribbed cotton-wefted ikat that had dominated production during the first half of the nineteenth century completely disappeared. There were brief resurgences in the production of hand-made fabrics just after the Revolution, during World War II and at other times during the twentieth century when it became difficult to obtain cloth from outside Central Asia. The making of all-silk ikat in both plain and satin weave continued during these periods of scarcity. The temporary revival of traditional workshop production preserved knowledge of many weaves that would otherwise have been lost. After the Revolution the individual craft workshops were actively discouraged. From 1917, the new Soviet administration attempted to organize weavers into large workshops, with only sporadic and temporary success. Most hand-weavers found other trades. In Bukhara, the textile wholesalers were squeezed first by the struggling Emirate and then by the chaotic economic situation of the early years of the Revolution.

The major silk-producing area of the Ferghana Valley suffered severe hardship at this time.[27] War, economic upheaval and general mismanagement all contributed to a series of famines between 1917 and 1920 that took the lives of a large proportion of the population of southern Central Asia.[28] In the process, traditional silk production in the Ferghana Valley was badly damaged, and most of the small silk workshops were replaced by factory combines. Workers' co-operatives supplanted extended family businesses, and more and more textile craftsmen and dyers moved into factory work. By 1929, there were seven dyers' co-operatives among the thirty-seven Jewish workers' co-operatives identified by L.M. Kantor in Uzbekistan. There was also one Jewish silk-reeling co-operative and one weaving co-operative in the Fergana district.[29] A similar re-organization affected Muslim textile craftsmen, many of whom were forced to work at home in secret.[30]

After a lengthy hiatus, a Soviet interest in "national crafts" allowed a revival of ikat weaving in the 1960s, and a new generation of weavers learned traditional ikat techniques. By the 1990s, the only remaining hand-weavers of ikat fabrics were a few craftsmen in the Marghilan area of the Ferghana Valley. Their production was limited to the very glossy all-silk *atlas* satin ikats.

For the most part, the "national fabric" of Uzbekistan came to be made by machines. The production of factory-made textiles within Uzbekistan increased rapidly after World War II. The Samarkand combine was established in the 1930s, the Marghilan combine in the 1940s. In addition to these large factories, a number of co-operative associations made silk fabrics. The combines began by using natural silks, but quickly moved into synthetic and artificial silks. In 1947 the combines

21 WALL-HANGING
Bukhara
mid-19th century
80" × 47" (203 × 119cm)
2 panels plus quarter panel in center, framed by solid and split indigo panels; 3 different ikats.
warp-faced plain weave
The designs of the center panel are a playful miniaturization of those on Turkoman carpets.

began producing printed silks in imitation of ikats. The methods used followed the earlier Russian and Soviet production of printed cottons with ikat designs made specifically for the Central Asian market.

The task of designing a machine-woven fabric with printed warps was carried out by artists who made blatant copies of existing patterns, or emphasized smaller patterns that could form a consistent repeat rather than larger, more monumental forms. New "faux-ikat" patterns based on Soviet motifs were introduced, and older designs were altered and given names like "Sputnik" and "Red Square". The post-Soviet patterns have non-traditional titles; one is named after a character in a Mexican soap opera shown on Uzbekistan television.

Across the border, in Chinese Xinjiang, similar machine-made textiles meet local demand for ikat-style fabrics, and a few silk-weavers make true ikats that are virtually identical to the current Marghilan hand-production. A radically different preservation of the ikat tradition took place in northern Afghanistan. From the third quarter of the nineteenth century, when Russian incursions into Central Asia captured large areas of steppeland, and during the forced collectivization of the 1930s, many Turkomans and Uzbeks moved southwards into Afghanistan. By the middle of the twentieth century much of northern Afghanistan was populated by immigrants from across the Amu Darya, from the borderlands of the former Bukharan Khanate. There have been occasional instances of immigrant masters who sustained their own ikat workshops in Afghanistan, but only one substantial individual production, in the city of Herat, has been documented.[31]

A more long-lasting revival began around 1930, when Turkomans from the Karaja subtribe of the Ersari settled in two small villages, Altibolak and Korshangi. The Turkomans wove simple cotton fabrics and made fine silk scarves. Two refugee Uzbek master craftsmen passed separately through the region soon after, and instructed the Turkomans in a much simplified method of weaving ikat. The 200 yard-long warps, of either white or yellow background, were reserve-dyed in very simple triangular patterns. The tied bundles were as thick as a man's arm, and the various dyed sections were only joined when they were set at the loom. Warps with the two different colored backgrounds were usually arranged on the loom to form four striped sections of alternating background color per fabric width, all with the same stepped triangle pattern. The process was one of arranging the reserve-dyed warps to make a pattern, rather than applying a total design to a single warp entity. Rayon replaced silk as the warp material after about 1970. This simple ikat-dyed fabric became extremely popular among the Turkoman, and was widely distributed throughout the north of Afghanistan. Until the 1970s, a cotton ikat fabric was made in Korshangi.[32] In 1991, a UNESCO project in Mazhar i Sharif, Afghanistan, reintroduced local weavers to the traditional Korshangi production.[33] The continuing Afghan war cut the UNESCO efforts short, and the project was abandoned.

The extraordinary expansion and development of the art of ikat weaving, which began in the early part of the nineteenth century, and reached its peak soon after, had faltered before the turn of the twentieth. Its evolution, and the dramatic changes in style, materials and technology throughout the nineteenth century were largely the result of commercial pressures. The periodic revivals in the twentieth century were based in the first instance on the scarcity of alternative fabrics, and subsequently on sentiment, and the contemporary fabrics are merely shadows of an earlier art.

4

THE MAKING OF IKAT

Beyond all inhabited places we find men called Scir, or Seres, who by a water process make a woolen cloth from the leaves and barks of trees...Our merchants...find on the banks of this river all manner of goods...and without any parlying, they look at one another, and with their eyes give the price of each thing.

Ser Bruno Latini, *Tresor*, c. 1260[1]

THE MIRACULOUS GENESIS AND PRACTICAL CARE OF SILKWORMS The medieval West was sure that silk was made by magic. The impossibly delicate, luminous fabric could only have been made by Chinese alchemists. Even in Central Asia, where every household had its mulberry tree, the hand of God – and the Devil – was present in the genesis of silk. The tale of Job is also the story of silk; this time with a twist that underlines the importance of women in the initial phase of silk production.

First the Devil burned down Job's house, making it impossible for his wife to cook for him. To obtain food for him, Job's wife cut off all her beautiful long hair to sell it for bread. The Devil mocked Job, saying that his wife had become ugly. Next the Devil caused Job's wife's body to become full of worms, but still Job thanked God that she was, at least, alive.

Then God spoke to Job, saying that since Job had faith, he would be healed. God caused a well of water to be in the ground, and told Job to wash himself and his wife in it.

Further, God said that they should take the last worms from their bodies, and cast them into the water, and they would have any wish they desired.

So Job cast the first worm, saying, "Let there be cotton", and cast the second, saying, "Let there be silk", and cast the third, saying, "Let this water be holy, and heal others", and in this way came about the well of Chashma Ayub in Holy Bokhara.

Interview with Yusuf Sharipov, a student of religion at the shrine of Bahauddin Naqshband in Bukhara, 1995

Better known in the West, and still current in Central Asia, is the story of the Chinese princess who married a barbarian nomad and brought silkworm eggs as her dowry. By carrying them to Central Asia on her person, the princess also performed the first step of the silk-raising process, warming and incubating the eggs with her body.

Within the nineteenth-century oases towns, women of almost every household raised the larvae of the silk moth, *Bombyx mori*, whose cocoon supplied the silk filaments for weaving and embroidery. The tiny eggs were sewn into little cotton bags and worn beneath each woman's clothing. The warmth of the women's bodies incubated the eggs, and as the silkworms hatched they were taken out, placed in shallow baskets lined with a strong-scented herb, and fed with tiny, fresh mulberry leaves.

At first delicate, the silkworms became voracious eaters, until entire branches had to be placed in the baskets every four hours. After four to seven weeks, the silkworms crawled upon the branches and spun their cocoons. As soon as spinning was complete, the cocoons were stripped from the branches and sorted. The finest cocoons were set aside to provide the following year's supply of eggs, and the others were placed in the sun to kill the larvae. Silkworm eggs could be purchased by the thimbleful in the market, but once production began eggs were saved from the previous year's laying. The mature moths emerged ten to fifteen days after spinning the cocoon, coupled, and laid their eggs soon after. The eggs were gathered and hung in bags near the ceiling until the next April, when the yearly cycle began again.

A traditional rite of spring was the exchange of silkworm eggs with neighbors and extended family. A silkworm egg disease called peprine that appeared in the 1870s spread rapidly as a result of the traditional egg exchange. Under Russian influence, several attempts were made to provide healthy eggs and inspect the eggs available locally. None of these measures was sufficient to check the spread of disease, and healthy eggs had to be imported from Europe, Turkey and even Japan through the end of the nineteenth century.[2]

The traditional users of silk were individual households, in which the silk preparation process was more primitive than that employed for commercial weaving. The majority of the silk prepared for household use was made from small or damaged cocoons, which provided carded and homespun silk wadding.[3] The broken threads of carded silk could still be spun into embroidery thread, but were unsuited for any kind of fine weaving.The rapid expansion of raw and finished-silk exports at the end of the nineteenth century placed much greater demand upon the household industry which supplied fresh cocoons to the markets. According to contemporary Russian sources, every mulberry tree in the Khanates was utilized to provide fodder for the silkworms – it took twenty mulberry trees to produce 120lb (54kg) of fresh cocoons. In 1909 Russian Turkestan produced almost 3,000 tons (3 million kg) of cocoons, by 1910 over 5,000 tons.[4] Total silk production reached almost 800 tons in the same period. Despite the huge volume, the basic process remained the same until silk was supplanted by artificial and synthetic fibers.

In Kokand it was formerly the custom to present the first cocoons to the Khan, who in return gave a "sarpai", or complete suit of clothes. When Shir Ali Khan, Khudayar's father, who had lived all his life among the Kirgiz, came to the throne, he was as usual presented with the first cocoons, and, supposing them to be some rare fruit, ate them with the greatest composure.
Eugene Schuyler, *Turkestan*, 1877

MAKING SILK THREAD The means of getting silk thread from a cocoon is not obvious, but it is simple. In much of Turkestan the most common method of reeling was to toss the unsorted cocoons into a cauldron of boiling water to dissolve the sticky sericin, which bound the threads of the cocoon. The cocoons were lightly brushed with a stick to which the separated filament ends would adhere. Then the filament ends were drawn directly from the pot and wound by hand into loose skeins. A more evenly tensioned thread was made by winding the skeined filaments on to a hand-turned wooden frame or cage-spool. Reeled silk ranged in quality from a strong, smooth, pure white thread that was used for the finest fabrics, to a mid-range thread for export, and finally to a very low grade, uneven thread, not suitable for anything but embroidery.[5] The best silkworms gave from 4 to 6 ounces (112–170g) of raw silk from each pound (453g) of cocoons.

As the individual silk filament is very fine, several had to be combined to make a usable thread. The reeled filaments were combined on a bobbin winder to make single and double plied strands. Then the thread was taken off the bobbins and placed on smaller spools. A skilled craftswoman using a simple treadle spinning-wheel could make about 62 small spools from two large bobbins each day. In the mid-nineteenth century the wife of the silk reeler did this work. By the turn of the century groups of women were hired by larger enterprises to work together in a special women's area of the house or workshop. Thread for silk wefts was often also made by women, who wound the weft from five spools through very smooth, glazed-pottery loops.[6]

PREPARING THE WARP In Central Asian ikat only one of the two interlacing yarn systems, the warp, is resist-dyed before weaving: the weft, which interlaces with the warp, is unpatterned. In most Central Asian towns, the same workshops prepared warps for the weavers of all kinds of silk fabrics. In late nineteenth-century Bukhara there were a number of workshops that specialized in making warps solely for ikat fabrics.

1

2

MAKING IKAT The ikat making process began with the preparation of a warp of about 210 yards (202.5 meters) in length. The twisted and divided threads for the warp were prepared on a wooden wheel with a circumference of about 7 yards (6.75 meters). A vertical frame held bobbins of silk, and the threads were drawn from the bobbins on to the wheel in a split pattern, forming the shed. The warp was boiled to whiten and firm it, then stretched and dried. In the *abr-bandi* workshop, the warp threads were separated, and placed through the holes of a pierced wooden board. The board had forty to sixty holes, and each hole held an equal number of threads. The use of the board maintained the tension of the warps and kept each group of threads separate. The warp threads were wrapped around wooden beams set into the ground two to three yards apart. The groups of threads formed the bundles into which the tied warps were divided for dyeing. The master designer, the *nishan-zan*, marked the outlines of the pattern on the stretched warps with charcoal. The marked sections of the warp bundles were wrapped tightly with cotton threads to prevent these areas of warp from coming into contact with the dyestuff. The warp was removed from the frame, wound on to a pole and carried to the dye house for the first of a series of dye baths. There the silk warps were wound loosely on sticks and dipped into vats of dye. The threads were rewound and dipped again to spread the color evenly. Hot and cold dyeing processes usually took place in separate workshops. Dye baths used to make red and yellow colors

3

1. Boiling cocoons to loosen the filaments. *Turkestanskii al'bom*, "Crafts Album", 1871–72. (Navoi Library, Tashkent.)
2. Making a silk warp. *Turkestanskii al'bom*, 1871–72. (Navoi Library, Tashkent.)
3. A Jewish spinner twisting silk filaments on a bobbin. *Turkestanskii al'bom*, 1871–72. (Navoi Library, Tashkent.)
4,5. The *abr-bandi* ikat binding workshop: the winding of the warp on the frame; the marking of the pattern. Photos: S.M. Dudin, 1901–02. (Archives of the State Museum of History, Tashkent.)

5

6

6. Dye house for silk. Photos: S.M. Dudin, 1901–02. (Archives of the State Museum of History, Tashkent.)
7. The *abr-bandi* ikat binding workshop: the preparation of a new set of bundles for dyeing. Photo: S.M. Dudin, 1901–02. (Archives of the State Museum of History, Tashkent.)
8. The insertion of warps through the loom harness. *Turkestanskii al'bom*,1871–72. (Archives of the State History Museum of History, Tashkent.)
9. Weaving ikat on a warp-weighted loom. *Turkestanskii al'bom*. "Crafts Album", 1871–72. (Navoi Library, Tashkent.)
10. Beating a completed half-silk fabric. *Turkestanskii al'bom*. "Crafts Album", 1871–72. (Navoi Library, Tashkent.)

7

were compounded in metal vessels and heated by means of hearths set below the vats. Indigo cold dye baths were stored in clay vessels. The warps were returned to the *abr-bandi* workshop and stretched on the tying frame between each dye bath. The old bundles were removed and new ones tied to expose the areas of warp that were to receive the next color. After the dyeing process was completed, the warps were rolled on a stick and brought to the harness maker. Harnesses were constructed of a wooden frame with loops of string to

8

hold the warps. The reed frame was made of bamboo, with fine split bamboo or rushes forming the blades. The ends of the warp threads were placed through the loops of the harnesses, one half of the warps in one, the second half in another, and then through the blades of the reed. Warps, harnesses and reed could be wound together into a bulky bundle, and brought to the weaving workshop. *Adras* ikat was woven on a simple, warp-weighted loom. The weaver either sat in a pit, or the warp beams were set into a low wall.

Treadles at the weaver's feet allowed him to raise one harness and pull down the other at the same time. The shuttle was passed by hand and the wefts flattened with a reed. The finished cloth was wound around a beam set near the weaver's waist. Beating the finished silk cloth gave it a brilliant, reflective shine. Both *adras* and other half-silk fabrics were beaten with a wooden hammer with a convex face, on to a similarly shaped base. A semi-sphere of glass was also used to polish the cloth. Finishes included the application of egg white to the fabric.

9

10

The thickness of the warp thread (that is, the number of filaments spun together in each thread) and the number of threads in the whole warp were dictated by the type of fabric to be woven. A single craftsman did the twisting of the silk threads for the warp on a giant wheel. Up to fifty bobbins of silk thread were placed on a vertical frame; in the early twentieth century, fifty threads formed a standard measurement called a *livit,* and four *livits* made up a *band.* It seems likely that in the nineteenth century, the standard number of threads in a *livit* was forty-eight, although the number may have varied between twenty-four and sixty threads. The threads were taken from the bobbins and were wound carefully, under even pressure, on to the wheel in an evenly split pattern to form the shed. The circumference of the wheel was about 7 yards (6.75 meters), and was used as the unit of measure of the total warp length, called a *davr.* The width of the warp was measured by the number of threads. If an order came in for a warp that was 30 *davrs* by 12 *band,* the prepared warp would have 2,400 threads across its width and be 202 meters in length, or 30 times the circumference of the drum. If no warping-wheel was available, warp threads could also be wound from bobbins on to a series of wooden pegs set into a long wall.

The warp was boiled for ten or fifteen minutes in a potash solution to make it white and firm, then boiled again in water along with a muslin bag of dried morel mushrooms.It was wound on a very smooth roller, the excess water was squeezed out, and it was returned to the owner, still wet.[7]

The next stage was to prepare the warp for tying and dyeing. This required a lot of space, so it was done in the street in the early morning hours, when there were not many people around. Up to eight men were required to handle the lengthy warp. The warp was dried and inspected, and any broken threads were knotted. If the warp was to be made into striped material, it was separated into sections so that each group of threads could be dyed separately. If the warp was for ikat fabric, it was wound into an elongated ball on a pole, and taken off to the warp-tying workshop.[8]

TYING THE WARP There were eight known *abr-bandi* ikat-binding workshops in Bokhara in the late nineteenth century. The tying of ikat warps required two specially skilled craftsmen. The pattern designer, called the *nishan-zan* or *nus-khazan,* made the marks on the warp for the design. The *abr-band* actually bound the warps, with a few assistants helping him.

A craftsman passed the warp through the openings in a special board a yard long, up to an inch and a quarter (3cm) thick and pierced with forty to sixty holes. Each *livit*, or group of threads, was passed through one hole in the board. If there were ten *band* in a warp, then forty of these holes would be used. The threads at one end of each *livit* were knotted. The craftsman put a black dot by each knot, and his assistant would then tie the warp at the dot with thick white threads. These bindings, which remained tied throughout the dyeing process, were an important reference point for the marking of the pattern and the final arrangement on the loom. The bindings appear at the end of each pattern repeat on the finished fabric; they form the distinctive white lines that occur at intervals across the width of all Central Asian ikats.

Two wooden beams, each a yard long, were attached by thick ropes to struts which were located eight to ten feet (2.5–3 m) from each other, about three feet off the ground. These formed the patterning frame, and the distance between the beams determined the length of

22 WALL-HANGING
Bukhara
third quarter 19th century
84" × 40" (213 × 102cm)
3 panels
silk velvet
An extremely rare example of a full-sized wall-hanging made of silk velvet. Silk velvet ikat was certainly far more costly than any other type and was used most often for dowry garments. This wall-hanging must have originally belonged to a person of substance.

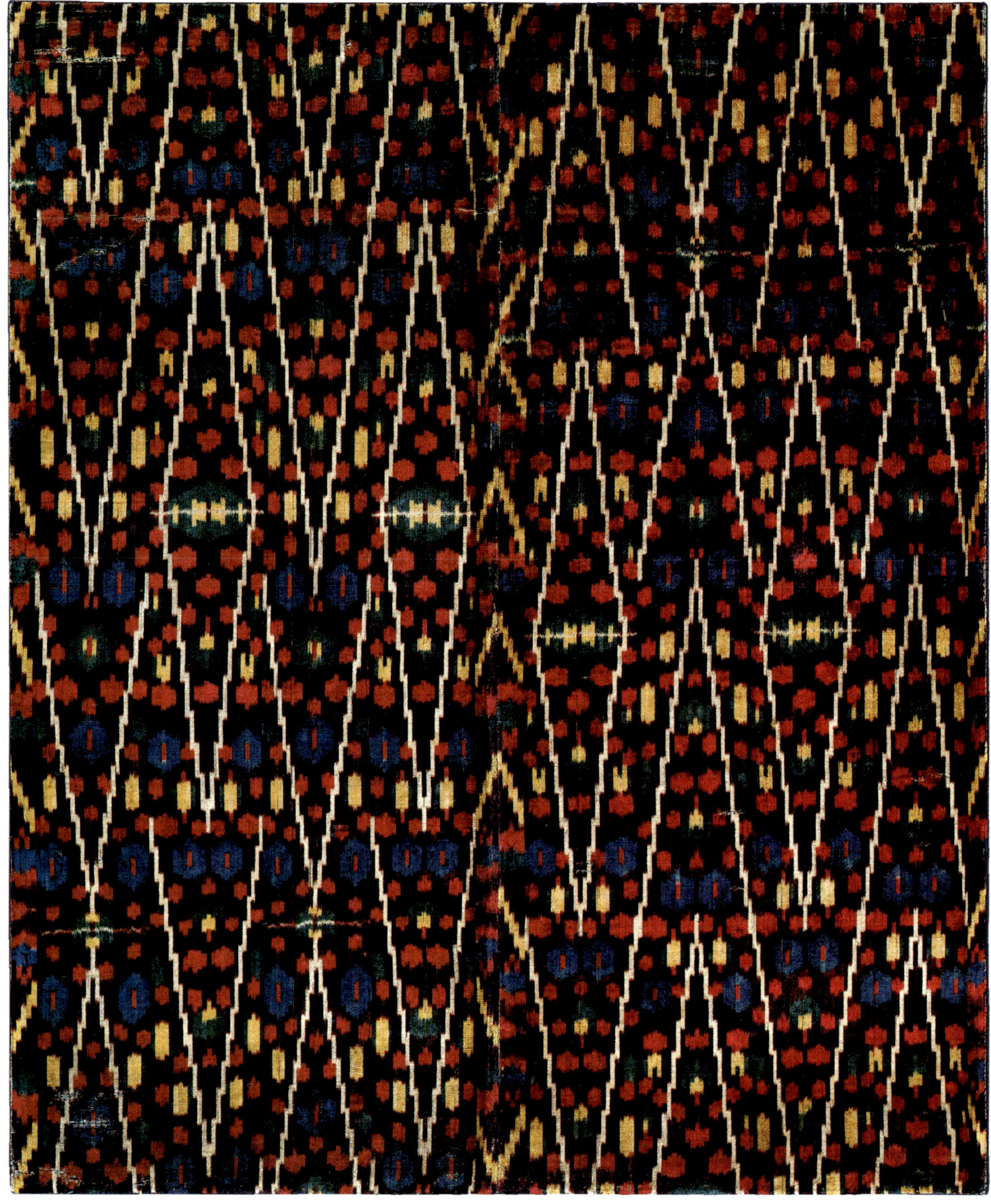

23 WALL-HANGING
Bukhara
mid-19th century
39" × 33" (99 × 84cm)
2 panels
silk velvet
This very unusual velvet pattern bears a close resemblance to the *adras* plain weave ikats of the first half of the 19th century. The modulated background color and deliberate asymmetry are very different from the later, rather stiff, large medallion compositions. Unfortunately there is no data on Central Asian velvet production in the early period; a conservative dating places this example at mid-century.

the pattern repeat. The craftsmen secured one end of the warp to one beam and then wound the entire length of the warp tightly on to the wooden beams, moving the threaded board around them to keep the *livits* in their correct place. A warp 260 yards (240m) long would form about eighty layers of warp on the beams. After winding the warp around the beams, the other ends of the *livits* were knotted and secured to the beam. The *nishan-zan* marked the outlines of the pattern on the upper surface of the warp with a little stick dipped in washable black dye or charcoal. In most early ikats the design is symmetrical along the central vertical axis, like a mirror image, although more than one axis will be present if the design repeats more than once across the width of the fabric. On to most ikat warps, the *nishan-zan* drew only one vertical half of the design. Only the final adjustment of the warps on the loom would reveal the complete pattern.

The *abr-band* tied up the warps into little bundles with a thick, waterproof cloth or a greasy cotton string as a resist. When the first tying was complete, the tied warp threads were carefully removed from the patterning frame, and brought to the dyer. The warp was given the first dye bath and then brought back to the *abr-bandi* workshop. Each additional color required another series of ties and another dye bath. The process was repeated until the *abr-band* had the pattern that he desired, and he would then untie and dry the warp.[9]

In late nineteenth-century Marghilan, as many as twenty warps would be prepared for the arrival of an itinerant master design-maker. The master would tie the warps between two trees or poles instead of using a patterning frame, and would apply the outlines of a different design to each one. While the *nishan-zan* knew all the patterns, the owner of the warp decided which design was to be drawn.[10]

DYEING THE TIED WARP In the making of ikat, the dyeing requires the most care, as it is essential to maintain a cohesive and beautiful pattern though a succession of dye baths. The brilliant colors must blend harmoniously, the dye must penetrate evenly without spreading to the tied areas, and the position of the warps relative to each other must be maintained.

The most prestigious and expensive type of early ikat fabric was the richly colored *haft-rang*, or seven-color ikat. Four separate dyeing operations were usually required, and additional colors could be created by over-dyeing one color on top of another. The number *haft*, seven, is not intended to be precise. Six-color ikat is also called *haft-rang*, as are the few rare fabrics in eight colors. Since the eleventh century, the expression *haft-rang* has denoted richness and luxury; and seven is a propitious number in Central Asia.[11]

Until the introduction of artificial dyes toward the end of the nineteenth century, purple, green and brown all required an over-dye sequence that included the application of blue. The usual process would be first to dye the yellows and reds, and then to apply the blue, both in its pure color and as an over-dye on top of the colors dyed previously. Central Asian folk belief held that indigo dye was not only the most colorfast, but that an indigo over-dye strengthened the combined colors, whereas over-dyeing on top of indigo would weaken them. It was thought that both the fabric and the colors applied to it were made more durable through contact with indigo.[12]

In Central Asia, where each craft had its own workshop, a genuine co-operation and understanding of the desired result was necessary to make a successful ikat fabric. In most instances, the application of even

The neighborhood's holy place was the grave of Sheikh Rangrez... His nickname is explained in a legend of a miracle that he performed here: he dyed three skeins of yarn three different colors by dipping them in a pond of clear water.

O.A. Sukhareva, 1976[13]

a few colors to a warp involved trips to two separate workshops. Tadjiks specialized in hot dyeing, making yellows and reds from vegetal dyes that required extreme heat during immersion of the fabric. Jews specialized in cold dyeing, primarily with indigo, in which the baths were not heated beyond hand-warmth.

The dyers' workshops were primitive and roughly built. The sign of the craft consisted of a scrap of cloth or hank of yarn dyed and hung at the entrance. The masters of the hot dye shops supervised several workers: one ground the dyestuffs, two others dipped the heavy, wet fabrics and warps, and another watched the fires. Each color was applied in a separate copper kettle. For two to three hours before dyeing, warps were generally soaked in alum, which acted as a mordant. When the warp was dyed, the alum reacted with the various dyestuffs to fix the colors and bind the dyes to the fibers. To make the warp easier to handle it was wrapped around a pole. It was dipped three times into the boiling dye solution, then rewound in the opposite direction and immersed again, to spread the color evenly. The warp was removed from the pole, and left to soak, sometimes for hours, in the dye solution.

The shops of the cold dyers who worked in indigo had a square floor plan. Two rows of giant clay vats, each holding about ten buckets of water, were set deep into the ground. These held the indigo baths, made of about 14 ounces (400g) of indigo, 7½ ounces each of lye and iron vitriol, and some dried mulberries. In winter, a trench beside the vessels gave access to hearths beneath them, to warm the vats. The only other equipment was a wooden spoon to stir the dye, and a three-foot-long stick to suspend loose warps or fabrics for dipping. Four of the indigo dye baths would be in use at one time. When these were exhausted, more dye ingredients would be added to the next four pots. The clay vessels were cleaned after two complete rounds of the dye baths, as the residue and impurities in the pots gave uneven results. The vessels were covered when not in use, to keep air out. The warp to be dyed was dipped in one indigo solution or in several successive solutions, depending on the depth of color desired. It was wrung out by hand and immediately returned to the customer. The excess dye remained in the material as the dyer did not rinse the warp. The dyer's fee depended upon the size of the item, the number of dippings and the depth of color desired.[14]

In the case of multicolored ikat fabrics, the dyed warp was returned to the warp-tying workshop, dried, stretched once again on the patterning frame, and retied to expose the areas to be dyed in the next color. It was taken again to the appropriate dye shop and the entire process was repeated. Several weeks might be required simply to complete the dyeing process for an ikat warp.

The last time the warp was stretched on the beams of the warp-tying workshop was to make a final arrangement of the pattern. The small groups of threads were once again placed through the pierced board and the pattern aligned by means of the permanent ties made where the black dots had been placed. To enable the weaver to unfold the two halves of the pattern to form a whole, each *livit* of dyed warp threads was separated into two groups of equal size: three threads were placed between each bundle to delineate each group of threads. When the warp arrived at the weaving workshop each divided *livit* was transferred to the loom, keeping their order in relation to the others. In this way the width of the warp was doubled and the design was reflected on either side of the midpoint. Most ikat warps were divided once along the vertical axis; but there were other methods of arranging the warps for weaving. The *livits* of one type of ikat-dyed warps were not divided at all, and the design of the finished fabric is not symmetrical along the vertical axis. Other warps were divided twice: their patterns have three vertical axes. In a few ikats a striped pattern was made by means of the insertion of solid colored warps between stripes of ikat-dyed warps.

THE WEAVING OF IKAT The standard Central Asian fabric loom was a simple treadle loom, although there were several variations: in Khodjent, looms were set into low mud walls, and the weaver sat on a board resting between them; in Bokhara the weaver sat on the ground, and the treadles were in a pit at his feet. Toward the front of the loom, a number of shafts were positioned across its width. These were attached to the treadles, and by moving them the weaver could lower the shafts. Straps connecting the shafts were passed over a beam and back to an alternate shaft to stabilize them. Each shaft consisted of a large number of vertical loops of thread (known as heddles) through which an individual warp thread had to be passed, one thread per loop. The craftsman who made the shafts was often responsible for threading the warp through them, and then, in groups of two or three, through spaces in the comb-like reed.[15] The reed had a sturdy frame of split bamboo and many fine teeth of bamboo or reed.[16] The warp, the reed and the shafts could be taken from the loom, rolled up and moved without displacing any of the warp threads. According to most accounts, when the warp arrived at the weaving workshop it was cut into numerous shorter lengths for weaving, sufficient to make only one item of clothing. Generally, two woven lengths were required for a substantial robe. Once threaded through the shafts and the reed, the warp was secured to a beam immediately in front of the weaver. Two shafts were needed to weave a plain weave fabric: as a treadle beneath the loom pulled down one harness, the other harness rose, to create a wide shed through which the weaver could pass the shuttle containing the weft. By pressing the other treadle, the alternate threads were raised, and by returning the weft to where it started, it interlaced with the warp to form a stable fabric. Satin required five to eight shafts depending on its fineness. Shuttles for silk-weaving were made of polished horn, so they did not catch on the fine warp. After the weft had been passed from one side of the warp to the other, the reed was pulled sharply toward the weaver to beat the warp into place. Another craft-worker made adjustments to the threads to keep the warp in line, and brushed them with a starch-like vegetable paste which enabled the fine silk threads to withstand the tensions and movements of weaving. This worker was assigned to either four looms of plain weave ikat or a single loom of velvet.

My heart's blood curdles from the sound of the loom.

My eyes are full of tears from broken threads.

From dawn to dusk I push my foot into the hole on which the loom stands.

I live as if walking on thistles and needles.

My heart is sad in the spring of my life.

Victor Beliaev, *Asulai bofandagi* (Weaver's Lament), Tadjikistan[17]

All ikat warps were woven in fairly narrow strips of between 9 and 24 inches (24–60cm) wide. In general, fabrics became slightly wider during the nineteenth century, though there were exceptions to that rule in all the major ikat weaving centers. Near the end of the nineteenth century it was common to find much wider fabrics from Bukhara, and much narrower ones from Khodjent. At the turn of the

24 SECTION OF LOOM LENGTH
Bukhara
third quarter 19th century
70" × 13" (178 × 33cm)
silk velvet
Large-scale medallions and patterns based on smaller forms which hang from a central stalk are the designs most characteristic of silk velvet ikat.

25 SECTION OF LOOM LENGTH
Bukhara
third quarter 19th century
56" × 14" (142 × 36cm)
silk velvet

century, a Khodjent weaver was credited with the invention of a partially mechanized loom which was used to weave ikat and other silk fabrics, the *paganyalki*.[18] In other respects similar to the traditional hand loom, the *paganyalki* had a mechanized shuttle, and allowed a single weaver to work a fabric more than a yard in width. This type of loom was twice as productive as the standard loom. Given the lengthy dyeing sequence and the complex adjustment of the warps in the loom, the weaving of a standard warp length of *adras* ikat (which was only a fraction of the total dyed warp), using the traditional hand loom, probably required between one and two months to complete.

FINISHES APPLIED TO IKAT FABRIC When the completed ikat was cut from the loom, the final step was to give the fabric a brilliant, reflective shine. Silk ikats woven with a cotton weft often seem to have been treated on only one side. The all-silk ikats remaining from the nineteenth century no longer carry a high shine, but are said to have had some kind of applied finish as well.[19] Satins, already glossy, were made even more so. The surface of the fabric was made shiny by the application of egg white or a special glue, or by thumping the surface with a wooden mallet. A watered effect was given by beating the fabric with a heavy wooden hammer with a convex face on to a convex working surface made from the same hard wood.[20] Light was reflected differently from the flattened sections of the cloth and produced a rippled or watered effect. The method of adding luster to silk ikat fabrics varied from place to place, as did the ethnic background of the craftsmen. In nineteenth-century Bukhara, two neighborhoods of Old Bukharan Tadjiks specialized in applying a variety of finishes to fabric.[21] In the Ferghana Valley, Uzbeks did glazing work with egg white. In Khiva, a heavy, semi-spherical glass bowl was used to polish the fabric, and as a result of such rubbing, even cottons became as shiny as silk. This glass sphere was also used on cotton-wefted and all-silk ikat fabrics.[22]

THE TYPES OF IKAT FABRIC All Central Asian ikat is warp ikat. The fact that the pattern was carried only on the warp threads meant that a great variety of fabrics could be made from the same type of ikat-dyed warp. Aside from the thickness of each warp thread and the density of the threads in the warp, the type of weave made a substantive difference in the appearance of the finished fabric. The ikats remaining from the earliest part of the nineteenth century are plain weave (also known as tabby) fabrics with a silk warp and a cotton weft, variously known as *adras* or *ishtope*. *Adras* ikat fabric used a thick silk warp thread drawn from 16 to 20 cocoons, and the number of threads generally ranged from 1600 to 2400 per warp width. A few rare examples are extremely dense, and use up to 3800 warps to form a fabric width. The early and mid-nineteenth-century fabrics were wefted with a hand-spun white cotton, but by the turn of the century a fine factory-produced cotton was used, sometimes dyed red. The compaction of the woven fabric on the loom gave a slightly ribbed appearance to the cloth. The result of the tension and compaction applied by the weaver was a fabric in which only the warp threads were visible on the surface.

All-silk plain weave ikat fabrics called *abr*, *kanaous* and *shahi* became common in the middle to third quarter of the century, and continued in production even beyond the 1917 Revolution, whereas the *adras* ikats were made only until the end of the nineteenth century. The all-silk fabrics have a lighter feel, due to their much thinner silk weft threads. White colors appear to be slightly pink, and other tones are reddened because the all-silk fabrics were balanced weaves, in which the weft and warp were both visible.

Toward the end of the nineteenth century and until the end of commercial hand-production in the 1930s, satin ikats called *atlas* and *khanatlas* became much more common. Ikat satin is another warp-faced fabric; unlike plain weave, the weft does not interlace with alternate warp threads but passes under four, five or seven warps, depending on the number of shafts being used on the loom. This creates a smooth, unbroken surface texture with a high gloss and a very clearly defined design on one fabric surface; the ikat design is barely visible on the reverse side.[23] A modern version of the glossy satin ikats, now almost entirely produced by machine, has become the official national fabric of Uzbekistan, and a garment made from it is referred to as a "national gown".

A few smaller towns developed regional weaving specialties that distinguished them from the more widespread production in the latter part of the nineteenth century. Both the warp and weft threads of ikats from the town of Hissar tend to be coarse and thick. The sections of warp were tied in far larger bundles for dyeing, and at times a single color extends the full width of the resist-dyed warp. The Hissar weavers often alternated different colored wefts in fabrics with wide, horizontal ikat-dyed stripes, and the coarser fabric allowed the colored wefts to be visible. An unusual type of ikat, made only in Khodjent at the end of the nineteenth and beginning of the twentieth centuries, was called *yalangdavron*. It was an all cotton fabric, with cotton warps resist-dyed in red, white and blue patterns.[24]

26 SECTION OF LOOM LENGTH
Bukhara
third quarter 19th century
25" × 13" (63 × 33cm)
silk velvet

27 SECTION OF LOOM LENGTH
Bukhara
third quarter 19th century
72" × 13" (183 × 33cm)
silk velvet

28 SECTION OF LOOM LENGTH
second half 19th century
62" × 15" (157 × 38cm)
warp-faced plain weave

It has been suggested that a late nineteenth-century group of all-silk ikats in brownish-pink and orange tones may have been made through the application of several different mordants.[25] The tying of a resist pattern on the warps would have remained the same, but instead of the warp being immersed in a dye bath after each set of ties, it would have been soaked in a mordant bath. After the warps were dried, a single madder dye bath would produce a pink, orange and white warp, as each mordanted section of warp reacted with the dyestuff to produce a different color.

Other fabrics are not well known, or only rarely dyed in resist technique. A light and fine all-silk fabric called *khalili* was sometimes produced as ikat. A few examples of all-silk scarves or sashes called *pokryvala* are also ikat-dyed. The *pokryvala* were twill-weave piece goods produced on broad-beam looms with a non-repeating ikat design framed with a border consisting of stripes of varying widths. These sheer scarves are between one and a half and two yards in width, far wider than any other type of ikat fabric. Certain fabrics that were not ordinarily resist-dyed might contain sections of ikat-dyed warp. At the end of the nineteenth century half-silk striped fabrics called *bekasabs* or *bekasam* effectively supplanted the *alacha* production of such fabrics.[26] In the dense *bekasabs* fabric, the number of threads per warp width ranged from around 2400 to as many as 4000. Each thread was drawn from 8 to 10 cocoons. Narrow sections of ikat-dyed warp were sometimes interspersed with plain dyed warps. In the case of *khalili* and *bekasabs*, the weave gave a fabric its name, whether or not the fabric contained ikat-dyed threads. Different terms may also apply to the same fabric in different localities. The cotton-weft ikat called *adras* in Bukhara and *dagir* in Marghilan was called *ishtope* in Afghanistan.

VELVET IKAT The last important type of Central Asian ikat was velvet ikat, *baghmal*. In making this, two warp systems are used: one is undyed and forms the foundation of the fabric, and one, resist dyed, forms the pile. The resist-dyed pile warp is substantially longer, and is woven in very precise loops over a wire or template to make the pile ikat pattern.The distance between the white lines that mark the pattern repeat is considerably reduced in the finished fabric because the resist-dyed warp is looped to form the pile. After every two or three passes of weft a wire or template is inserted instead of the weft. This causes the threads of the pile warp to be raised over it, forming tight loops, and then more weft is passed to secure the wire. When several wires have been woven into the fabric, a knife is run along them to cut the loops and free the wires. Central Asian *baghmal* velvets are similar in construction to the Persian *makhmal* velvets, although the nineteenth-century Persian fabrics tend to be much wider.[27]

The Guido Goldman Collection includes an extremely rare complete length of velvet ikat, more than twenty-two feet (6.7m) long.This complete bolt of ikat velvet has seven white lines marking the pattern repeat between the two finished ends; the resist-dyed warp needed to produce the velvet pile was likely to be two to three times the length of the finished fabric.[28] Velvet weave was extremely difficult and time-consuming to make, and of all the ikat fabrics, it was produced for the briefest period, probably only from the late 1860s to about 1910. It was also the most limited in production geographically, and seems only to have been made in Bukhara.[29] Although velvet ikat was too expensive to produce in the hinterlands, robes made of Bukharan *baghmal* were important prestige items throughout Central Asia.

29 SECTION OF LOOM LENGTH
Bukhara
fourth quarter 19th century
53" × 13" (135 × 33cm)
silk velvet
This late Animal Skin pattern is essentially a novelty that draws on influences from outside Central Asia, perhaps Europe (Russia) or the Far East.

5

IKAT DESIGN: SOURCES & INFLUENCES

"You see the mountains – you think them firm, yet they move like clouds." Abu'l-Qasim Muhammad al-Junayd's response to Nuri, "who objected to his sitting quietly while the Sufis performed their whirling dance".

Annemarie Schimmel, 1975[1]

The extraordinarily light and brilliant *adras* ikat fabrics carry a weighty burden. Their complex motifs are drawn from a vast repertory of Central Asian pattern, their dynamic lines and rich handling of color are founded in Central Asia's lengthy and vital artistic tradition. The sources of ikat design must be sought far from the urban workshops of the nineteenth century, in the influence of the open steppes and the art of the ancient past.

It would seem that there was little in common but language between a horse-breeding nomad of the plains and an Uzbek silk-weaver in Bukhara. In fact, the most durable connection between steppe and city lay in a shared visual aesthetic. The materials and techniques of nomadic art were different – wool rather than cotton, and silk embroidery instead of complex weaves – but the styles of ornamentation had much in common. The gift from the steppe to the city, renewed again and again, was a determined rigor and a strength that was often lacking in the urban arts of nearby Iran. Within the art of the steppes, decoration is subservient to function. Craft does not become an end in itself, and sentiment is refreshingly absent. A vigorous line, assertive color, a rendering of images that are always abstracted from nature, not drawn from it – these are equally to be found in steppe and oasis art. Beyond all this, Central Asian art is characterized by the imposition of two-dimensional patterns upon even sculptural form, and by the equality of negative and positive space within a composition.

12

The subject matter of urban art was also influenced by the surrounding steppes.The presence of the nomad tribes was a constant reminder of the cycle and flow of a life directed by nature's actions. Central Asia's cities were tiny, shining islands in the vast sea of the steppes. Their bustling streets were crammed with caravans, and their bazaars full of dusty men, whose parched lips and ragged clothes spoke of their recent arrival from the deserts beyond. Man was a fragile creature on the face of the steppe. Every form of life was a miracle; the wild tulips and lush grasses of spring were paid for with the harsh snows of winter. A reverence for the chaotic energy of nature, a healthy regard for her power, a mystical response to the phenomenon of life; all these informed the urban arts.

The artistic connection between steppe and town was reinforced by daily contact. An implicit social contract between the urban and steppe peoples required co-operation from every element of the complex Central Asian society. The nomads relied upon the wealth of the cities, and the cities depended on the nomads for animal products, slaves, and their military skills as mercenaries. Rulers relied upon merchants to supply goods and provide revenue. Merchants depended upon the ruler's ability to maintain a stable environment by imposing order on the settled population, and by negotiating with and manipulating the nomads. It may be too simple to say that the decentralized character of kingship and authority in Central Asia was the foundation for her non-iconic and open-ended artistic tradition, or that the constant influx of different cultures created a medley, a fortuitous and unique mix. A marked

13

12, 13. Bronze belt studs from Northern Afghanistan. Central Asian Bronze Age, 2200–1500 BC.
12. Woman with goats.
13. Woman with griffins.
14. Detail of Sogdian mural depicting a frieze of banquettes. Pendjikent. (from *Sogdian Painting: The Pictorial Epic in Oriental Art*. G. Azarpay. University of California Press, 1981.)

artistic freedom and invention go back to the urban settlements of the Bronze Age, before the movement of peoples along the Silk Road began. A look at the evolution of successive Central Asian styles may help to serve as a key to understanding the ways in which ikat design echoes and reflects the past.

ANCIENT AND PRE-ISLAMIC INFLUENCES For thousands of years, Central Asian art, from the Bronze Age to the Sogdian kingdoms and on throughout the Islamic period, has been characterized by a dramatic style that leaned heavily toward abstraction. Though capable of naturalistic rendering, the artists of 2000 BC took greater interest in abstracting animal and floral forms, in using an element of a creature's body to represent its potency and strength. The ram's horns, the scorpion's tail, the falcon's claw and beak embody the animal's essence. These creatures, as well as purely abstract forms, are the most common subjects of the earliest Central Asian art. Their attributes are borrowed by human figures who may be gods: winged men and women poised between opposing animals (figs 12, 13). Bronze Age art

14

Royal life in Sogdiana was not an expression of official grandeur, but a reflection of the luxurious life of affluent men.

A.M. Belenitsky and B.I. Marshak, *Sogdian Painting*, 1981[3]

celebrates the success of man, who coaxes nature to enrich him. Man does not dominate, he brings natural forces into balance through his new skills. The graphic abilities of the artist are best seen in the bronze belt-studs of 2000 BC. The stylized human, animal and floral forms were usually framed within a medallion, and the tendency toward reticulation is very strong. The arrangement of opposing figures within a medallion is one of the most enduring conventions in Central Asian art, and occurs frequently in later carpets and textiles.

Much of the later Animal Style art of the Scythians and Sarmatians of the steppe has its antecedents in the energetic stylization of the Bronze Age. The textile remains from the Pazyryk tombs demonstrate a kinship between design in the durable media of wood and metal – of which numerous objects remain – and more fragile felts and woven fabrics. The winged animals, lions, eagles and griffins of Pazyryk are closely related to the fantastic creatures of the Bronze Age.[2]

The period of the Kushan, from the first century BC to the third century AD, brought together native traditions of monumental sculpture and the influences of Roman art. Central Asia's brief flirtation with

30 WALL-HANGING
Bukhara
first half 19th century
74" × 56" (189 × 142cm)
5 panels
warp-faced plain weave

naturalism at this time was tempered by her traditional artistic concerns. The kingdoms of ancient Sogd, which followed closely upon those of the Kushan, best illustrate the cosmopolitan atmosphere and adaptive character of urban society – and the arts – in Central Asia. In the Sogdian period, urban life had much in common with contemporary concerns.The bustle of the city, the calculations of merchants, the palpable sense of expansion, of business being done and life lived – these are all familiar to the modern world.

Sogdian art was about pleasure, about the joy of seeing, and delight in the good life. The trappings of wealth were not limited to the royal elite, they were equally to be found in the homes of prosperous men whose business contributed to the success of the state. The dynastic propaganda of Iran is not paralleled in Sogdian art. Vessels are decorated with beautiful women and succulent fruits, not the heads of crowned kings.

Household decoration in this period, albeit through fresco remains and not silk, has been clearly delineated. The walls of ancient Sogd were her canvases. The wall-paintings at court and in the homes of merchants or wealthy farmers were very similar. Their subjects were predominantly secular, and they often dwelt on enjoyment. Aside from depictions of daily life, including court and religious ritual, the wall-paintings illustrated incidents from Central Asian epics, fairy-tales and fables. Elegantly dressed heroes and heroines ate and drank rich foods from fine vessels. They amused themselves with music, dance, and the hunt. They fought fiends, risked life and limb in battle. Sogdian art is full of grace and gesture, of the precise moment captured.

A curious feature of these decorative programs in both tile mosaic and banna'i is the consistent absence of a progression toward a decorative climax... These sheathing devices created new ambient environments, and the effect was abstract and transcendental.

Thomas W. Lentz and Glenn D. Lowry, *Timur and the Princely Vision*, 1989[4]

The local fabrics depicted on the costumed figures of the wall-paintings have large roundels in horizontal rows, alternating with smaller interstitial designs; in this respect, many are similar in composition to later Central Asian carpets and textiles. The roundels enclose figures, sometimes simple geometric patterns, but often elaborate compositions of opposed animals or mythical beasts. These rampant animals are usually separated by a tree or a linear, floral design. There are many striking parallels between the Sogdian motifs and Central Asian ikat designs. Although the panel width of Sogdian fabrics is far greater than that of nineteenth-century ikats, the repeating vertical rows of medallions suggest the multiple-panel arrangements of ikat wall-hangings.

15

15. Marbled paper illustration of a princess carrying a peacock. The Deccan. c. 1650. (Free Library of Philadelphia.)

ISLAM Islam brought science, art and theology into partnership. Since the time of Al Biruni, scientific knowledge has been a path to God. The universe was a puzzle placed before man by God, and the study of nature expressed reverence for God's work. Artists made a conscious effort to describe the pattern of the universe through pure geometry. The great, tile-covered mosques of Bukhara and Samarkand honor the faith of Islam, but each encapsulated section of pattern also represents a distillation of the infinite. Mysticism and science are joined in the flow of pattern beyond the boundaries of solid architecture.

These enormous, glittering buildings carry two messages for all who come to see them. One combines politics and spirituality: God lives *here*, and a *very* great king built me. The enormous size of the buildings, and the magnificence of their decoration, speak of temporal power and of empire as surely as the intricate patterning and elegant scale invite and enhance spiritual contemplation. The other message is more subtle, more abstract. The tilework decoration is a lesson in a new way of seeing. The eye does not focus on a single element, but is pulled from one pattern to the next. There is no central focus, no compositional nexus, no absolute direction.

16

16. Detail of facade of a mausoleum at the *Shah i Zindeh* complex, Samarkand. 14th century. (Robert Harding Picture Library.)

The influence of such architecture on the art of the nineteenth century may have been subconscious, but is there all the same. These buildings are so big and so beautiful that they take one's breath away. No one, country bumpkin or nomad, shopkeeper or artisan, could ignore them. Only the very late ikats from the close of the nineteenth and early twentieth centuries actually imitate tilework patterns. In these later ikats, there is a deliberate attempt to incorporate elements taken directly from other arts. The earliest ikats took more subtle lessons from architectural decoration, in deliberate combination and juxtaposition of patterns. The complex patterns of unglazed brick in buildings of the tenth century also give rise to questions of surface and texture in weaving, and carved stucco lends to ikat a number of its exuberant forms.

Other Islamic arts may also have contributed to the evolution of ikat design. The term *'abr,* or cloud, associated with ikat technique, was also used for the making of marbled paper, an art that was practiced in Central Asia from the thirteenth century AD.[5] Marbling continued to be popular whenever there was a demand for luxury paper. Nineteenth-century Central Asians associated marbled paper with the Turkish court, a much admired model for traditional Islamic government. The Ottoman style was considered refined as well as respectable, and when it was possible, the Bukharan rulers imitated the costume and ceremony of the imperial Turkish court. It is not known to what extent the taste for Turkish materials extended throughout the Central Asian community, but Ottoman marbled paper may have been familiar to many artisans.

The influence of marbled paper on fabric design was necessarily limited: some types of marbled paper are visually very similar to ikat, but there is no technical relationship between the two. While ikat designers may have seen marbled paper, the paper patterns could only have influenced fabric design after the textile technique was well advanced.

The emphasis on ornament and surface within Islamic art is an inherent part of fabric design. In Central Asia, the primary use to which fabrics were put was surface decoration. Carpets and hangings made large rectangles on walls and floors. The voluminous robes of the nineteenth century were worn one atop the other; they framed and boxed the figure. People look very similar when they are wearing five full-length coats at a time. What one saw was pattern, cut and clipped and juxtaposed in a way that challenged the eye.

The roots of all Central Asian art are clearly stated within her textiles: abstraction from nature, emphatic and defined color, vigorous line, a love of pattern and, above all, a willingness to play around. Ikat makers could not resist any of these opportunities for design, especially the open invitation to change, to try a new pattern with every warp. Each component within the design of an ikat echoed the ancient culture of Central Asia.

SYMBOL Attaching meaning to a recurring image in Central Asian art can be risky. What does it signify that for four thousand years the images of goat horns, scorpions, snakes, and birds of prey have appeared with the greatest frequency in Central Asian art? There is no single language, no religion, no political structure or economic entity that spans that lengthy period; there are many. It has most often been the case that no one culture has been entirely dominant in the area at one time. How can a symbol retain its meaning under such relentless pressure for change? Any symbolic value attached to an image must be

31 WALL-HANGING
Bukhara or Samarkand
first half 19th century
88" × 63" (223 × 159cm)
5.5 panels
warp-faced plain weave
The predominant diamond motif is framed by cypress tree and scorpion forms.

32 WALL-HANGING
probably Ferghana Valley
third quarter 19th century
84" × 54" (215 × 137cm)
5 panels
warp-faced plain weave
The motifs descending from the vertical stalks in this wall-hanging depict *tumar*, triangular talismans with many small pendants.

17

18

17. *Tumar*, amulet container. Niello on silver. Central Asia. 19th century. Triangular *tumar* pendants made in a variety of materials were worn as talismans throughout Central Asia (see plate 32). (Private Collection.)

18. *Pish auz*, breast ornament. Silver with glass insets. Central Asia. 19th century. Bell-shaped ornaments with multiple drops were worn at the breast or hung by a chain from a woman's belt or sash. (Private Collection.)

either very bland or very vague in order to survive for this length of time. An image must say "good luck" or "power" or "money", not "my clan is the falcon" or "Buddhism is best". The images within art appear again and again, but the use to which they are put is variable. If they have a specific meaning, then the meaning must change frequently, and with ease.

Certainly there are folk beliefs that are associated with many of these images, particularly those of animals. Folk belief often parallels the material, but there is no adequate bridge between a belief and an image. No source from the nineteenth century has ever said about ikat, "We put *this* here because it means *that*". Folk belief associates certain animals or shapes with amuletic or talismanic qualities. Ikats are not talismans, but it is appropriate to include positive images within them.

There are no familiar sayings or folk tales to support the notion that the scorpion is a protective image for urban garments or wall-hangings; there are only vague associations with shamanic traditions of the underground world, and the common use of the scorpion pattern in nomadic embroidery (plates 31, 49).

Many ikats contain triangular patterns with pendant teeth or dangling elements that are variously identified as "combs" or "amulets" (plate 32, 70). The "comb" design, which has the shape of a weft beating tool, is well known as one of the minor pattern elements of Central Asian carpets. This simple, highly abstracted design is also indistinguishable from the *tumar* form used to represent the ubiquitous triangular talisman worn by all Turkic peoples to ward off evil. *Tumar* wrought in gold and silver are common elements in women's jewelry, and a familiar image for urban Central Asians (fig. 17).

The most easily identified image in ikats is also the most seemingly innocuous. The *aftaba* is a water-jug brought to guests along with a basin, to facilitate the washing of hands before eating. It is a simple symbol of hospitality, an appropriate decoration for the walls of a guest room. Along with fruits and flowers, *aftaba* were often illustrated in wall-paintings in nineteenth-century homes. These water-jugs appear on ikats made throughout the nineteenth century, but always as minor elements within a composition. If the general effect of a design is floral, they hang from a branch like an accidental, oddly shaped fruit, a flourish to show the designer's skill (plate 18). The water-jug pattern makes its appearance in textiles well before the advent of Islam. A peaked cap of *zandaniji* from an archeological excavation at the Moschevaja ravine is made of a Sogdian fabric with a design of pearl roundels enclosing two jugs (fig. 20).[6]

Beneath the banality of this easily recognizable ikat design lurk other possibilities of interpretation. Lisa Golombek's study of landscape imagery within a small group of funerary monuments in Samarkand and Damascus from the fifteenth century raises the issue of an "iconographic program" that is also found in the ikats of the nineteenth century.[7] She notes the repeated combination of the paradisiac vision of a living landscape with various forms of water-jugs in both tilework and fresco in these monuments. The joining of the two elements may be an oblique reference to Sufism, and the jugs may represent the human vessel, which wishes to be filled with the Divine spirit.

One of Central Asia's major contributions to the Islamic world was the development of metaphysical speculation and Islamic mysticism. Central Asia has been home to more Sufi schools than the rest of the Islamic world combined. Sufism was an important element in the life of nineteenth-century Central Asians; most of the Muslim craftsmen

33 WALL-HANGING
mid-19th century
72" × 46" (183 × 117cm)
4 panels
warp-faced plain weave
The wide fabric width and warp density of this ikat possibly relate this hanging to other striped part-silk fabrics, such as *bekasab*, which seldom contain ikat-dyed warps. In this instance, there is also a strong similarity in design to the heavily ribbed ikats made in the town of Hissar in the last quarter of the 19th century.

34 WALL-HANGING
mid-19th century
41" × 35" (104 × 89cm)
3 panels
warp-faced plain weave
There are three striped sections in each panel width. Each dyed section of the warp has been split and the sections have been alternated to form an elaborately patterned row of eleven stripes on each panel. The alternating stripes have the same colors, and were probably warped, tied and dyed in groups, then arranged on the loom, with the patterns staggered at a distance of about a quarter of an inch.

35 WALL-HANGING
Ferghana Valley
second to third quarter
19th century
80" × 67" (203 × 171cm)
6 panels
warp-faced plain weave
The hooked motif on this wall-hanging is one of the clearest renderings of a gül borrowed from carpet design.

producing ikat and other luxury textiles were allied with one Sufi school or another. Despite the importance of Sufism in society there was no visual art related explicitly to the mystical experience. Neither the poetic traditions of Sufism, nor the secular epic tales preserved in memory by professional storytellers appear to have contributed directly to the imagery of textiles.

Like other Islamic arts, ikat design can only be defined by its treatment of form, not by its iconography. Within the most overtly Islamic of all decoration, calligraphic tilework on mosques, the script is often contorted and abstracted to the point of illegibility. In textiles as in tilework, the tendency is always to subordinate individual elements to create a harmonious overall pattern.

For many Central Asians, it would not have been comfortable to recognize a specific cult or magical meaning within a design. A garment or urban wall-hanging was not the proper context for such symbolic meaning. The well-known, and often misunderstood, prohibition against the depiction of religious images in art affected notions of propriety and taste within the general community; but the claim that the representation of living forms in art is forbidden by the Koran is not applicable to textiles. Unlike sculpture and painting, textiles have always been neutral ground for images. Wall-hangings and tents with pictures of both humans and animals have been used in the Islamic world since the time of the Prophet Muhammad. The lack of interest in depicting specific images in Central Asian ikats derives primarily from the fact that geometric pattern and abstracted form have had far greater importance than figuration in Central Asian art.

20

Ikat may be the most hermetic of all the arts of Central Asia. Many ikat patterns are dissolved, fragmented, turned around and upside down. They can only be called patterns because there are so many variants on a basic shape, not because the general shape can be identified with its figural or floral origin. Central Asians would see no difficulty in an ambiguous rendering of designs; it would be entirely to their taste. Within ikats, the designers have abstracted potent and symbolic images to the point where they are almost unrecognizable, and then combined these shapes in a bewildering variety of patterns. As is the case in other arts of the Islamic world, designs which at one time had a symbolic character are combined with others without symbolic content. In ikat, the symbolic elements of the pattern are no longer invested with their original meaning. One may question whether the highly abstracted designs any longer even represent the objects they were drawn from. Even when a naturalistically rendered object is found within a composition, this element does not dominate or give meaning to the piece.

The combination of images cannot be read, like a story. One cannot describe what is going on in an ikat. There is no presumption of understanding for the viewer. For the nineteenth-century owners of these garments and wall-hangings, the message was not specific – it was general. Representation did not equal symbolism, meaning was implicit rather than explicit. Ikat not only included familiar images from Central Asian culture; in its method of combining and transforming those images, it was a resonance, a response to the culture itself.

19

19. *Aftaba*, water-vessel. Brass with hammered and engraved design. Bukhara. 19th century. Depictions of water-vessels, especially *aftaba*, are often found on both ikat and embroidery in Central Asia. (Private Collection.)
20. Man's helmet. Leather lined with linen, covered with Sogdian silk showing a pair of affronting jugs in roundels. 8th century. (State Hermitage, St Petersburg.)

TECHNICAL BASES AND OPPORTUNITIES In comparison to ikats made in other areas of the world, Central Asian fabrics display the least regard for the technical and conceptual difficulties inherent in the technique. If the material that remains is representative, then it seems that ikat designers were willing and able to make up a new pattern for virtually every warp. The rejection of design formulae in a technique where the end results cannot be readily seen during the dye process is remarkable, but it is tied to the very nature of Central Asian pattern. Indeed, a degree of uncertainty about the exact end result may have been an accepted part of the design process. The rapid changes in ikat pattern during the nineteenth century may have been spurred on in part by the temptations offered to the ikat designers by this lack of predictability.

The greatest art of ikat design was in the working of pure color. The variety of patterns is endless precisely because the designer was less interested in rendering a specific shape than in experimenting with color itself. The shapes were there to draw upon, in a kind of general vocabulary of Central Asian design that also applied to carpets and embroidery and ceramic. Artistry lay in the interplay of one color against another, in blending and contrast. The virtuoso performances of the ikat dyers can be better appreciated in this textile technique than in any other type of weaving or embroidery.

The ikat binding technique softens and blurs the edges of shapes and areas of color. Because bindings for resist-dyeing were reapplied throughout the dyeing process, one color sometimes overlaps another, producing an effect rather like an out-of-register print. This is most often visible in areas in which two separate dye baths were used to make purple or green.

21

21. Detail of an ikat from the Guido Goldman Collection, showing warp manipulation in which the two half-sections of warp yarns have been laid side by side, rather than being divided to form a mirror image along the central axis of the fabric.

Another distortion of the pattern took place in the preparation for weaving. A very slight realignment always occurred between the original binding of the warps and the final placement on the loom. Extreme examples of this distortion may be found in ikat panels, in which the pattern takes a sudden slant. In the early part of the nineteenth century, a deliberately staggered pattern was sometimes made in the warps that would form border stripes. In the ikats of the later period, this type of warp manipulation became a useful method for making a simple design more complex.

Narrow sections of ikat-dyed warp in contrasting patterns could be combined to make vertiginous striped panels (plates 13, 17). In the finished fabric, the number of warp threads within each section of color is very small. In some instances it is likely that the dyed groups of warps, or bundles, were divided more than once when the warps were prepared for the loom, in order to achieve the sharp geometric figures and narrow stripes that form the pattern. It seems probable that the different stripes were designed, tied and dyed separately, then joined only when readied for the loom; one example has only half the standard number of threads per bundle in certain of the sections of striped warp (plate 34). This small group of very finely patterned ikats may have been influenced by the striped *alacha* fabrics of the seventeenth and eighteenth centuries. The most brilliant and complex examples were made in the earlier part of the nineteenth century, and do not appear to be related to the late nineteenth-century striped ikats that were made in the city of Hissar.

Most Central Asian ikat fabrics are symmetrical on either side of the central vertical axis of each panel. The warps are doubled for the purpose of outlining the pattern, binding and dyeing, then divided only when they are prepared for the loom. A few ikats exhibit unusual types of warp manipulation. In one wall-hanging from the Guido Goldman Collection (fig. 21), the two half-sections of dyed warps were separated and one of the sections was rotated 180 degrees, so that what

36 WALL-HANGING
Bukhara
first quarter 19th century
82" × 45" (210 × 114cm)
4 panels
warp-faced plain weave
A pattern type with large medallions interspersed with branch-like designs is characteristic of a small group of ikats from the early 19th century.

37 WALL-HANGING
Bukhara
first half 19th century
97" × 83" (246 × 211cm)
6 panels in center, split ikat panels framing field
warp-faced plain weave
The exceptionally intricate design was probably achieved by dividing the dyed warps twice before arranging them on the loom. The simple, two-color ikat that frames the field is probably of the same age as the much more complex center.

would have been the center became the outside border. The two half-sections of warp are identical, but serve to repeat, rather than mirror each other.

Among the group of ikats that bear patterns relating to certain Turkoman bag-faces of the Amu Darya or Ersari type is a subgroup in which the warps were not divided along the vertical axis. The bundles of warp yarns typically contain twice the number of warps of other ikats of the period. This indicates that the warping technique remained the same, with the exception of the final splitting of the warps. A large-scale pattern was made possible by using this warping technique, but in the eventual construction of the wall-hangings no attempt appears to have been made to join the panels of cloth so that the design would be symmetrical.

23

INFLUENCES OF CARPETS AND KILIMS This distinctive mid-nineteenth-century ikat group is very closely related in design to Turkoman tribal carpets from the Amu Darya area. The unusual technical arrangement of the ikat warps, and the radical change in the scale of the pattern suggest that a specific type of asymmetrical ikat design evolved in imitation of the carpet pattern. In many cases, there appears to have been a greater impact upon carpet design by ikats, rather than the other way round.

22

22. Turkoman saddlebags. 24" × 47" (61 × 119cm). Probably Burdalyk area. 19th century. (Private Collection.)
23. Kizilayak carpet. Probably Kunduz, northern Afghanistan. 19th or early 20th century. 38" × 48" (97 × 122cm). (Private Collection.)
24. Ersari carpet. Amu Darya. 19th century. 86"×116"(218×295cm). (from *Central Asian Rugs*, Ulrich Shürman. Verlag Osterrieth, Frankfurt am Main, 1969.)

Relatively early examples of Amu Darya carpets echo ikat design. In a pair of Turkoman saddlebags (fig. 22), the selvedge of an ikat panel is represented by a solid line of blue knots, and the overall pattern imitates the random alignment of ikat panels. Increasingly fragmented and geometrically rendered ikat designs occur frequently in the smaller-scale narrow tent-bags of the Amu Darya Turkomans. A group of Turkoman carpets in which the field is broken into a grid, and either floral or, more rarely, scorpion motifs are repeated may be related to ikat design.

A group of late nineteenth-century Turkoman and Kizilayak carpets have motifs inspired by the patterns of ikat velvet. Some of these rugs also imitate the often haphazard arrangement of ikat panels (fig. 23). Another notable borrowing of designs occurs in a group of ikats whose patterns closely relate to the large, rectangular Turkoman storage bags with latticework designs (plate 11). The motifs of a further group are strikingly similar to those used in Turkoman and Uzbek kilims.The borrowing of urban designs by rug weavers was a continuing phenomenon throughout the nineteenth and twentieth centuries; nomadic art welcomed this urban influence.

24

The large group of ikats in which the field is filled with saturated reds and blues bears a less direct design relationship to nomadic carpets, but the influence of the Amu Darya type of Turkoman rugs seems clear in the working of color and the choice of palette. The similarity to rug design within ikat lies primarily in the interplay and relationship of color. The blurred edges of over-dye on ikat are a fortuitous result of the dyeing process, but the visual effect is similar to the Turkoman technique of edging a mass of color with a border of slightly brighter or darker tone. The effect in both ikat and carpets is to define the pattern, and make all the colors appear richer.

Motifs that occur as minor elements within carpet design are scattered like confetti throughout these ikats. An ikat with a "cloud band" pattern may be based on similar carpet designs, especially as these appear in rugs from Eastern Turkestan, although the pattern could derive from tilework or pottery (plate 5). Hanging pomegranates, a

25

minor design element in the case of carpets, become the dominant motifs of many ikats. It might be claimed that the white field Beshir-type prayer rugs influenced ikat design in the case of early nineteenth-century white field ikat wall-hangings (plates 2, 36). The reverse could also be argued – that the carpet design was based on the patterns of both ikat and suzani. Occasional, rather rare, occurrences of borrowing from rug design take place much later in the nineteenth century. In other ikat wall-hangings with large medallion and multiple prayer-arch patterns, the palette of the carpet weavers is abandoned and only rug motifs are incorporated (plate 35).

38 WALL-HANGING
Bukhara
first half 19th century
83" × 58" (212 × 147cm)
4 panels
warp-faced plain weave

The disregard for the alignment of the ikat panels within finished garments or wall-hangings may stem from a nomadic weaving tradition. Woven woolen bands were made by yurt-dwelling Uzbeks and other steppe people to ornament and secure the yurt structure. Very similar bands were also stitched together to make floor rugs and brazier covers. The intricate geometric pattern of the forty-foot (12m) band may remain consistent along its length, but it more often changes about once every foot.

26

27

25–28. Details of ikats from the Guido Goldman Collection which illustrate floral designs extending from vase-like bases.

The warp-float technique, *gazhery*, has given its name to the widely distributed Central Asian kilims which are made up of these woven bands. When the narrow bands were stitched together to make a rug, there was little or no interest taken in aligning the patterns. The eye-dazzling effect was achieved in part by the choice of where to cut and where to sew.

Even the most expensive and luxurious ikat fabrics were handled in this arbitrary fashion. Silk velvet ikat panels are often arranged in garments with the pile lying in opposing directions on adjacent strips of fabric. It is not uncommon to find wall-hangings in which two ikats, sometimes of similar design, are combined. To the Central Asian eye, the arbitrary linking of patterns adds visual interest. It seems that the designer and the eventual consumer were not concerned with matching up patterns in a coat or a wall-hanging. They were more interested in the complex design that resulted from *not* matching the panels. In addition, while Central Asians were fond of masses of fabric, they were also thrifty, and no material was wasted in composing a garment or wall-hanging in this manner.

28

INFLUENCES OF OTHER URBAN TEXTILE ARTS The most common forms of household decoration in the Central Asian Khanates were the hand-embroidered wall-hangings and bed and bolster covers known as suzanis. Although some suzanis had large circular patterns popularly called "suns and moons", the motifs were essentially floral. Suzani design was more conservative than ikat design; domestic embroidery was a traditional art, not a commercial one. Suzani patterns were drawn by older women, and conservative professional designers; young girls had to argue with their grandmothers over the addition of new colors or patterns.[8] In contrast, the ikat makers were male artisans on a deliberately experimental path: they borrowed antique motifs and adapted them.

Many early nineteenth-century ikats may draw on the abstracted floral patterns of suzanis, although the flowering buds float free of tendril attachments. Floral ikat patterns more clearly imitate wall-paintings of flowers arranged in vases and pots (plates 38, 45). The composition of ikat floral patterns is the result of the tying process, and every image becomes a vertical repeat. This sequence of ikat fabrics, made throughout the nineteenth century, demonstrates the simplification and stylization of the ikat patterns over time (figs 25–28). One of the most common early twentieth-century ikat patterns (fig. 30) appears to be related to a late style of suzani, but its antecedents can be traced back to the early years of ikat production (plate 2). The suzanis of Tashkent and nearby Urgench have the same giant roundels and swirling patterns of these later ikats.

Rose and mirror and sun and moon – what are they?

Wherever we looked, there was always Thy face.

Mir, eighteenth-century Urdu poet[10]

Central Asian ikat designers borrowed the static, single cypress image of Persian textiles and transformed it into a lively, highly abstract pattern repeat. Although the cypress has also been a common design element in Central Asian textiles for centuries, the Persian style clearly influenced the composition of certain Central Asian ikats. The exterior lines of the cypress remain from the Persian original, but the interiors of the Central Asian trees are vividly colored and electric in design (plates 31, 39).

29

29. Detail of Pskent suzani. 19th century. (The Textile Gallery, London.)
30. Wall-hanging. Bukhara, last quarter 19th century. 91" × 59" (231 × 150cm), 3.5 panels. Warp-faced plain weave. (Guido Goldman Collection.)

REMNANTS OF ANTIQUE ELEMENTS IN LATER IKAT DESIGN The Uzbek scholar Sayora Mahkamova has emphasized the ancient traditions within ikat design, specifically the motif of the tree of life between two animals that is found in Sogdian fabrics. The pearl roundels and concentric circles surrounding rosettes that were found in Sogdian fabrics are commonly found in ikats. This tendency to transform minor design elements from other media into central figures within Sogdian textiles occurs frequently in ikat design. Small jugs, branching horned figures and many other designs can be identified in fabrics of both the Sogdian period and nineteenth-century Central Asia. Certainly these familiar forms have not the same "meaning" within the modern fabrics. In Central Asia, it is the versatility, not the age or the symbolic import of a design that is important.

In the 1930s, V.K. Rozvadovsky collected ikat patterns from the town of Maghilan for a book of thirty designs published in 1941.[9] While the ikats show the continuing influence of nineteenth-century patterns, the designs are static, and they exhibit the constrained, deliberate qualities of the ikats of the twentieth century. At the time of collection, ikat patterns for popular fabrics were drawn by artists who were associated with the major silk combines as well as by the traditional masters. The ikats of this period represent the very end of individual workshop production.

TOWARD ESTABLISHING A CHRONOLOGY The basis for a chronology of Central Asian ikats is, to a degree, subjective and circumstantial. All the sources of information – documented materials and anecdotal history, technical analysis and economic data – must be balanced and compared. In the end, there are likely suppositions to be made regarding the period before the 1860s, and limited but valuable documentary sources for ikat production after that time.

Ikats may be categorized in technical terms by the structure of warp and weft, by the number of bundles used in tying, by the manipulation of the warp, by the type of dyes used, and by the weaving technique employed to produce the finished fabric. They can be grouped by design similarities, and by the manner in which colors and motifs are handled. This type of categorization also reflects local tastes and may be helpful in establishing a geographic provenance for certain types of ikats. Tendencies toward simplification, elaboration, and the preference for certain color groups also provide clues to their age.

Both the marketplace and public collections have supplied a large body of materials from which to group ikats within these guidelines. These sources also allow for an estimate of the relative scarcity or abundance of the different types of ikats. Rarity is certainly no guarantee of age, but it seems reasonable to assume that, if supported by technical and design characteristics and by other comparative documentary evidence, the present rarity of certain ikat groups may offer some indication of their age.

Regrettably, the factory-produced imported cottons used to line ikat wall-hangings and robes are not a reliable tool for dating purposes. Backing fabrics can be identified and dated in many cases, but it has been common practice to reassemble and reline ikats, and old backing fabrics were much admired in Central Asia. A late nineteenth-century ikat could be lined with a mid-nineteenth-century cotton, or the other way round.

Ethnographic photographs from the early period of photography show the popularity of ikat, and its wide dissemination throughout the Khanates. The photographs also make it clear that a broad range of designs was popular at the same time, and that tastes and fashions altered only very slowly until a few decades before the turn of the century. Western travelers were entranced by the costumes of Central Asia, and a rash of late nineteenth-century travel books carry illustrations of natives in exotic dress. Itinerant Russian photographers took pictures of yurt-dwelling nomads, dervishes and minstrels, as well as making more traditional family portraits.

Some of the most valuable documentary evidence comes from the photographs commissioned by the Russian General K.P. von Kaufman in 1871 and 1872.[11] The six volumes of the *Turkestanskii al'bom* include well over a thousand photographs of Central Asian commercial, social and family life. The Kaufman photographs establish a baseline for the production of certain ikats, and provide detailed information on both textile processes and the use of finished fabrics in domestic decoration and family ceremonies.

30

The reopening of a case of ikat garments in the early 1990s at the Ashmolean Museum in Oxford led the curator Ruth Barnes on a quest for its origin. Painstaking detective work enabled her to identify the material as having been collected in 1868 by Robert Shaw, an English tea planter. Shaw had traveled to Kashgar and Yarkand in the hope of establishing a trade relationship with its new ruler, Yacub Beg, who had recently ousted the Chinese authorities in Eastern Turkestan. Shaw reported that at his first audience with the ruler, the court was filled with retainers in brilliantly colored silk robes. In keeping with Central Asian courtesy, Shaw was presented with a rich pink satin robe by Yacub Beg himself at their first meeting.[12]

The Ashmolean collection contains the earliest provenanced ikats from Central Asia. Because the year in which they were collected in Asia is known, it allows for the setting of an absolute date for the production of certain ikat fabrics. The Shaw material included twelve ikat robes of Central Asian cut, in a style characteristic of the Ferghana Valley.[13] There were seven robes of *adras* cotton-wefted ikat, one of *atlas* satin, two tabby-woven all-silk robes, one of *bekasam* (a striped fabric that often includes areas of ikat warp), and one with simple striped patterns in Surkhandarya[14] style. There was, in addition, a reversible coat in Chinese cut, made of cotton-wefted ikat on one side, and all-silk ikat on the other. The coats display a wide variety of designs and colors, and the use of scraps of ikat fabric to form the lapse on the lining of the garments provides more than twenty examples of ikat from 1868 or before.[15]

A larger collection of similar ikat fabrics of various lengths was acquired by the Victoria and Albert Museum in London in 1880 through the India Office, but no documentation regarding the ikats has yet been discovered. The Victoria and Albert ikat panels are almost entirely lengths of unsewn fabric, and the materials show few signs of wear. As in the case of the Shaw materials, there is a wide range of fabrics, colors and weaves. An unusual feature of a number of the museum's fabrics is the variety of colors in the selvages. The majority of the ikat fabrics remaining from the nineteenth century have blue selvages, while many of the fabrics in the Victoria and Albert collection have yellow, green or white selvages, which set them apart from the standard Bukharan production.

TECHNICAL BASES The pressures of the marketplace have always affected fabric production. It is a more expensive and time-consuming process to tie a warp into many tiny bundles and dye it in four or more dye baths than it is to tie fewer bundles and dye it twice. Anecdotal evidence suggests that the price of a fabric was in large part based on the number of colors it had. Very early ikats were not necessarily many-colored. A large wall-hanging of tulip-like pattern has six colors in the fabric of the field, yet is bordered with sections of two-colored ikat. The two fabrics are virtually identical in construction; the warps are of equal density, and the bundles are of relatively small size (plate 37).

The warp threads of the early ikats may have been thinner, that is, composed of fewer filament strands. There was a general tendency toward a narrower fabric in the early years, and a correspondingly wider cloth towards the end of ikat production. The complexity and detail of the early ikats give the impression that the warp bundles are composed of fewer threads. In most cases, however, the intricacy results from the number of ties, rather than the number of threads in the bundles. The number of threads per warp bundle remained fairly consistent throughout most of the nineteenth century, then increased dramatically at the turn of the century.

39 WALL-HANGING
Bukhara
first half 19th century
61" × 33" (154 × 84cm)
3 panels
warp-faced plain weave

40 WALL-HANGING
Bukhara
first half 19th century
82" × 37" (208 × 95cm)
2.5 panels
warp-faced plain weave

41 WALL-HANGING
first half 19th century
90" × 15" (229 × 39cm)
2 panels
warp-faced plain weave
Narrow loom and bundle width, the balanced but intricate design, and saturated colors all place this ikat in the very early period. Its unusual palette distinguishes it from all but a few other early ikats.

Technique is by nature conservative. A production process is difficult to change; habits must be broken and many adjustments made. The easiest way of lowering the cost of a fabric was by varying the number of dye baths to which it was subject. Changing the structure of the warp or the tying process was more difficult. Radical changes in the ikat-making process took place only in the last quarter of the nineteenth century, when local fabrics came under extreme pressure from imports, and it became essential to reduce the cost of production. The introduction of chemical dyes resulted in a dramatic change in both ikat colors and the handling of pattern. Chemical dyes were officially banned in Bukhara until the twentieth century, but could easily have reached dyers within the Emirate through unofficial channels after the late 1860s. Most nineteenth-century sources indicate that natural dyestuffs dominated the markets of Bukhara and the Russian Protectorate until the 1880s, and that many were widely available until after the turn of the century.

The weaving of tabby-woven *shohi* all-silk ikat fabrics and *atlas* ikat satins became common by the 1860s. There is no evidence, based on comparative design, that they were made any earlier. Silk velvet ikat probably began to be made at about the same time. Velvets with comparatively simple patterns and a limited palette continued in production beyond the turn of the century, but velvet ikat production appears to have been completely abandoned by the time of the 1917 Revolution.

CHRONOLOGY AND DESIGN There is no fixed date for the inception of *adras* ikat production in Central Asia. The technique of ikat dyeing in simple stripes had been known for centuries throughout the region, but the early *adras* cotton-wefted ikat, with its explosive patterning and dramatic scale, is not known until the beginning of the nineteenth century. The earliest reference to *adras* ikat fabric is from the 1813 report of a British spy regarding Bukharan trade with Kabul. The report mentions the export of robes made from "*adras*, *ulecha-muslin* and *norka-kub*".[16] The name of *adras* does not occur among the many fabrics mentioned in the Russian customs records of the seventeenth or eighteenth century.[17] The economic and social changes that began to take place at the turn of the nineteenth century support the hypothesis that *adras* ikat was first made at that time. These same factors also suggest Bukhara as the most likely place in which ikat-dyed cloth underwent a revolutionary change from a simple, striped material to an elaborately patterned luxury fabric.

The oldest *adras* ikats appear to be the finely detailed fabrics with a white field and tiny spots of color (plates 9, 36, 37), and the equally complex *adras* of mottled blue/green background and highly saturated color. These two early design types have the richest tones, the least fabric width, and consistent, small bundles, and they are also the rarest of the Central Asian ikats that remain. Neither of these two design types appears among the dated materials in public collections. Among these ikats of elaborate pattern and restricted width are extraordinary examples of inventive design by the early ikat makers (plates 30, 41). The extremely fine striped ikats may belong to the latter part of this period of experiment and invention.

A somewhat larger group of ikat styles developed around or before the middle of the nineteenth century, and at this time certain regional differences appeared. These mid-nineteenth-century ikats were still cotton-wefted, with a heavy, ribbed appearance. The widest range of patterns probably belonged to Bukhara, while ikats tending toward a more geometric design and pinker tones are now thought to have been made in Samarkand. Among the ikats that may be ascribed to Samarkand workshops are an unusual group of *adras* ikats with solid backgrounds that range from rich gold to a pale, clear yellow (plates 42, 70), and another group with simple geometric patterns on a white field (plate 1). These yellow or white background ikats share certain design characteristics; although they have the saturated colors of the ikats of the early period, they are also uncluttered, and the main design elements float freely on the solid colored field, rather than interlocking with many other small elements.

Around the middle of the nineteenth century, ikat patterns became even more varied. New designs and patterns appeared; colors were still rich, but the designs were slightly less intricate. The material that remains from this period is more abundant, and rather than unique examples, there are numerous variations on the same design. One large group has patterns based on hanging pomegranates (plate 18), a common design element within embroidery; others relate to carpet design. The Guido Goldman Collection contains many examples of these complex-patterned ikats of rich red tone, and it is possible to appreciate the success of the designer in bringing oft-repeated Central Asian motifs into a new and uniquely harmonious relationship within each fabric (plate 37).

Deep blue indigo-dyed fabrics with thin, white, branching patterns in *adras* technique make their appearance by the middle of the nineteenth century (plate 63). The importance of the indigo fabrics as mourning robes ensured their longevity in the local marketplace. Anecdotal information from numerous ethnic studies made in the early twentieth century indicates that these indigo-dyed ikats were considered proper attire for older women in many areas of Central Asia. The wide distribution of Jewish indigo dyers throughout Central Asia would have made production of dark blue ikats possible in any of the ikat-making cities. The ikats with indigo background continued to be made in *adras* until almost the end of the century, with only a slight loss of color saturation and tone, while brighter fabrics were increasingly made in all-silk plain weaves and satins. The simple, narrow patterns of the ikats with an indigo background are not found on *adras* ikats in any other color range.

42 WALL-HANGING
possibly Samarkand
third quarter 19th century
80" × 55" (204 × 140cm)
5 panels
warp-faced plain weave

31

31. Wall-hanging. c.1900. 80" × 56" (203 × 142cm), 4 panels. Warp-faced plain weave; silk warp and weft. The designs of turn-of-the-century ikats are often bolder and larger in scale than those of earlier periods. (Guido Goldman Collection.)

IKATS FROM THE FERGHANA VALLEY Compelling economic and ethnological evidence from the end of the nineteenth century makes it clear that the Ferghana Valley, the center of the Khanate of Kokand and the area closest to China, became at least the equal of Bukhara in the magnitude of its silk production. The change took place as a result of the movement of capital and entrepreneurial activity to Russian-held territories and the emigration of many Jewish dyers from Bukhara to the area of the Ferghana Valley. Tashkent, a hundred miles west of the valley, was considered part of Kokand's sphere of influence. Samarkand, much further to the southwest, was at times included within the same economic area, although it was more often closely allied with Bukhara.

Ikat production probably spread to the Ferghana Valley by the late 1850s; it was well established there by the 1860s. The branching horn designs emanating from a central stalk are widely associated with the Ferghana Valley. The small town of Khodjent, at the western end of the area of the Ferghana Valley, would soon establish a conservative, local tradition based on this branching pattern and the use of an unusual palette that included an acidic green and turquoise.

Ethnological studies have cited a taste for darker, more sober colors in the Ferghana area, and the all-silk ikats with an iridescent purple background from the latter part of the nineteenth century have often been given a Ferghana provenance on that basis. However, the studies related to male costume, and the all-silk fabrics were most often worn by women, who were not subject to the same social pressures of public dress. Blue warps and red wefts gave this all-silk cloth its purplish hue. A similar fabric was also made in Bukhara,[18] and robes of what appear to be this type of material are seen in photographs from Bukhara and Samarkand.

There is insufficient evidence to state which region developed the linear, branching patterns that are the most common type of ikat produced in the last third of the nineteenth century. The conservative, regional variants found within the Ferghana area suggest that the pattern may have originated there. Certainly, by the end of the nineteenth century, the Ferghana Valley had become at least the equal of Bukhara in the volume of production.

LATE NINETEENTH-CENTURY IKATS Samarkand is generally credited as being the source of another large group of *adras* cotton-wefted ikats from the last third of the nineteenth century which were woven in simple patterns of red, white, and either yellow or pink. These geometrically based patterns are similar to a style that was established in mid-nineteenth-century Samarkand; the rich rose colors of the early period were replaced by pale pinks and flat reds. This group can be reliably attributed to Samarkand, through both early ethnographic studies and materials collected in the twentieth century from local owners by the Samarkand Museum and other regional public collections.[19]

The town of Hissar developed a regional style based on simple chevrons and striped and plaid designs. The late nineteenth-century Hissar materials are cotton-wefted, with a thick, ribbed appearance. After the turn of the century a loose weave using unboiled warps and a silk weft produced a fabric that was rough and coarse to the touch. A variety of colored wefts was used in some of the late nineteenth- and early twentieth-century Hissar ikat fabrics. While they were popular imports in Bukhara, the Hissar fabrics were not imitated elsewhere.

Plain or tabby-woven all-silk ikats in vertical, branching patterns typical of the third quarter of the nineteenth century continued to be made at least up until the late 1880s and gradually replaced the half-silk *adras* as a fabric for traditional costume. By 1890, commercial pressure from competing, imported cloth forced ikat makers to produce a less expensive fabric, with interesting results. Rather than make a complex pattern badly, the designers took a simple design that required fewer ties and fewer dye baths, and did it very well.

In the Ferghana Valley the existing floral branching patterns and vase-and-flower designs were simplified and the palette was reduced, often to just three colors. Fabrics in subdued green and brown tones became common in the Ferghana area; in Bukhara, shocking pinks and purples vied with brilliant yellows and greens. Even these garish colors were given a muddied tone by the visible red wefting. In both regions the scale of antique patterns was radically altered. In Bukhara, traditional motifs tripled and quadrupled in size. The very large motifs and vivid, if sometimes acid, colors of the final phase of Central Asian ikats are testimony to the designer's skill and represent the last inventive leap of the Central Asian textile arts.

WALL-HANGINGS & HOUSEHOLD DECORATION

When starching the warp on the looms they would say, "In God's good heaven there are always flowering gardens, and in them eternal streams. God is pleased with them and they are for God's sake. This is for he who fears his God."

A prayer to accompany weaving, N.O. Tursunov[1]

HOUSEHOLD CONSTRUCTION AND DECORATION The role of textiles in the private lives of the oases dwellers was not just considerable, it was exaggerated.[2] In the street, a man's clothing defined his status in society. In the home, the place of honor was filled with the richest textiles. The rites of family life, from the entertainment of entire clans in outdoor festivals, to the most intimate rituals of marriage, were celebrated in surroundings made beautiful with fabrics – at times within silken tents.

Custom demanded the exclusion of outsiders from this private ceremonial. The life of the family was *pardah*, veiled. It was difficult enough for strangers to reach the hidden lands of the Khanates, to visit Bukhara, and to carry the tale back home. It was impossible to see into the private lives of its citizens. Half the population rarely ventured out of doors. When women did go out into the streets, they were cloaked from head to toe, and veiled with a heavy net of black horsehair. They moved like ghosts through the man's world of the town. Until the twentieth century the lives of Central Asian women were centered almost entirely on the extended family. Most households were large,

32. "Humay and Humayun on the Day after their Wedding", from a Diwan of Khwaju Kirmani. Baghdad. Inscribed AH Jumada I 798 (March 1396). (British Library, London.)

32

43 WALL-HANGING
Bukhara
first half 19th century
67" × 34" (169 × 86cm)
3 panels
warp-faced plain weave
The central figures are neither roundels nor tulip-shaped, but something in between. This hanging belongs to a group of early red-field ikats which share a repertory of ancient Central Asian designs and consistent color relationship, and display a playful, musical and infinitely varied composition.

44 WALL-HANGING
Bukhara
first half 19th century
68" × 44" (174 × 113cm)
3 solid panels, 1 split panel
warp-faced plain weave
This is one of a very rare group of early, large-medallion ikats.

45 WALL-HANGING
Bukhara or Samarkand
first half 19th century
80" × 48" (204 × 123cm)
4.5 panels
warp-faced plain weave
Though this floral pattern becomes common in later years, an unusual palette and delicately applied color distinguish this luminous, early ikat.

46 WALL-HANGING
third quarter 19th century
81" × 61" (207 × 156cm)
5.5 panels
warp-faced plain weave

and included grandparents, uncles and their wives and children. The eldest women were invested with absolute authority within the home; young brides worked the hardest, sharing among themselves the tasks of cleaning, cooking and raising children. Their lives were active and fulfilling, but their world was circumscribed by the walls that surrounded each home.

Typically, houses were made of sun-baked brick, whitewashed or mud-plastered in the various shades of the steppe. High walls enclosed a courtyard, where women washed clothes, dried fruit from the family orchard, and baked flat breads in a low oven. On summer evenings, beds could be placed on the flat roof of the house to catch a cooling breeze. The world within the walls was invisible to all but the closest family. Male visitors called out from the gate to alert those inside – the women vanished into private rooms, and a small child led the visitor through a high-columned porch to the guest room, the largest and best appointed in the household.

In the humblest of the oases homes, the only furnishings might be a scrap of bright, printed cloth over a doorway, and a few colorful patchwork mattresses. In the houses of the wealthy, the wall-hangings and bedding-quilts were multiplied a hundredfold, and the materials used were the richest and most brilliant silks and satins. The finest handiwork of the women was displayed in the guest room, where all the furnishings were made of textiles. Heavy cotton quilts and embroidered bolsters lined the walls, and a long carpet ran down the center of the room. In the daytime, the piles of bedding were hidden beneath a bright cover, often made of ikat silk. The walls held arched recesses with many shelves, filled with the best teapots and bowls belonging to the family. Ikat silks or embroidered curtains covered niches and doors, and bouquets of flowers were painted on the walls and ceiling.

When visitors arrived, a child brought a ewer and basin, and poured water over the hands of each guest in turn. Food was brought to just behind the curtained doorway by women, passed to a child or male server, and placed on a carpet or cloth set on the ground. When women entertained each other, men were banished from that part of the household. During large family gatherings, such as weddings or funerals, a tent-like structure was built in the courtyard of carpets, embroideries or ikat silks. Uzbek families who still had memories of life on the steppes sometimes built a raised circular platform inside the walls of the courtyard, and erected a yurt on it. The men gathered in the yurt or pavilion, and the women were entertained inside the house.

The effect and intent of all the textile decoration was to create the atmosphere of a garden.[3] In the Khanates, the garden was the ideal setting for the good life. The walled orchards outside the town were not merely to supply fruits and vegetables to the families that owned them; in spring and summer they were the family park and place of recreation. Going out to the gardens was a joyful occasion for the entire family, and certainly the moment of greatest freedom for the women.

It was important that the symbolic life of the garden should be part of the everyday world. The significant moments of a person's life were to be lived within this idealized garden, created not by Nature, but in woven and embroidered silks. The marking of the New Year, the celebration of a wedding, the welcoming of a birth – all were sanctified and given deeper meaning in the surroundings of the artificial paradise. In the chill of winter, and indeed, all year inside the dusty town, the garden was made to live again through the embroidery work of women, and the spring-like colors of the rich ikat silks.

33

33. Landscape from a poetic anthology, copied by Mansur Bibihani. Watercolor, ink and gold on paper. Iran. Dated AH Istanbul, Muharram 801 (September 1398). (Turk ve Islam Eseleri Müzesi.)

The citizens, rich and poor, went to walk therein and found no retreat more wonderful or beautiful than those and no resting place more agreeable and secure; and its sweetest fruits were common to all.

Ahmed ibn Arabshah on Timur's gardens in Samarkand, fifteenth century.[4]

47 WALL-HANGING
third quarter 19th century
86" × 59" (218 × 151cm)
5.25 panels
warp-faced plain weave
The free-flowing patterns of the early 19th century become more rigid in later years. Although the colors are still rich, and the pattern complex, the continuous vertical lines of this ikat prefigure the more static designs of the last quarter of the century.

48 WALL-HANGING
probably Samarkand
third quarter 19th century
84" × 60" (213 × 152cm)
4 panels
warp-faced plain weave
This is more complex in pattern and richer in color than the rigid geometric ikats made in late 19th-century Samarkand. The forms are reminiscent of kilim design; the clean lines of the double repeat were made possible by dividing the ikat-dyed warp twice along the vertical axis.

WALL-HANGINGS OF IKAT AND SUZANI Two types of wall-hangings were important prestige items in the Khanates. Aside from clothing, the essential items in a woman's dowry were the embroidered wall-hangings she made before her marriage. These suzanis played an important part in many private rituals. They decorated the walls during festivals, lay on the marriage bed, and in some towns, covered a woman's bier when her body was taken for burial. Although some suzanis have arched-shaped borders like a *mihrab*,[5] inscriptions are far more often poetic than religious, and the essential nature of these hangings is secular. The decorations on suzanis are most often abstractly rendered floral designs, bouquets, or overall patterns of flowers connected by running stems. Urban suzanis were embroidered on narrow panels before they were joined, and in many embroideries there was not much concern that the floral pattern of the panels should match in the final assembly.

Wall-hangings made of panels of silk ikat were the other important type of urban wall decoration. The general term *pardah*, meaning curtain or veil, was used for these wall-hangings. The word

49 WALL-HANGING
Bukhara
first half 19th century
74" × 54" (189 × 137cm)
5 panels
warp-faced plain weave
Highly stylized scorpions are integrated into a complex design that includes abstracted floral and jewelry patterns. The colors are keyed and balanced so perfectly that each element of the pattern is well defined, yet blends with the other motifs in a unified composition.

34

34. Ceremonial tent. A variety of ikat panels decorate the enclosure; Kirgiz carpets cover the steps. Described on the back of the photograph as "a typical tent for greeting officials". Photo: Melik Sarkisian. c. 1900. (Archives of the State Museum of Uzbekistan, Tashkent.)

pardah was also applied to any type of drapery, including that used to cover bedding piles or unsightly household utensils. The same name was given to the silk panels used to make pavilions outside the house.

To make an ikat *pardah*, a number of panels of fabric, usually from four to six, or even eight, were joined together and sewn to a cotton backing. Wall-hangings made of ikat were usually longer than they were wide. At times, a border of ikat cloth surrounded a rectangle of plain silk or cotton, or one type of ikat fabric formed a frame for another group of panels in the center. Often, strips of unmatched ikat fabrics were joined in the same wall-hanging. In most hangings, the individual lengths of fabric were sewn together without regard to the alignment of the pattern, and the arrangement of the panels was vertical. The selvedge formed the sides of the hanging, and the lengths of fabric usually ran from ceiling to floor. Small loops were sometimes sewn to a strip of edging along the top to facilitate hanging the ikats as curtains or for the construction of pavilions. More often, stretching or wear along one of the sides indicates the manner in which an older piece was hung.

50 WALL-HANGING
Bukhara
mid-19th century
64" × 37" (163 × 95cm)
2 solid panels, 2 half panels
warp-faced plain weave
One of a very rare group of ikats which combine richly detailed areas of design with solid masses of suffused color. The monumental scale of later Bukharan ikats is prefigured in this mid-century group.

51 WALL-HANGING
Bukhara
first half 19th century
83" × 65" (211 × 166cm)
6 panels
warp-faced plain weave

52 WALL-HANGING
Bukhara
mid-19th century
76" × 48" (193 × 122cm)
2 full panels, 1 split panel
warp-faced plain weave
Monumental scale and an experimental palette characterize a small ikat group that includes plate 53.

53 WALL-HANGING
Bukhara
mid-19th century
83" × 47" (210 × 121cm)
3 panels
warp-faced plain weave
The designs on this ikat and on plate 52 are based on a medallion form so large that it can barely be seen in its entirety within the fabric length; its edges extend to the cut lengths of each panel.

35

35. Tadjik wedding ceremony. Bride and groom stand on a quilt beneath a canopy of printed cloth. The groom is offered a drinking bowl, and a mirror is held before the bride. *Turkestanskii al'bom*, 1871–72. (Navoi Library, Tashkent.)

The most elaborate arrangement of fabrics was in quilts or wall-hangings of patchworked triangles called *caroq*.[6] The patchwork construction of these hangings had a talismanic, protective significance. Harmful spirits which might injure a young mother or child, or an evil-eye curse cast on some member of the household, could not enter a home decorated with these materials. The patchworked hangings acted as a trap: the evil spirits would become entangled in the many seams and divisions in the cloth. This triangular shaping of fabrics is found in many amuletic objects from Central Asia, notably the *doga*, the ubiquitous triangular talisman.

BACKING MATERIALS AND LININGS Ikat wall-hangings were usually lined with a cotton fabric to give the hanging weight and strength. The center section of the backing was usually made of an inexpensive cotton. A thin strip of material, usually a cotton calico, a scrap of another ikat fabric, or an *alacha* striped cotton cut on the bias, formed a lapse on the edge of the backing, and whereas the lapse might be four to sixteen inches (10–40cm) wide on the back, only an inch or so was visible from the front. At times, a thin filling of cotton wadding was quilted in vertical sections on to the linings. Coverlets and mattresses contained a much thicker mat of cotton.

Until the third quarter of the nineteenth century, the most common lining fabrics for Central Asian ikats were locally made cottons.These were not considered as stylish as imported cotton goods, but they were less expensive and perfectly suited for backings. Fabrics ranged from plain tabby-woven coarse cotton to finer plain weave fabrics, striped warp-faced cottons, and block-printed textiles.

Of the block-printed fabrics used to line ikats, the most basic were mordant-dyed cotton *chit*. *Chit* fabrics have a long history in Central Asia; the oldest known weavers' guild ritual text, which dates to the eighteenth century, pertains to this craft.[7] The fawn-colored background of most block-printed cottons was produced by dyeing the fabric before printing began in a solution that included pomegranate rind; an indigo bath was used to make a medium blue background. A resist of wax or clay could be applied to reserve areas of white for later printing. After the initial dye bath the reserve material was removed. In the most common mordant-printed

54 WALL-HANGING
Bukhara
mid-19th century
57" × 31" (145 × 79cm)
4 panels
warp-faced plain weave
A medallion form with a delicate, spotted outline has been stretched and then twisted in this unusual blue-toned ikat. The lines of the medallion flow around the smaller design elements rather than containing them.

fabrics, alum and iron vitriol solutions were applied to the cloth with patterned woodblock templates, and the material was dried and then taken for dyeing. These mordants fixed the dye on the fabric by combining with the dyestuff to form an insoluble compound which would not wash out. A single dyestuff, madder, reacted with the first mordant to make a black pattern, and the second to make a red one. The most common pattern applied to mordant-print cottons was a repeat of small floral or paisley shapes.

Imported cottons, primarily from Persia and Russia, were also used to line ikat robes and wall-hangings. English and French printed cottons were expensive in comparison to Persian or Russian manufactures, but were also sporadically available in the Central Asian bazaars.The most common, simple Persian fabrics were virtually identical to Central Asian *chit* mordant prints.[8] The bulk of the Russian cottons exported to Central Asia were produced in the town of Ivanovo, located about 165 miles northeast of Moscow. Ivanovo and its surrounding towns were originally famed for their hand-printed woodblock cotton materials designed for the peasant market. The Ivanovo factories had expanded and mechanized production to become major centers of the Russian textile industry by the third quarter of the nineteenth century.[9]

As early as the seventeenth century, the Ivanovo hand-printed cottons borrowed designs from the luxury fabrics of Central Asia and Persia. Among these were woodblock-printed fabrics in imitation of *dorogi*, the Russian term for a Persian or Bukharan fabric with ikat-dyed warps. Traders from Ivanovo began to sell printed cloth in Astrakhan in the second half of the eighteenth century, and many designs were adapted to suit Eastern tastes. Some of the first mass-produced Ivanovo prints utilized the designs of Bukharan fabrics, but the most widely distributed materials were "oriental-style" patterns which included birds amidst luxuriant vegetation and floral sprays on striped backgrounds, patterns that derived from eighteenth- and early nineteenth-century printed textiles from Europe.[10]

A vogue for roller-printed cottons influenced by Kashmiri shawl designs had begun in England in the 1830s. Soon after, a virtually identical style of printed cotton fabric became very popular in Russia, where the authentic shawls were much prized by the female aristocracy. Engravers were employed to cut the delicate paisley patterns on to metal cylinders, a more effective means of achieving the detailed shawl designs than woodblock printing. Paisley and floral patterned cloths from the Ivanovo region were the most popular imported fabrics used for ikat backings in the first half of the nineteenth century. In a few instances, these patterns were provided with complementary stripes or background patterns that were clearly in imitation of the Central Asian silk ikat fabrics.[11] By the latter part of the nineteenth century, machine-printed "faux ikat" fabrics were made in Ivanovo specifically for the Central Asian market.

Ikat silk was itself used as a backing material in some instances. Wealthy women could afford to use the valuable cloth to line the backs of dowry suzanis, and ikat linings are often found on rich saddlecloths. Ikat fabric turns up in unexpected places: in the linings of antique books, as a backing material for traditional nomadic tent decorations, in the form of mirror cases and wrappings for the Holy Koran, even for use as sock-like slippers.[12] Ikat fabric was used to add richness, and to honor the object that it embellished.

7

COSTUME, FASHION & FABRIC

After this I was allowed to go, being nearly stifled, from having to wear three heavy robes, one above the other, the gift of the King this afternoon; such is the custom of the country. I forgot to say that when I entered, the king wished me "Moobarak" (or happy) on putting on the new robes.

Robert Shaw, on receiving gifts of robes of honor from the ruler Yacub Beg in Kashgar, 1868[1]

Much of the nineteenth-century ikat fabric that remains is in the form of costume. Men's robes and women's dresses and distinctive head coverings served important functions in Central Asian society. A person's clothing said very plainly who he or she was; it defined social rank, domestic role and tribal affiliation or geographic origin. A glance at the evolution of Central Asian dress gives primacy to the role of fabric, for all along the Silk Road, it was the cloth that made the man.

ANCIENT CENTRAL ASIAN COSTUME You cannot ride a horse in a toga. Trousers were among the many gifts brought from the East by the nomad hordes. With trousers go tunics, and a tunic slit down the front is a robe. Whether turning to loose an arrow from a galloping horse, hiking up a trouser leg to plow a muddy field, or lounging cross-legged to puff a hookah, these are serviceable, comfortable and versatile garments.

This costume of tunic and trousers has an ancient history in Central Asia, both as worn by nomadic people and by the aristocratic descendants of warrior horsemen. The Saka, a nomadic people from Central Asia related to the Scythians, are depicted on stone wall-reliefs in Persepolis. The men of the procession wear tunics, breeches, and long-sleeved coats in cape fashion, and bring robes as gifts to the Persian king. Herodotus makes special note of the trousers and tall caps worn by the Saka in the army of Xerxes. Other wall reliefs at Persepolis depict Median noblemen wearing the *candys*, a long-sleeved coat hung over the shoulders as a mantle.[3] Xenophon remarks that the Persian cavalry only put their arms into the sleeves on inspection days.[4] Not only is the robe ancient, but the style of wearing it is the same as that of the nineteenth century.

36

Thou art about, my king, to make war against men who wear leathern trousers.

Sandanis, the Lydian, attempting to dissuade Croesus from making war on Cyrus, Herodotus I, 71[2]

The earliest clothes that remain from Central Asia were found in royal tombs in the Altai Mountains, far to the northeast. Among the treasures of the *kurgans* of Pazyryk and Bashdar II were complete costumes, preserved in ice for more than two thousand years.[5] The Altaian finds included a short hempen tunic, soft embroidered boots, and several striking robes with long, narrow sleeves. There are many parallels between ancient Altaic and modern Central Asian clothing, both in the essential items of dress and in their specific cut.

Throughout the early centuries AD, from the arrival of the Kushan on the western steppe to the establishment of the Sogdian kingdoms, this sporting style of clothing was worn by the nobility. The elite members of Central Asian society had the time and leisure to hunt; they were people whose heroic occupation was battle, and who had only recently left behind a life of active conquest. Toward the end of the first millennium AD the same basic cut of clothing came to be worn by people at every level of society. The nomad's furs and leather breeches were far too coarse for a shopkeeper, and an affront to a court rich in silks, but each villager and town dweller came to wear the same basic style as the ancient horseman. The difference between the costume of the different classes in society lay primarily in the richness of the materials and in minor elements of trim.

Only fragments of excavated textiles remain from the Sogdian period: the cut of early costume is best known from wall-paintings. Murals from the seventh- to eighth-century city of Pendjikent show men wearing fitted robes with very tight sleeves and cuffs. Narrow side panels cut on the bias gave the robes width at the hem. They were worn closed, with one side folded over the other, or with the edges turned slightly back to form a lapel. A trim was sewn to cuffs, edges and hem. Belts were ornamented with metal plaques, and small pouches attached to them held personal items. Women's costumes from the Balalyk Tepe murals show both open, flowing garments that were thrown over the shoulder, and sewn, fitted robes like those worn by men. The fitted dresses had either very wide sleeves or sleeves with narrow ornamented cuffs. Trousers were made of two types of fabric, one above the thighs and one below. They narrowed at the ankle, and were identical to the nineteenth-century pattern.

36. Prince's coat. Weft-faced compound silk twill; lining silk damask. China, Sogdiana. 8th century. 19" × 32" (48 × 83cm). (The Cleveland Museum of Art, purchased from the J.H. Wade Fund, 1996.2a.)

37. "Hatim Tay and the Thorn Gatherer", from a Gulistan of Sa'di. Bukhara. Dated AH 954 (AD 1547). The miniature illustrates the costume worn by both laborers and the elite. (Bodmer Foundation, Geneva.)

37

Of our company was that Tartar envoy whom Timur had sent to the King of Castile, but at his present appearance his friends laughed very much for he was dressed by us in the manner and fashion of a gentleman of Spain.

Clavijo, describing his reception at the court of Tamerlane, 1403–06[6]

FASHIONS OF THE LAST THOUSAND YEARS With the arrival of the Turkic tribes on the steppe, tunic, trousers and robe came to prevail entirely over draped and tucked garments. These three articles of clothing became the basic costume for men, women and children in Central Asia. At times they fit tightly to the body, at times they were worn in loose folds, some years they were worn long, some years short. Nomad or shopkeeper, grandmother or bride – everyone wore them.

The dervish's coat and the Emir's silk robe had the same cut. The difference between rags and raiment lay in the material.

Few surviving Central Asian costumes predate the nineteenth century. There is no tradition of preserving clothing in Central Asia, no treasury of royal garments. Information on clothing must come from illustrated manuscripts, or be drawn from written sources. The paintings of the Bukharan School, dating from the fifteenth to seventeenth centuries, confirm and define the continuing style. Robes are longer than before, and are sometimes worn like a cape over the shoulders. Active young men often wear short-sleeved robes over thin tunics. Older men and scholars, who led sedentary lives, wore the style closest to that of the nineteenth century. Their long sleeves were pushed up to expose the hands for riding, or were draped politely below them (especially over the left, the unclean hand) on formal social occasions.

According to sixteenth-century written sources, a complete man's costume consisted of a cotton shirt, a simple, robe-like overshirt, and a more formal outer robe. The clothing of the poorer classes consisted of the same undershirts and belted robe, but these were made of coarser materials and worn shorter, only to the knees. A wealthy man's outer robe was a long-sleeved, sober, scholar's coat, or a more brilliant robe of red cloth. The collars of the thirteenth to fifteenth centuries, a remnant of Mongol tradition, have disappeared. Narrow sleeves ended at the forearm or at the center of the palm. The outer robes worn by the aristocracy were embroidered with silk and studded with precious stones.[7] Sets of clothing could be extremely valuable, and were used for payment or in trade by the oases lords, who, like other Islamic rulers, considered them equivalent to currency. A rich costume was negotiable anywhere in the world.

ROBES OF HONOR The fabric and finish of a man's clothes defined his place in society. Within Central Asia, the close relationship between dress and rank goes far back, to before Islam came to the steppes. Writing in the tenth century, Narshakhi described the daily assembly before the regent queen known as Khatun in the seventh century AD. Her courtiers, eunuchs and nobility attended her, and a troop of youths, girded with gold belts and carrying swords, stood by. Khatun "issued orders and prohibitions, and gave a robe of honor to whomsoever she wished and punishment to whom she wished".[8]

Clothing was a tool of the social and political system throughout the Islamic world.[9] Social status was bestowed and confirmed through gifts of robes of honor. In nineteenth-century Central Asia, robes were a kind of social currency. Gifts of robes were made in recognition of services, as a reward for achievement in battle or in sport, as a way of marking the holidays, and as a form of payment or a bribe. The retinue of a powerful person was equipped through the yearly bestowal of *sar o pa*, head-to-foot costumes. The choice of fabric in presentation robes sent a clear message to the receiver. Both parties to the transaction were sophisticated and knowledgeable consumers, knew the value of each fabric, could assess the quality of the material, and understood by the gift their respective positions in society.

Western travelers were often bemused by this archaic, "oriental" habit. When Henri Moser traveled to Central Asia in 1882–83, in the suite of the Prince of Wittgenstein, he received gifts of 140 robes and 17 horses complete with trappings and harness. It was expected that he should turn these gifts to his advantage by selling them. Merchants came daily to his compound to purchase the gifts the embassy received.

55 WOMAN'S ROBE
third quarter
19th century
collar to hem length
52" (132cm)
sleeve length cuff to cuff
80" (203cm)
warp-faced plain weave

56 WOMAN'S ROBE
third quarter 19th century
collar to hem length 53" (135cm)
sleeve length cuff to cuff 65" (165cm)
warp-faced plain weave
The dark background color of this *adras* ikat made it as suitable for an older woman's festive garment as for a bride's wedding robe.

57 WOMAN'S MUNISAK ROBE
third quarter 19th century
collar to hem length 65" (165cm)
sleeve length cuff to cuff 48" (122cm)
silk velvet

By placing his seal upon the lining of robes that he returned to the market, Moser discovered that the same items were presented to him more than once.

Moser found Bukharan costume gorgeous and picturesque. At the Wittgenstein mission's official reception in Bukhara, the Emir's courtiers lined the entrance to the throne room in order of their importance, and Moser noted the various fabrics worn by each functionary. Courtiers of lower rank wore robes of all-silk ikat, velvet, satin and cashmere. He states that the courtiers of highest rank wore robes of gold brocade, although it seems more likely that he refers to the *gulduzi*, gold embroidery on satin and velvet, that was popular at the court.[10] Moser also describes the Emir's disapproving reaction to the wearing of a luxurious robe by one of the embassy's native servants. Moser claimed that in Bukhara, wearing a robe unsuitable to one's rank was cause for summary corporal punishment and the imposition of a severe fine.

The traveler Arminius Vambery described the payment to Turkoman mercenaries in robes by the Khan of Khiva in 1863. Each soldier had brought the heads of slain enemies along with him in a sack. A clerk counted the heads as they were spilled out on the ground and dispensed a receipt to be exchanged at the treasury for coats to the value of ten, twelve, twenty or forty heads, as was warranted.[11] Unfortunately, no description of the coats is given. There was far greater latitude in dress among the various nomad tribes, and many Western travelers describe the Turkoman and Kazakh chiefs as wearing brilliant and luxurious silks. In 1883, Edmond O'Donovan, reporting on the clash between the Tekke Turkoman and Russian forces from within the Tekke camp, described a coat that was clearly made from ikat: "...Aman Niaz presented me with a robe similar to the singular one he himself usually wore, in which all the colors of the rainbow, and especially vermilion, yellow and purple, were splashed in irregular dashes".[12]

In the early Islamic period, certain types of fabric came to be seen as either sanctioned or forbidden by religious tradition. While certain proscriptions in regard to excess and luxury did exist, there were no codified sumptuary laws as such, merely accepted practices.[13] The best known of these was the prohibition against the wearing of pure silk next to the body. The half-silk materials with cotton wefts met the criteria of *mashru'*, "legal" or permitted fabrics, even though the cotton weft was completely hidden within the silk warp.

Nineteenth-century Western travelers and twentieth-century Soviet field researchers have often noted that the common people were forbidden to wear silk. At times the names given to fabrics are cited as a basis for this proscription. *Shahi* and *padshahi* both refer to all-silk ikat fabrics; both names mean "of the king". These fabrics, however, appear late in the nineteenth century, and probably owe their elegant names to marketing tactics, rather than to a literal definition. The Emirs did not wear *shahi*, they wore Italian and French velvets and gold brocade. Numerous family photographs from the nineteenth century show women and children of well-to-do families, including many Jews, dressed in *shahi*. It would be more accurate to say that in Bukhara, all who could afford silk or part-silk fabric wore it, at least at home.

MEN'S GARMENTS For the ordinary oasis dweller, the style of a robe was based on locale. Slight differences in the cut of the robe were typical of certain towns. So were certain kinds of fabric, especially for men's robes. A town stripe was a distinctive marker, rather like a school tie in the West, and men wore fabrics that were appropriate to their occupation. In general, costume was less a matter of personal taste than an indication of social rank and geographic origin.

Bukhara was full of dandies. Old photographs show loungers about the mosques and water cisterns in padded robes of brilliant striped cottons and silks. Even Uzbek farmers from the villages surrounding the city might be found wearing robes of brightly colored imported calico with an oversized floral pattern. It is difficult to imagine how the wealthiest Bukharan men could move on formal occasions. The rich dressed in layers, wearing up to ten robes, and were weighed down by a turban of as many yards. Such a complicated outfit was unusual, but it was common for the well-to-do to wear three or four robes, especially in winter.

The belt was an essential item of male clothing. Poor men wore a simple twisted cloth sash around their waists, while the upper classes sported magnificent wide belts of cross-stitched, braided or woven silk, studded with silver plaques that were chased, enameled or set with turquoise. Private citizens wore their belts over their under-robe, and left the outer robe loose, often hanging from the shoulders as a cape. The Emir and court officials wore belts on top of their outer robes.

The Oriental, only here to be met with in his original purity and peculiarity, is fond of the tchakh-tchukh, *or rustling tone of the dress. It was always an object of great delight to me to see the seller* [buyer] *parading up and down a few paces in the new* tchapan [dress] *to ascertain whether it gave out the orthodox tone.*

The Hungarian linguist and adventurer Arminius Vambery, *Travels in Central Asia*, 1865 [14]

The most common and basic type of man's robe was the *chapan*, or *khalat*.[15] Throughout Turkestan these words refer to the standard, lightly padded, lined male outer-robe of silk or cotton. Both terms are also used as a generic expression for all types of men's and women's robes. The *yaktak* or *degdeh* was a thin lined robe. The *chakman* was a robe of a heavy coarse cloth, usually without a lining.

Robes were lined with cotton cloth, either a simple plain woven local fabric, or a bright printed cotton of Persian, Russian or English manufacture. A decorative edge or lapse, usually between two and ten inches (5–25cm) in width, ran along the sides and hem of the lining. In many cases, this edging was of a luxurious silk cloth in a contrasting color to the main fabric. It was often made of an *adras*, cotton-wefted ikat that was much older than the outer part of the coat. The trim flashed as the wearer walked or rode, to great effect.

Its collar is annihilation of intercourse, its two sleeves are observance and continence, its two gussets are poverty and purity, its belt is persistence in contemplation, its hem is tranquility in [God's] *presence, and its fringe is settlement in the abode of union.*

Hujwiri, with reference to the mystical interpretation of dervish garb, mid-eleventh century[16].

58 WOMAN'S MUNISAK ROBE
third quarter 19th century
collar to hem length 52" (132cm)
sleeve length cuff to cuff 63" (160cm)
silk velvet

The well-dressed Bukharan man wore fabrics that only women could wear in other towns. Bold patterns in bright colors were considered perfectly suitable, and the effect of several brilliant robes tucked into very wide leather riding breeches (for no man walked who could ride), and topped by a mighty turban, was rather more striking than ridiculous. The voluminous Bukharan robes were cut in a firm T-shape, with wide trapezoidal wedges forming the sides. Hems were long and sleeves were up to eighteen inches (46cm) wide at the ends. There was no attached collar. Often, a thin edging of loop-manipulated or needle-woven trim was sewn completely around the robe, along sides, hem, neck and cuffs.[17]

The men of Samarkand dressed with more restraint than did those of Bukhara. Robes were full, but not extravagantly wide. Sleeves were long, and narrowed at the cuff. A quilted collar of the same material as the robe reached to just below the breastbone. The base of the collar had two narrow ribbons that were tied during prayers.

Ferghana and Tashkent costume was even more conservative. Robes were close-fitting and shorter than were those of other towns. The trapezoidal side wedges were far narrower, and sleeves were straight. Dark, sober sateens in black and green tones were the most popular fabrics. In Khwarazm, robes were also more restrained in cut; they were very narrow, with long, tight sleeves. A vertical slash was cut in the end of the sleeve so that the hand could be put out for working, and the sleeve rolled up. The men of Khwarazm preferred red-toned fabric with thin stripes.The most common fabric worn by men in all the oasis towns was *alacha*, a name that applied to an all-cotton warp-faced striped cloth as well as to a fabric in which only a few stripes of the warp were made of silk, and the rest of cotton.[19]

If he is a man [showing predominantly male characteristics] *then wearing a garment with a seam is indecent; ... if he is a woman* [showing predominantly female characteristics] *he should wear a garment with a seam, like a woman.*

The twelfth-century *Hidaya* of Burkhaneddin-Ali Marginani of Marghilan, from the section detailing the clothing suitable for different types of hermaphrodites.[18]

38

GENDER AND DRESS In Central Asia there was great similarity, not only of all men's clothing, and all women's garments, but of the two conjoined. The layered undergarments, robe and over-robe worn by men in the early Islamic period are also seen in many portraits of women. A long dress with a closed seam was the only garment specifically for women.[20] Because clothing was otherwise so similar, it was thought proper to define precisely the boundaries of male and female garments. The *Hidaya*, a compendium of Islamic law written in the twelfth century, included a section spelling out the garments appropriate for the subtlest of gender differences. This work of jurisprudence was well known and widely used in nineteenth-century Central Asia, but the various proscriptions regarding dress were no longer strictly observed. Men outside the Ferghana Valley area sometimes wore seamed garments, and by the end of the nineteenth century, only old men still wore robe-like undergarments.

WOMEN'S DRESS Early Western travelers rarely had the opportunity to meet with Central Asian women. Muslim women of good reputation would not have been seen by strangers, and visitors to private homes would be served by the men or the children of the house. Jewish women could meet with men from outside their immediate family, and numerous photographs of them in sumptuous "at home" dress remain from the last quarter of the nineteenth century. Similarly, nomad women went unveiled, and their habits and costume are better known than those of urban women from the early part of the nineteenth century.

39

The camzol *is green but the cabbage soup isn't salted.*

A saying reflecting upon the vanity and improvidence of women.

38. Uzbek woman, Khimet-ai. The vertically cut collar of the ikat dress is characteristic of the costume of a married urban woman. *Turkestanskii al'bom*, 1871–72. (Navoi Library, Tashkent.)
39. Nomad woman seated outside her yurt. (Paul M. Fekula and Walter P. Fekula Collection.)

Once the Russians were firmly established in Central Asia, their families came to join them, and social commerce was possible between the women. But for the most part, the descriptions of travelers like Moser are based on the appearance of women on the street or from hearsay. Early twentieth-century sources are considerably more detailed. Many of the finest ethnographers of the early Soviet period were women, and their work with older informants is the primary source for nineteenth-century women's costume in Central Asia.

Among the poorer classes, women's costume was similar in many ways to that of men. A closed dress with a front seam was worn in place of an under-robe, for women did not usually wear belts. A poor person usually had only a single shift dress. Many women are said to have simply borrowed a male relative's *chapan*-style robe to wear over their heads if they ventured outside. Women in small farming villages would not have had the luxury of going veiled.[21]

Moser speaks of the oasis women as very vain. According to him, a hand mirror was held constantly in the palm, and a woman's toilette was her sole pastime. This may have been true of women whose wealth

59 WOMAN'S MUNISAK ROBE
third quarter 19th century
collar to hem length 65" (165cm)
sleeve length cuff to cuff 48" (122cm)
silk velvet

or occupation allowed them the appearance of total leisure. In most of Central Asia extended family households were the norm, and women shared the tasks of raising children, preparing food and housekeeping. Younger women and new brides were at the bottom of the family power structure, and were expected to work the hardest, albeit in their best clothes.

Those who could afford richer clothing seem to have indulged themselves. In Bukhara, layers of silk dresses were worn atop one another, the full sleeves allowing each dress to be displayed to advantage. Shifts worn by unmarried women and girls sometimes had horizontal collars, with a button closure at each side of the neck. Dresses for married women had a long vertical neckline that ran to below the breastbone along the seam. Long, vertical embroidered silk collars of trim between two and four inches (5–10cm) in width were simply laid on top of garments or tacked very lightly to women's dresses.

Gold-embroidered silk headbands, breastbands and bits of trim for cuff and hem were added to the basic costume. On special occasions a tiara of filigree work studded with garnets, glass or turquoises held hair and scarf in place. The ubiquitous scarf was worn by all women and by girls who had reached adolescence. It was wound over the head or looped at the breast. Dresses could be left unfinished at the neckline because the area was disguised by the scarf. Soft leather boots were worn indoors. In the street, women covered their boots with curly-toed leather galoshes with iron fittings.

It is more difficult to identify a woman's dress as coming from a certain area than it is to identify a male robe. Throughout the nineteenth century, women's clothing became more uniform. There was a very effective distribution of fabrics throughout Central Asia, and depending on what they could afford, women wore fabrics from many producing centers other than their own.

The early Soviet ethnographers, notably O.A. Sukhareva, collected valuable information on women's dress from elderly people between the 1920s and 1950s. Individual informants could provide details from their own recollections of dowry materials and ceremonial costume. In early nineteenth-century Nurata, for example, exceptionally long, bias-cut sleeves were very wide at the shoulder and so narrow at the cuff that a slash had to be cut in the material so that the hands

60 WOMAN'S ROBE
Bukhara
first half 19th century
collar to hem length
54" (137cm)
sleeve length cuff to cuff
73" (185cm)
warp-faced plain weave
This extraordinarily finely patterned robe has the same cut as a man's *chapan*-style robe, but its size and color were appropriate only for a boy or a young woman.

40

40. Kirgiz woman on horseback. Late 19th-century postcard print. (Private Collection.)

could be freed to work. By the 1890s sleeves were ten inches (25cm) wide; by 1915, sixteen inches (40cm) wide. When wider sleeves became fashionable, dresses became fuller, to bring the dress into aesthetic balance. Bukharan dresses, always full and with few bias cuts, retained the same style longer than those of other areas, and by the turn of the century they became a widely recognized standard of traditional clothing, as opposed to modern, Western-influenced fashions.

Most women's robes were identical in style to male coats. The generic robe, the *khalat* or *chapan*, was of the same cut and style as that of men. Other types of outer robes are specifically female – the *munisak*, the *pishvo* and the *parandja*. The *munisak* had very accentuated feminine lines. It had no collar, and the sides of the robe curved over the breast and flared outwards. Either material was gathered in folds under the arms, or gores were added to give fullness. The shape of sleeves varied, from very long, narrow ones with a slash at the wrist and pleated ends that fell a foot (30cm) below the hands, to wider sleeves cut to normal wrist length and edged with a bit of trim. The *pishvo* was very possibly the precursor to the *munisak*. The term *pishvo*, meaning a robe, was used only by very elderly informants. By the end of the nineteenth century the related term *pishvon* meant a scarf worn over the head of a bride, and gradually the word applied to anything that was worn over the head. The *pishvo* robe was made of cotton-wefted silk *adras* ikat fabric, without a lining, and seems to have had the same distinctly feminine cut as the *munisak*.

Both the *munisak* and *pishvo* were made to be worn during the important rites of passage in a woman's life. Although the *pishvo* had completely disappeared by the end of the nineteenth century, and the *munisak* was considered a relic of the bad old days of oppression after the Bolshevik Revolution, these garments continued to mean a great deal to the women of Central Asia. The first use for both garments was as dowry. In the early part of the nineteenth century, it was proper for a woman to have several *pishvo* robes in her trousseau, the material to make them being sent from the house of the groom. When the wedding was celebrated, the bride was brought to her new home wearing the *pishvo* as a head covering. As the richest of all her dowry clothing, the *pishvo* was worn atop all other garments, over her head. A newly married woman held the sleeves in her teeth while doing chores, so that it would not fall off.

61 WOMAN'S MUNISAK ROBE
second half 19th century
collar to hem length
48" (122cm)
sleeve length cuff to cuff
59" (150cm)

The *munisak* robe, which had the same feminine cut as the *pishvo*, but might be lined or unlined, was widely distributed throughout Central Asia in the mid-nineteenth century. *Munisak* robes were given as dowry and worn by the new bride. They were considered the proper attire for attendance at family festivals and funerals. In Samarkand, in the second half of the nineteenth century, a woman wore a *munisak* over her head on the day after her wedding, so that she could not see, or be seen by, her father-in-law or her husband's brothers. The manner of wearing *munisak* and *pishvo* robes related to traditional attitudes regarding the role of women in society. A ritually expressed shyness and delicacy was considered extremely good manners for women in Central Asia. With the exception of the nomadic women, a formal submissiveness was the only proper behavior for the nineteenth-century bride. She did not know, and certainly did not choose her husband. He and his friends came (by prearrangement) to "steal" her by force from her home on the day of her wedding. She was expected to wail at being torn from her family, and the bride who raised her head once during the day-and-night-long wedding ceremony shamed herself and her relatives.

It was as important to have a *munisak* at a funeral as it was at a wedding. A specific type of dress was considered proper funeral attire for both mourners and the deceased. In Muslim Central Asia the body was washed and wrapped in a shroud. It was placed on an ordinary bed, and this bier was carried by family members to the graveyard. If the body was that of a woman, either one or two *munisak* robes from her dowry were placed on the bier as a covering.[22] After the funeral the *munisak* robes were ritually purified, and given either to the woman's daughter or to the woman who had washed the body. It was essential that some kind of *munisak* be given to the body washer, as it was thought quite possible that if a male-style *chapan* was given, the deceased might rise at the Day of Judgment in the form of a man. On the second day after the burial, the family put on their blue or black mourning robes.[23] If they had no special mourning robes, they turned their ordinary robes inside out, and wore them with the seams outward. In the twentieth century the *munisak* virtually disappeared as a dowry robe, and as a consequence, *parandja* robes were substituted for bier coverings. It is natural that the role played by the *munisak* in the funeral ceremony lasted longer than its function as a dowry garment, as it was the women who had received such garments decades before, at their weddings, who would expect to have them as bier coverings.

41

41. Tadjik women. Embroidered caps, jewelry and braid ornaments complement ikat dresses and robes. *Turkestanskii al'bom*, 1871–72. (Navoi Library, Tashkent.)

42. Tadjik women. Women also wore robes on top of their heads, and veiled themselves by drawing the edge of the robe across their faces. *Turkestanskii al'bom*, 1871–72. (Navoi Library, Tashkent.)

The *parandja* was the only strictly feminine robe that continued in use well into the twentieth century. *Parandja* robes were worn on top of all other clothing when outside the home; they were draped from the top of the head to the heel, like a cape, and were worn in conjunction with a heavy horsehair veil. The sleeves narrowed so sharply that it was not possible to insert the arms fully; the ends of the sleeves were often closed, and sometimes joined together at the back of the robe by an embroidered panel or loop-woven trim.

A hostess made her feelings about a guest clear by the manner in which she took her *parandja*, honoring her by placing it up high, or insulting her by laying it down. A guest who wore her *parandja* inside a home made a gesture of extreme ill will, amounting to wishing death on the household, as only corpse washers could wear one indoors. When the *parandja* came to be substituted for the *munisak* at funerals, the robe that lay on the bier was brought home and hung on a wooden peg. Only the robes of the dead were hung on pegs. To hang your own *parandja* that way was regarded as being very dangerous, and might bring about your death.

Many nineteenth-century travelers described the appearance of women on the street as hideous. The rough, impenetrable black veil gave them a sightless, voided look disturbing to European eyes. Further, only well-to-do women could afford the elegant *parandja*, and many women wore an old, worn out *chapan* as an outer robe. Wealthy young women of Samarkand or Bukhara might wear a pink and white *adras* ikat *parandja*. Other oasis towns were more conservative. In the latter part of the nineteenth century the most common fabrics used for *parandja* robes were striped or moiré half-silk cloths in which gray and silvery blue colors predominated. The twentieth century brought violet, green and yellow velvets into fashion. The *parandja* began to be decorated with tassels and trim. The lining of a *parandja* was made of inexpensive printed cloth, but a lapse of brilliant silk half a yard in width gave the lining a luxurious appearance.

42

The choice of fabrics for other garments was also determined by a woman's age and status, as a maiden, bride or matron – as hostess, guest or mourner. In general, young women wore bright colors and the largest patterns, women of middle age dressed more soberly, and older women wore dark blues and blacks. A family's means limited a woman to home-made, locally produced or imported fabrics. Most Central Asian women wore dresses made from inexpensive native cottons. The dresses of the wealthy were made of all-silk and cotton-wefted ikat fabrics and other rich locally made textiles. (Imported cloth from England, France, Turkey and India was also available in the bazaars, as were massive amounts of Russian cotton expressly designed for the Central Asian market, in particular a red calico for dresses.) Rich fabrics that were used for many types of garments in Bukhara were considered proper only for *munisak* robes in other cities. Bukharan silk velvet ikat in particular is found most often in the *munisak*, the most sumptuous garment in a bride's trousseau. The dark blue background cotton-wefted *adras* ikat was also used almost exclusively in *munisak* robes and in non-garment items, as the sober colors of this fabric were entirely appropriate for funeral wear.

Underclothes were not worn, so trousers were an essential item of dress. Women's trousers were constructed of two fabrics, a cotton one above the thigh, and the best they could afford below. They were cut wide, and drawn together with a woven cotton string. Only very well-to-do women could afford all-silk trousers. Red calico, bright chintz and plain and satin-weave ikat silks were mixed with abandon. The Western concept of clothes that match never found favor in women's clothing in Central Asia. Fabrics that contrasted were much more pleasing to local tastes.

Both women and children received gifts of clothing at the New Year, which fell at the spring solstice in Central Asia. Early Russian sources indicate that women were expected to use less clothing than men, and the fabric weights given suggest that one suit of clothes per year was the norm.[24] Few items of children's clothing remain from the nineteenth century. Those that do are very like adult clothing in miniature. Young children were considered exempt from geographic, class and sumptuary restrictions. Nineteenth-century photographic portraits show well-off young children dressed like little princes; ikat dresses and robes are much in evidence. Several Soviet period ethnographers working outside the major towns have noted that *shahi* all-silk ikat fabrics were considered proper only for children, as the brilliant and cheerful colors of these ikat fabrics were most suitable for the very young.

WESTERN-STYLE CLOTHING By the end of the nineteenth century, the style and cut of clothing began to display the influence of Western, "foreign" fashions. Innovations in dress appeared first in the addition of decorative elements. Pockets, collars, buttons and bits of trim were added to otherwise traditional Central Asian clothing. Later, Western garments were adapted to Central Asian tastes; vests, camisoles and short-sleeved shift dresses were borrowed from Western fashions, but were constructed of locally popular fabrics.

Women were screened from the effects of modernization in the man's world of the bazaar. While urban men quickly adopted Russian styles after the Revolution, traditions of all kinds were retained longer in the woman's sphere. It is possible that the trend toward fitted garments resulted in part from economic hardship, for they utilized less cloth and were cheaper to make. Ordinary, everyday clothing was more likely to reflect a Western influence. Widespread and radical changes in women's garments for family ceremonial took place only in the early part of the twentieth century, a time of severe economic distress and scarcity. The luxury of a beautiful wedding dress and the propriety of garments for a feast day or a funeral were not trifling matters in a society preoccupied with textiles. The assimilation of Western styles into Central Asian women's costume began with the addition of collars to traditionally collarless clothing. By the turn of the century a stand-up collar was worn by the youngest women. At the same time, robes and dresses began to be tailored to the body, and pockets and lapels appeared occasionally on garments of the period. The *camzol*, a long, sleeveless open vest, appeared as early as the late 1880s in areas with more Western contact. The *camzol* was usually made of dark-colored, heavy velvet or plush, and in the twentieth century began to be embellished with garish bits of gold and silver trim.

Women's clothing was made by neighborhood seamstresses or by the family of the person who was to wear it. Nineteenth-century photographs of robe sellers indicate that men's robes were often sold ready-made. In the early nineteenth century, seamstresses rarely cut fabric with scissors; cloth was cut with a knife, and sewn along selvedges rather than cut and sewn to a pattern. All measurements were taken by fingers, and based on a standard clothing size, so fit was determined by the luck of the day.[25] The arrival of sewing machines coincided with the introduction of modern dress styles at the turn of the century. By the 1930s a simple calf-length shift with a Western-style collar and sleeves was popular with younger women, and with the addition of full pantaloons, became the standard dress for the rural population. Western styles are now worn by Uzbek professional women and the urban working class, though many still prefer the *atlas* ikat satins for home and festive wear.

CENTRAL ASIAN JEWS & THE SILK TRADE

According to the tradition preserved by the old Jews of Bukhara, there reigned in Bukhara fifteen hundred years ago a great Khan... While in a good mood, that ruler said unto his ministers: "My land is large, and all I need is Jews; I had better send a courier to Persia to bring me ten Jews there from". From a letter to A. Druyanoff, recounted by Samuel Komissaroff of Bukhara, 1914[1]

The place of the Central Asian Jews within the silk trade, and their influence upon it, has always been disproportionate to their small numbers. The integral role of the Jews within a vital textile tradition in the Islamic world requires some explanation, as the history of the Jewish community in Central Asia is less familiar than that of other elements of the Diaspora. For many centuries, Jewish merchants were prominent in the international trade in silk fabrics throughout the Muslim world. The Jews' access to rare and precious dyestuffs, their closely held knowledge of the dyeing methods, and their skill as weavers of luxury fabrics kept them at the center of the silk industry throughout its history. This lengthy background in the silk trade allowed the nineteenth-century Bukharan Jewish community, after several centuries of declining prosperity, to take an important part in the trade in ikat fabrics.

An explanation of the position held by Jews in Central Asian society demonstrates the social separation between the workers in each textile craft, and lays stress upon the multiple skills – and the inter-ethnic co-operation – required to make a complex textile such as ikat. While the two communities remained largely in opposition, individuals within the majority Muslim and minority Jewish population allied their talents in the production of ikat.

Finally, a genuine understanding of Central Asian society's obsession with textiles is only possible within the context of family life. The role of ikat fabric as not only the stuff of commerce, but as the seal and symbol of the family contract, can be seen through the examination of Jewish family rites. The relative ease of access to the homes and private lives of Central Asian Jews allowed early ethnographers to observe many customs, often held in common with the Muslim population, that would otherwise be known only through hearsay. Most compelling for this study are the details of dowry and marriage arrangements involving silk fabrics, and the use of textiles in intimate family rituals. To a large extent, the function of luxury textiles within the Jewish community reflected their place in the lives of the urban population as a whole – for which no comparable data exists. A study of the minority community helps to define the essentially popular nature, and the common social functions, of *adras* ikat fabric within an extremely diverse society.

JEWS WITHIN THE ISLAMIC WORLD Many would argue that, until the nineteenth century, the Islamic world was one of the best places to be a Jew. Especially in the early medieval period, when Islam felt its power unchallenged, there was far greater tolerance for minorities than in the West. The Jews, unlike the Christians, constituted no political threat to the Muslim state. In comparison with the general population, there were many learned people and skilled craftsmen among the Jews. The wealthy among them offered a source of ready cash, the poor would take jobs that no one else would have. Jewish merchants were willing to risk their lives and fortunes on the seas and the caravan roads to expand trade. They brought home the rarest commodities – spices, dyes and rich textiles – from the very boundaries of the known world. A sensible government saw the advantages of making a place for a Jewish minority in the Islamic community.

Islamic law formally recognized the place of the Jews as *dhimmi*, outsiders with a protected status within the Muslim state. They were subject to a separate system of taxation, they were supposed to follow certain sumptuary restrictions, and limits were set with regard to the rank and power they could achieve. In return, their lives, property and rights of religious observance were guaranteed. In theory, their position compared very favorably with that of the Jews of Europe.

In practice, it did not always work out so well. At times, legal restrictions were applied unfairly and with undue severity. Taxation became so burdensome as to impoverish whole communities. In periods of unrest, Jews became scapegoats; their riches were exaggerated and their occupations reviled. Yet through much of Islamic history, Jews found life in the Muslim community more tolerable than among Christians.

The center of the Islamic world was often a safer and more secure home to Jewish communities than the Muslim states of the periphery. Especially in Iran, a center of schismatic and messianic Islam, Jews periodically faced terrible persecution, even massacre. They fared somewhat better in Central Asia, where pragmatism usually acted to check violent and extreme acts of oppression. Many individuals suffered, but the Central Asian Jewish community was maintained.

SETTLEMENT AND TRADE ALONG THE SILK ROAD There is evidence of Jewish communities within Central Asia well before the early Islamic period. After Babylon was taken by the Achaemenids in the sixth century BC, elements of its large Jewish community spread northward and eastward. According to the Book of Esther, compiled around the first century BC, Jews were to be found at the farthest reaches of the Persian empire. Evidence of long-established Jewish communities within Central Asia comes from the visit to Merv by the fourth-century Jewish traveler, Semu'el bar Bisena, who reported that the Mervan Jews had been separated for too long from the greater Jewish community, and had become neglectful of religious observance.[2] Modern excavations at Dandan-oilik, in present-day Xinjiang Province, have revealed an eighth-century letter from a trader, written in Judaeo-Persian, indicating that there were Jews with regular business relationships extending as far as China by that time.

Despite numerous instances of conversion, many small Jewish communities persisted throughout the early Islamic period.[3] Trade, especially in textiles, greatly increased. A network of Jewish merchants extended from North Africa into southern India, where there were substantial Jewish communities, and reached as far into the hinterlands as China and Central Asia. In *The Book of the Routes and the Kingdoms*, written between AD 846 and 886, Ibn Khurradadhbah describes the routes of the Jewish merchants he called *al-radhaniyya*, "guides, or those skilled in the ways".[4] "These merchants speak Arabic, Persian, Roman, Frankish, Spanish and Slavonic. They travel from the East to the West and from the West to the East by land and by sea."[5] Throughout the Middle Ages, Jews are described not only as dyers, but as the primary traders in silks and dyestuffs within the Islamic world.

Some found riches, as the Jewish merchant of Oman who brought back a vase of black porcelain, gold lidded, in it, "...a golden fish, with ruby eyes, garnished with musk of the finest quality. The contents of the vase was worth fifty thousand dinars."

Edward H. Schafer, *The Golden Peaches of Samarkand,* 1963[6]

EVOLUTION OF THE NINETEENTH-CENTURY JEWISH COMMUNITY The Mongol invasion of the thirteenth century shattered the Central Asian economy, and flattened some of its great cities. The extraordinary revitalization and reorganization achieved under the "pax Mongolica" and subsequent Chengizid rulers were first a matter of picking up the pieces. The Jewish population was not completely destroyed, but war and forced conversions splintered the community and severely reduced its numbers. The impact of the Mongol invasion was such that many nineteenth-century Bukharan Jews believed that their present community dated only to the beginning of the fifteenth century, when the ruler Timur Leng (Tamerlane) sent large numbers of Jewish silk-weavers and other skilled textile workers back to Central Asia after conquering Baghdad and Shiraz.

In the sixteenth and seventeenth centuries, religious persecution in Iran brought many Iranian Jewish immigrants to Bukhara, but isolation and economic stagnation took the community into a decline. The Rabbi Yosef Maman Magrebi traveled to Bukhara in 1793, and was so appalled by the state of religious observance that he determined to settle there. His sixty-year effort succeeded in invigorating the community, in reforming and introducing religious rites,[7] and in establishing contacts with Jews in Palestine and European Russia.

The first three quarters of the nineteenth century were a time of relative stability and quiet expansion for the Jewish communities in Central Asia. Emigration from Iran continued in the early part of the nineteenth century, and after forced conversions took place in 1839 in Meshed, many Jews moved to Merv, Samarkand and other Central

43

We are not eager after gold, or silver, or jewels, or any wordly pleasures, but to hear the word of our Lord. We have, however, no manuscripts, no books nor anything pertaining to the Law.

Letter from Rabbi Magrebi to "all parts of Poland and Turkey" requesting books, early nineteenth century[10]

43. First lessons in Samarkand. *Turkestanskii al'bom.* 1871–72. (Navoi Library, Tashkent.)

Asian cities.[8] Although population estimates vary widely, it is likely that in the early nineteenth century, there were about ten thousand Jews in Bukhara, the town with the largest Jewish population.[9]

THE JEWISH AND CHALA COMMUNITIES As in other areas of the Islamic world, social restrictions were applied to non-Muslim minorities. The need to distinguish non-Muslims by means of their dress had been a protection for the Muslim minority in the early Islamic period, and subsequent restrictions evolved as a politically expedient means of demonstrating Muslim superiority and domination.[11] In Central Asia, Jewish public dress was restricted to robes of cotton and wool. They wore short earlocks, shaving the rest of the head. They were not allowed to wear the turban; a sheepskin cap usually covered a smaller round cloth cap. Jews were prohibited from wearing the elaborate belts favored by well-to-do Central Asians; a simple rope bound their robes. They were not allowed to ride either horses or donkeys within the city walls, which was a major inconvenience in the muddy streets. Jewish women veiled themselves

62 WALL-HANGING
Bukhara
first half 19th century
83" × 44" (211 × 112cm)
3 full panels, 1 split panel
warp-faced plain weave
Few indigo-background ikats have such richly colored patterns or such elaborate motifs. The central panels have much in common with the intricate, red-field ikats of the early 19th century.

63 WALL-HANGING
mid-19th century
54" × 38" (138 × 93cm)
4 panels
warp-faced plain weave
This ikat has the simple white branching pattern that is most characteristic of this ikat group. The sober colors of indigo ikats were considered appropriate for older women's garments and for funeral wear.

64 WALL-HANGING
mid-19th century
probably Bukhara
78" × 55" (199 × 140cm)
5 panels (central 3-panel rectangle framed by complete ikat panels)
warp-faced plain weave
Two ikats of similar palette and scale are joined in a frame-like composition. The center-field ikat is only approximately symmetrical along the vertical axis; the pattern has been applied across the full fabric width.

to avoid harassment when they went out of doors, and lived and worked within the same restricted environment of home and family garden as women of the Muslim faith.

Small settlements of Central Asian Jews existed in most large towns, and individual Jewish dyers resided in many smaller villages. The center of Central Asian Jewish culture was in Bukhara. The Bukharan Jewish community was headed by an administrator appointed by the Emir from the Jewish elite, and by the chief rabbi. Legal matters were dealt with as much as possible within the community, as there were special dangers in coming before the Muslim courts. The word of a Jew was not equal to that of a Muslim, and Jews charged with capital crimes could only escape death by abjuring their faith. False accusations were sometimes encouraged by the authorities. A Jew who submitted to Islam was separated from his family and his neighbors, and moved to one of the communities of Muslim Jews known as Chala. The Chala were often described as the most miserable of the Khanate's residents. They were closely observed to prevent their secretly maintaining the Jewish religion, neither able to return to their relatives, nor accepted into the greater Muslim community.

In the early nineteenth century, Bukharan Jews were allowed to live only in the neighborhood called Mahallai Kohna (Old Neighborhood), in the quarter named after Sheikh Rangrez, the Venerable Dyer. As a result of severe overcrowding, permission was given to build a second settlement on some very expensive bog land in the Turki Djangi quarter that the Jews were obliged to purchase from the Emir. These neighborhoods, Mahallai Nau (New Neighborhood) and Amirobad, were the poorest of the Jewish quarters and the least desirable residence because of the prevalence of malaria. Several neighborhoods near Mahallai Kohna were inhabited by Chala, Muslim Jews. In the 1830s the Chala represented about thirteen per cent of the total Jewish population.[12] Although the two communities lived in close proximity to one another, social interaction was forbidden by the Muslim authorities.

JEWISH OCCUPATIONS In the early part of the nineteenth century, most Jews worked as dyers and small traders. Others wove fine fabrics made from raw silk, making the diaphanous kerchief fabric called *khalili.*[13] There are no records indicating that Jews wove ikat-dyed fabrics until the late nineteenth century, when they are noted as weavers of ikat-dyed scarves of pure silk. The principal roles of the Jews in the ikat process were as dyers and as distributors of finished fabrics. Chala also worked as dyers and traders in silk and cotton yarns.[14]

Modern Central Asian scholars have asserted that yellow and white silks were preferred by the Jewish community, and these colors are often seen on the transparent silks used to make women's dresses.[15] A heavily ribbed yellow and white silk *adras* ikat has been identified as a "Jewish" fabric, on the basis of the ancient stipulation that members of the Jewish community should dress in yellow,[16] but this association is not supported by the nineteenth-century photographic record, in which Jews wear the same types of ikats as members of the Muslim population.

DYEING AND SOCIAL STATUS The role of the dyer was not an illustrious one. There was no caste system in traditional Islam, but there were well-defined social classes. Within Central Asia, certain occupations were considered necessary, but undesirable because they

65 WALL-HANGING
probably Samarkand
mid-19th century
73" × 51" (185 × 129cm)
5 panels
warp-faced plain weave
Much of the earliest Samarkand production is characterized by the use of consistent, medium-scale designs on shimmering white and yellow backgrounds.

66 WALL-HANGING
Ferghana Valley
third quarter 19th century
86" × 56" (220 × 142cm)
5 panels
warp-faced plain weave
The muted background colors and strong, vertical composition of this type of ikat are often associated with the Ferghana Valley area.

involved some kind of pollution, either physical or spiritual. Contact with unpleasant or ritually unclean materials gave a person a status similar to an untouchable. Status was passed, along with occupation, from father to son, and marriages were usually contracted within the same occupational class. People who worked with dead animal products had low social status, whether they were butchers, tanners, or even rope-makers who worked with wool. Barbers held a very low social position, as did trash collectors, but the lowest rank within the community was reserved for dyers.

In a study conducted by the French anthropologist C.J. Charpentier in the 1970s in the bazaar of Tashkurgan, in northern Afghanistan, almost every informant stated that he would not eat with a dyer. Some mentioned the stains on the dyers' hands as the reason for their prejudice. In a society that ate with their hands, often from a communal plate, these stained hands were offensive. Social ranking in other occupations could change if the members of a craft became richer or poorer, but this was a temporary, localized phenomenon, and of all the crafts, the dyer's had the least variance in status.[17] The Jews in nineteenth-century Central Asia could not have been more compromised in the eyes of their neighbors. Not only were they members of a despised, minority faith, but their primary occupation was one in which even Muslim practitioners suffered gross discrimination.

INDIGO DYEING In the nineteenth century, the indigo trade in Central Asia was entirely in Jewish hands. Indigo was obtained from Baghdadi Jewish merchants living in India, shipped by Herati Jewish traders, and finally used by Jewish dyers in Bukhara and other Central Asian towns.[18] Indigo dye came to the Khanates from India via Afghanistan, carried on pack animals over the mountain passes and across the steppes.

The virtual monopoly of the Jews in indigo dyeing at least assured them a relatively stable place in the economic life of the Khanates. Materials and methods were considered trade secrets in Central Asia, and a closely knit community could best monopolize these skills. Although an uneven dye quality was often caused by impurities in the vats and mechanical defects in the dyeing process, these flaws were compensated for by the cheapness of the work, and the easy availability of local dyers to re-dye materials that had faded.

Dyeing was not the sole profession of the Jews. In 1825 Jakovlew wrote that "they carry on commerce, follow different trades, manufacture silk stuffs, and are distinguished as goldsmiths, tinkers and smiths... The Jews alone have the permission to make wine and brandy; they drink these liquors themselves, and sell them in secret to the Bucharians, by which they make large profits."[19]

THE TRADE IN FABRICS Early nineteenth-century evidence for the Jewish role in the wholesale textile trade is fragmentary. In the 1820s several "large wholesale" merchants were exporting goods from Bukhara and importing Russian products in exchange,[20] but specific merchants are not identified with specific wares. The expansion of Jewish trade seems to coincide with the increased volume of importation of Russian cotton goods. By the middle of the nineteenth century, Bukharan Jews were permitted to become members of Russian merchant guilds, and allowed to trade in the great fairs at Orenburg and Nizhni Novgorod.[21] These concessions made possible a rapid growth in Central Asian Jewish business with Russia, and by the late nineteenth century, Jews were described as dominating the wholesale market in textiles. The large quantities of silks and cottons carried back and forth by caravans between the Khanates and Persia, Russia and China were often distributed on arrival by Jewish merchants, who often took up temporary residence in the smaller towns in order to sell their wares.

67 WALL-HANGING
third quarter 19th century
82" × 65" (208 × 166cm)
6 panels
warp-faced plain weave
This ikat may be identified as coming from the Samarkand area by means of its white background, its evenly scaled motifs, and the use of large areas of blue and green in close proximity.

JEWS UNDER THE RUSSIAN PROTECTORATE Many of the most influential Jewish families supported the Tsarist efforts to annex Turkestan. The Russians initially saw the Jews as a sympathetic element in the local population; there was little love lost between the Khanates' native administrations and the indigenous Jewish communities. In the Russian protectorate the restrictions on dress and property ownership were relaxed, and Chala Muslims who had been forced to convert to Islam were able to return to Judaism. The Emir of Bukhara forbade the Jews to leave the city, but many fled, either abandoning their property, or leaving it in the hands of officials as heavy bribes.

Between the early 1870s and the late 1880s the Jewish population in many cities outside Bukhara increased to five times their previous numbers. As the Jewish population of the Ferghana Valley swelled, Russian anti-Semitism found expression in restrictions on Jewish immigration. Chala were also denied permission to settle although they were nominally Muslim. The official effort to keep Jews in Bukhara failed. Immigrant Jews from Bukhara were allowed to live only in a few smaller cities, but the Russian merchant community preferred to trade with the Jews, and objected, and bribes were paid by Jews to government officials to allow them to stay.[22]

Within the Russian-held areas of Turkestan, cotton production and processing became major industries, and several Jewish families were prominent among the cotton manufacturers.[23] The majority of Jewish immigrants were poor, and with the introduction of new chemical dyes in the marketplace, many found their skills unwanted. Hairdressing and shoe repair became important new occupations for Jews; these activities, as well as barbering and working with leather (the product of dead animals), were regarded as polluting occupations.

MOVEMENT OF DYERS TO THE FERGHANA VALLEY Jewish emigration from Bukhara was the final element needed for the Ferghana Valley to rival Bukhara as a center for silk, and particularly silk ikat production. Samarkand's role as a silk producer expanded as well, but by the third quarter of the nineteenth century, the technical and material resources required for commercial production were concentrated in the Ferghana Valley. Russian trade was centered there, and the economy was booming. Entrepreneurs were looking for businesses to establish, and the raw materials were ready to hand. A wide range of textile manufactories was organized, and as the Jewish population grew, the number of dye shops increased proportionately.

There are quite detailed studies available for the town of Khodjent, on the far western edge of the Ferghana Valley area. In 1871 there were 23 dye shops in Khodjent, which employed a total of 42 people. By the early twentieth century there were 13 cold-dyeing workshops alone in four neighborhoods of the city, in which all the dyeing was done by Jews. There were also 27 hot-dyeing workshops in five neighborhoods scattered throughout the town which employed both Jewish and Tadjik dyers.[24] Khodjent was a far smaller and less active silk-weaving community than the larger town of Marghilan, at the valley's

68 WALL-HANGING
probably Samarkand
mid-19th century
86" × 64" (218 × 163cm)
4 panels
warp-faced plain weave
Two closely related ikat fabrics are joined in this wall-hanging, which is part of a very rare group of dark palette, large medallion designs.

center. In the late nineteenth and early twentieth centuries, dyeing in Marghilan was also done by Bukharan Jews.[25]

No single factor can account for the dispersal and expansion of the silk industry in the last half of the nineteenth century. The tumultuous changes in political and economic life in Central Asia altered, but by no means ended traditional production. Trade, skilled workers and raw materials were only one part of the equation. While the native cotton production collapsed, silk-weaving adapted to new demands and expanded in the face of increased competition. Imported goods, even those designed for the Central Asian market, replaced only the less prestigious domestic fabrics. A major reason for the continuing production of ikat silks was the important part that the indigenous textiles played in social and family life.

JEWISH FAMILY LIFE AND THE ROLE OF SILKS A passion for textiles informed the whole culture of the Khanates. Among the Jews, who were bound by restrictive covenants of dress in public, this preoccupation with silks was all the more striking. Because of the limited land allocated to the community, Bukharan Jewish homes were often overcrowded and cramped. Even the wealthy had few luxuries, the exceptions being household decorations and garments of silk. Inside Jewish homes sumptuary restrictions were cast off. In virtually all the photographs of affluent Jews in this region taken in the nineteenth century, families were dressed entirely in silks, usually made of *adras* and *shahi* ikat fabrics, and men wore heavily ornamented silver belts.

Jewish homes were decorated in the same manner as those of Muslims. They were almost entirely without furniture, and used wall-paintings and textiles for decoration. The family sat and slept on padded cotton and silk quilts. Ikat hangings appear in photographs of the early 1870s as decoration for the stacks of quilted bedding. The use of ikat textile decoration for the home was not determined by ethnic background or religion; it was an urban style, and the choice of pattern and form was decided by the fashion of the town in which the textiles were made.[27]

All you have sent, my lord, is fine, but I wish to ask you to buy everything all over again, for the three robes striped with curved lines, as well as the white robe which I wanted to have for me as a mantle, were taken from me by a man who imposed on me. Present circumstances make such things necessary: I cannot go into detail about this. May God save us from what we fear. All I could say was that those garments were for sale.

A letter from the correspondence of two merchant families from Cairo, AD 1010[26]

BETROTHAL AND MARRIAGE RITES Detailed information on certain aspects of Jewish family organization, particularly those which

44

44. At the Kudo-bini ceremony, the groom has an opportunity to steal a glance at his bride-to-be. She sits in an adjoining room, and while both families discreetly look the other way, he passes her a tray of sweets and glasses of wine, which she rearranges and passes back. *Turkestanskii al'bom*, 1871–72. (Navoi Library, Tashkent.)

involve marriage and dowry arrangements, is available through the work of Z.L. Amitin-Shapiro, who made extensive ethnographic studies and collected Jewish materials in the region in the 1920s and 1930s. His work makes abundantly clear the importance of silk textiles in Jewish family life. The degree to which Jewish rituals paralleled Muslim customs cannot be assessed with certainty; there is simply no similar source of information for the wider community. The fragmentary information that is available on Muslim customs of the period indicates many similarities to Jewish traditions. Some folk customs known from Amitin-Shapiro's work are preserved in Muslim ceremonies even today.[28]

Among both Jewish and Muslim families, the right to give children in marriage belonged to the father. At times, marriages were arranged even before the children were born. More typical arrangements were initiated by the father of a son of marriageable age, who would send a relative or friend to sound out the prospective bride's family. Within the Jewish community, a positive response resulted in a series of discussions on bride price and dowry between an official matchmaker and

45

45. The inspection of the dowry by relatives of the bride and groom. The display of dowry goods, or *takhta zanon*, lasted four days, and was an important part of the marriage ritual. *Turkestanskii al'bom*, 1871–72. (Navoi Library, Tashkent.)

the two fathers. Among late nineteenth-century urban families, Muslim or Jewish, in which wives were not income producers, bride price was a minimal, relatively symbolic payment, and was often returned as part of the dowry if the bride was not easy on the eye, or was approaching the status of an old maid.[29]

According to Amitin-Shapiro, once agreement on the dowry was reached, the fathers met in the first official ceremony of betrothal, the *shrina-khury*, the repast of sweetmeats. The groom's father sent large trays of sugar and sweets to the house of the bride, then arrived with his relatives and neighbors. The rabbi, or the oldest man present, divided the sugar and gave pieces to each of the fathers, saying *siman tov*, a good omen, and then passed sugar to the guests, who wrapped the lumps in cloth to take home. On the evening of the day after the *shrina-khury*, a piece of silk was sent to the home of the bride, a part was kept, and the rest returned to the house of the groom.[30]

The viewing of the bride and groom by each other's families took place in a ceremony called the *kudo-bini*. Again, gift trays were sent to the house of the bride, but this time in a procession with musicians,

69 WALL-HANGING
Samarkand or Ferghana Valley
mid-19th century
74" × 47" (188 × 119cm)
5 panels
warp-faced plain weave
The regular, vertical arrangement of comb and branching horn motifs becomes characteristic of the Ferghana Valley production in the last half of the 19th century, particularly in the Khojent area. This earlier example has the saturated colors and balanced composition of Samarkand ikats.

70 WALL-HANGING
Samarkand
mid-19th century
81" × 62" (206 × 159cm)
6 panels
warp-faced plain weave
The secondary motifs are delicate renderings of women's jewelry ornaments – earrings and triangular talisman-shaped pendants.

46

46. The *shvi dukhtaron* was a merry, prenuptial celebration with music and dancing for the bride, her girlfriends and female relatives. The bride, seated at the center, wears an ikat dress and floral kerchief. *Turkestanskii al'bom*, 1871–72. (Navoi Library, Tashkent.)

and with richer presents. The groom's parents arrived with the bride price, which generally consisted of money and silk garments. These were displayed on a low table with the trays of sweets, so that all could see that a respectable value had been placed on the girl. The bride sat in a room just beyond the one in which the presents were displayed. The groom arrived stealthily, and was seated near a door left slightly ajar. He passed a tray of sweets with a glass of wine through the door to the bride, who rearranged the items and returned the tray to him. The groom was not supposed to peek, but no one blamed him for doing so.

In the weeks or months that followed, the groom made periodic visits to the bride's house, bringing gifts of sweets or cloth. It was a time for getting to know the bride's family, and demonstrated the groom's financial commitment to the marriage. The custom of *bakshido bazi* that took place in this period was in complete contrast to the generally modest relationship between bride and groom. The groom was invited to stay over at the home of the bride, and when the girl was asleep, or pretending to be, he was allowed to kiss and caress her and whisper sweet nothings – all under the close supervision of his future mother-in-law.[31]

As the wedding approached, a series of ceremonies took place. The viewing of the dowry, *takhta zanon*, lasted for several days. The entire dowry, which was made up principally of textiles, was displayed on a balcony or hung in a room. A woman was hired to announce the value of each item, inflating it several times over. A party for the bride's unmarried girlfriends, the *shvi dukhtaron*, gave the groom's friends a chance to sneak a look at the available bride-stock, and the *dzuvanon*, a farewell party to bachelor life, was held for the groom.

THE KETUBA, DOWRY AND BRIDE PRICE The writing of the *ketuba*, the marriage contract, took place the day before the wedding. All negotiations on the contract prior to this were verbal arrangements between the matchmaker and the bride's father. It was possible, but very unusual, for the wedding to be canceled if the parties could not agree on the valuation of the objects in the dowry. The standard formula of the *ketuba* was written in Aramaic, which few Central Asian Jews understood. Another part of the *ketuba* was written in colloquial Judaeo-Persian in Hebrew script, and contained a very detailed list of all the items in the dowry, the items included in the bride price, and their value.

The oldest *ketuba* Amitin-Shapiro saw was dated 1818, and related to families in straitened circumstances. The primary role of textiles in the marriage contract is clear. The bride's dowry consisted of a mirror and mirror-case, five dresses and five vests, three mourning robes, pieces of fabric for robes, a washstand with basin and candle-holder, and a large pot. The groom's bride price was: gifts, 50 *tillah* (a gold coin) in cash, 22 *tillah* still owing, sandals with overshoes, a brocade scarf, a waistcoat, three mourning robes, and an over-robe. In this early *ketuba* the valuation of the bride price is considerably higher than the dowry. Later the equation began to change, and in a ketuba from 1874, the dowry was five times larger than the bride price.

The 1874 dowry included various household utensils and small furnishings, but consisted primarily of garments and fabrics of various kinds. Among the items listed were "...twenty *adras* garments, one garment of French [foreign] silk, an open brocade garment, twenty pieces of marquisette [a very fine net material], eleven mourning robes, a fur coat, twenty-nine turbans, a brocade turban, twenty-nine pairs of trousers, one brocade pair, two embroidered pieces of suzani

47

47. Conclusion of the wedding agreement, *kashi-katua*. The *ketuba*, wedding contract, is completed by the man seated second from the left. Both the groom and an older woman standing beside him wear ikat robes, and the bride is veiled by a satin robe. A *talit* prayer shawl is draped over the heads of bride and groom. *Turkestanskii al'bom*, 1871–72. (Navoi Library, Tashkent.)

and one of colored calico, two night canopies, two long pillows – one of velvet, one of silk – eleven bolts of fabric for robes, two towels, three pairs of stockings, two pairs of sandals with overshoes, two *parandja*, four pairs [sic] of silk robes for the groom, one scarf and a shawl to tie around an iron trunk, eleven skull caps, cords with golden ends (to attach to hair braids), two pairs of earrings, one pair of chain-style bracelets, a gold ring, a pair of necklaces, a pair of temple ornaments, a necklace of twenty-six gold chains with coral, a coral chain, and a nose ring".

The bride price given by the groom was "nine robes, one garment of French silk, one brocade waistcoat, a silk garment, two *adras* mourning robes, sandals with gold-embroidered overshoes, and a bathing apron".[32] It is very likely that the term "mourning robes", used by Amitin-Shapiro, referred to the distinctively cut *munisak* robes that were essential for both wedding and funeral wear throughout urban Central Asia.

Specific dowry lists for Muslim brides are of a date substantially later than those for Jewish brides given by Amitin-Shapiro. Textiles form an equally important component of these later, Muslim, dowry lists, but the type of fabric has changed to the cloth that was popular at the turn of the century and beyond. In Bukhara, the 1897 dowry of a thirteen-year-old Muslim girl included ten dresses of *ferangi* (imported fabrics) and *atlas*, and two *munisak* robes, one of dark cherry velvet and one of brocade. In 1906 the dowry of a fifteen-year-old middle-class Muslim girl included forty dresses, all of factory-made or inexpensive materials, and two *munisak* robes, one of green factory-made velvet and one of silk brocade. In 1911, a seventeen-year-old Muslim girl married a wealthy jeweler, who provided half of the dowry dress materials. She had forty dresses and a sleeveless brocade vest.[33]

THE WEDDING CEREMONY In the wedding ceremony, the Jewish bride and groom stood under a *talit*, a prayer shawl, while in the Muslim ceremony an embroidered wall-hanging was used for the same purpose. The Jewish groom placed a ring on the bride's finger or gave her a coin. He made a set declaration, the couple drank wine from a glass over which the rabbi had pronounced seven blessings, and the

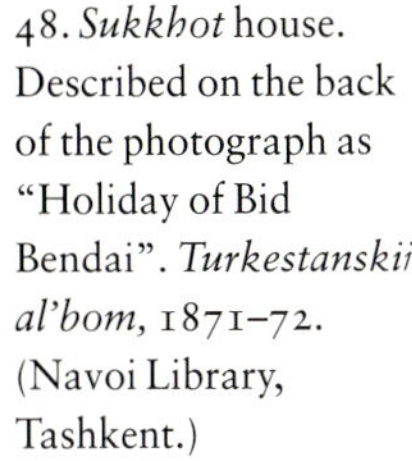

48. *Sukkhot* house. Described on the back of the photograph as "Holiday of Bid Bendai". *Turkestanskii al'bom*, 1871–72. (Navoi Library, Tashkent.)

48

marriage contract was read aloud. In both Muslim and Jewish ceremonies great care was taken to be sure that no one present acted to hinder the couple's happiness. Attendance was restricted to close family to prevent anyone from secretly closing a lock during the ceremony, which would have the effect of preventing the couple from achieving sexual union. One of the women present would thrust a threaded needle through the groom's robe at the culmination of the marriage rite, to ensure that he would perform his first husbandly duty with ease.[34] A plate was broken, and congratulations bestowed all round. Celebratory feasts followed, and lastly, the *nishala* ceremony was held, at which the bride's mother "proved" the virginity of the bride, presumably by displaying the soiled wedding bed-cover.

In most marriage rites and customs, Muslim and Jewish ceremonies differed only in the religious elements of the ritual, in which scriptures were read or chanted. Urban Central Asians of both religions shared many folk beliefs and superstitions, and the same steps were taken to ward off evil influences and encourage a propitious outcome to the marriage. The desired result of any union was the birth of children,

49

49. *Adras* ikat wall-hanging with chain-stitch silk suzani embroidery. Warp-faced plain weave. Bukhara, third quarter 19th century. 32" × 51" (81 × 129cm). (Guido Goldman Collection.)
50. Suzani on ikat foundation. Bukhara, 19th century. The Hebrew inscription is embroidered on a separate panel added within the arch. (Israel Museum, Jerusalem, formerly in the collection of the Baba-Tamah Bokharan Synagogue in Jerusalem.)

especially male children. For that reason, barren women might be divorced, and there were a few instances documented among the Central Asian Jews, in which a second wife was taken.[35] According to Amitin-Shapiro, separate households had to be maintained for each wife, and only the rich could afford the expense.

TEXTILES IN RELIGIOUS SETTINGS Silk hangings and embroideries that the West has tended to associate solely with Muslim culture were also used by Central Asian Jews in explicitly religious ritual contexts. The decoration of a *sukkhot*[36] house (a booth-like, temporary edifice constructed of textiles and decorated with the fruits of the harvest) with an embroidered suzani is an example of the use of these textiles in a household ceremony. Within the synagogue, carpets and embroideries covered the walls and floor, and textile gifts from the congregation supplied the curtains for the Ark and the wrappings for Torah cases. A suzani embroidered on ikat fabric in the traditional "Islamic" prayer-arch style, but with a later addition of an embroidered Hebrew inscription, served as an Ark curtain in a Bukharan synagogue in Jerusalem. This same prayer-arch was a common form in the architecture and ornamentation of Central Asian synagogues and religious schools. A set of ikat-covered *teffilin*, small boxes tied on the hands during prayer, were collected by Amitin-Shapiro with other household goods and ritual objects.[37] In more sober, private ceremonies, the influence of the wider urban culture determined the appropriate costume for the women who attended. The inclusion in the dowry of many coats named specifically as mourning robes suggests that they were not only the bride's richest garments, but that they were expected to last her entire life. Their dark colors were considered suitable both for mourning, and as ceremonial wear for an older woman.

50

In all matters concerned with textiles – in their use as garments, household decorations, and furnishings – Muslim Central Asian customs were similar to Judaic traditions. Within family ceremonial, the origin of specific elements within the two traditions may sometimes be found in the influence of one community upon the other. More often, similarities in observance may be ascribed to the development of patterns in common by both communities over the centuries.[38] Rites, customs and folk beliefs were not so much borrowed, as shared. For both Muslim and Jewish communities, the role of textiles within the primary events of family life was paramount.

At the end of the nineteenth century, and beginning of the twentieth, the Jewish community was continually challenged to maintain its distinct identity and way of life. Persistent discrimination on the part of the Tsarist administration encouraged the first wave of immigration to Palestine, where Bukharan Jews established their own quarter in Jerusalem.[39] Direct intervention in Jewish affairs by the Bolshevik authorities took place soon after the Revolution. Strife between the traditional heads of the Jewish community and the new communist leadership ended in the collapse of the communal administration, and the arrest of many of its members.[40] Only a few synagogues were allowed to remain in each city,[41] and every effort was made to enforce assimilation into the Soviet community. A second wave of Jewish emigration, first to Afghanistan and Iran, and then on to Palestine, took place from 1924 to 1935, when the Soviets succeeded in closing the borders. The entire population of Afghan Jews emigrated to Israel and the United States after the Soviet invasion of Afghanistan in 1979.

Once I was in the presence of Mutawaffak, the son of Al-Mutawakkil, and I saw him feel a garment over with his hand, then he said to me, "Hasan, this stuff pleases me. How much have we in the stores?" Thereupon I brought out of my boot a little roll in which was set forth the total of goods and stuffs in the stores, given in detail. Therein I found 6,000 pieces of this kind of stuff. "Hasan," said Al-Mutawaffak to me, "we have nothing to wear. Write to the country [of origin] *to make 30,000 pieces of this kind of fabric, and to send them with the least possible delay."*

'Ibn Al-Tiktaka [1]

CONCLUSION

The transformation of Central Asian ikat from an experimental craft founded on a mighty textile art tradition, to a commercially driven, sentimental echo of an era that had passed, paralleled the turbulent history of the nineteenth-century Khanates. The ikat revival began in the relative quiet and prosperity of the early nineteenth century, a time of political and social renewal. Ikat designers and producers were able to call upon the technical skills and artistic capabilities of the diverse population of the Central Asian Khanates: the fusion of many vital artistic traditions, ancient, urban and nomadic, yielded astoundingly beautiful results. The demand for ikat was immediate and widespread. One can only imagine the excitement caused by the appearance of a new fabric in the bazaar, the murmured approbation of courtiers as robes of honor were presented, the delight of the newly arrayed bride. The degree of visual pleasure afforded by ikat fabric allowed it to transcend the ordinary role of a commercial textile. It was an art that all could share: by the 1870s, the photographic record shows that ikats were as prominent in the decor of nomad yurts as they were in the homes of Bukhara's elite.

Throughout the nineteenth century the evolution of ikat design in Central Asia did not falter. The range of materials created within a hundred years was astonishing. Ikat was not merely decorative, in the Western sense of the word. It was not an overlay on a sumptuous fabric: without the brilliant color and the vibrant pattern, the fabric, the garment, was nothing. All the artistic concerns traditional to Central Asia were present in the gorgeous *adras* ikat silks, but there was no single art which was antecedent to ikat. There was not, as with metalwork, or miniature, a comparable art from a neighboring region which could define, or provide a larger context for the Central Asian style. The ikats of Iran, India and Turkey had little in common with those of Central Asia. Ikat design was both firmly rooted in Central Asian tradition, and uniquely experimental.

Ikat weaving was the most compelling art that sprang from the brief Central Asian urban renaissance, but it was only one of several luxury crafts that were revived and re-examined by local artisans between 1800 and 1880. The commercial weavers of the time were inspired to produce other rich fabrics – new types of heavy, ribbed silks in stripes and checks, sheer scarves and the shimmering fabric called *paripasha*, "wings of fairies". Other craftsmen – metalworkers, potters and jewelers – also developed new styles that drew on traditional forms and techniques, but experimented with surface, texture and ornamentation. A remarkable degree of creativity was expressed within locally based, traditional styles.

The circumstances in which these arts evolved were unparalleled within the Islamic world. Throughout the first half of the nineteenth century, Central Asia remained relatively isolated during a period of European expansion. In many Islamic kingdoms the crafts simply collapsed under pressure from European imports. Other nations, notably Qajar Iran, which also evolved a distinctive style in the nineteenth century, experienced a degree of cultural influence that radically affected the local arts and resulted, too often, in heavy-handed attempts to merge Eastern and Western styles or an uninspired search for historical roots in the grandeur of former empire.

The success of the early ikats encouraged the development of local variants and regional styles, and as Bukhara's economic importance diminished, these new silk-weaving centers drew advantage from increased contact with the West. Although ikat production expanded in the second half of the nineteenth century, commercial pressures forced changes in the weaving process and the character of design. The *adras* cotton-wefted ikats were replaced by chemically dyed silks and satins in bold but simplified designs.

My spinning wheel throws off the thread, flower

garden Foretelling some misfortune...

From the Uzbek women's work song

"Charkh" (Spinning Wheel)[2]

The art of Central Asian ikat did not long survive the oasis kingdoms. Events in the world outside made a languorous exit impossible; the craftsman's art ran headlong into the twentieth century and stopped cold, a victim of commercial and political pressures beyond Central Asia's control. Denied traditional sources of production, local consumers naturally sought a replacement, and the wearing of formalized, factory-made ikat came to express national identity in Uzbek Central Asia.

The high art of ikat weaving was blessed with an explosive birth, a vigorous middle age, and a rapid demise. Each great period and regional style of ikat weaving may be found in its full range within the Guido Goldman Collection – among them many of the most beautiful ikats ever woven. Within this remarkable and comprehensive collection is the essential, the defining art of an eventful century.

APPENDIX

Notes on nineteenth-century dye recipes

The hu *of the Western countries take its blood for dyeing their woolen rugs; its color is clean and will not turn black. Some say that when you prick it for its blood, if you ask, "How much will you give me?" the hsing-hsing will say, "Would two pints be truly enough?" In order to add to this amount, you thrash it with a whip before asking, and it will go along with an increase, so that you can obtain up to a gallon.*

Method of obtaining the dye called "gibbon's blood", P'ei Yen, Preface to "Hsing-hsing ming"[1]

The dyer's stock-in-trade was his secret knowledge; both Jewish and Muslim dyers of the nineteenth century closely guarded their recipes. It is quite difficult, even in technically advanced circumstances, to produce beautiful and colorfast fabrics from the action of plant and mineral dyes. Central Asian dye workshops were primitive: cauldrons of clay or metal were set into the earth, and only a rough stick was used to manipulate the articles in the baths. Pigments were made by the dyer from the best minerals and plants available, their quality dependent on the raw materials to hand. The brilliant, saturated colors of the ikats, embroideries and carpets of the period are testimony to the dyer's remarkable skills.

The introduction of artificial and synthetic dyes in the last quarter of the nineteenth century severely damaged the local dyeing industry, and many dyers found other occupations. Though banned in Bukhara by the Emir, small quantities of the first coal-tar dyes undoubtedly found their way to the local dyers soon after the end of the 1860s. By the end of the century, dyestuffs described as "fuchsin, green, Congo [red], and benzopurpurine"[2] were commonly found in Central Asian bazaars. Within the former Khanates, the political and economic rigors of the early twentieth century rapidly broke down craft organizations of all kinds, and few remembered the old skills. In parts of Central Asia outside Russian influence, the antique methods, used primarily for dyeing silk thread for embroidery, were retained for much longer.[3]

Two collections of dye recipes from early Russian sources have preserved some of the antique formulae. They follow here, without comparative analysis or comment except for the bracketed notes, mostly regarding relative weights and measures. The Persian and Uzbek names given for dyestuffs and colors are transliterated through the Cyrillic.

Ivan Krauze's essay, "Zametki o krasil'nom iskusstve tuzemtsev"(Notes on the painters' and dyers' art among the indigenous inhabitants) appeared in Moscow in 1872.[4] Krauze's valuable notes form the most comprehensive early record of Central Asian traditional dyestuffs and methods.

VEGETABLE DYES

1 *Ruyan* – madder, grown locally, especially plentiful in Kokand. Also grows wild. Used for silk and *mata*, plain cotton cloth.

2 *Isparak* – yellow delphinium [staphisagria], grows wild in abundance on the outskirts of Tashkent and elsewhere. Gives a good yellow color, used for silk and [silk] thread.

3 *Pugak* – a sponge that grows on mulberry trees. Used to dye sheepskin coats a dirty yellow-green. Brought in large quantities from Kokand.

4 *Tukhmak* – flowers of saphora japonica, a tree cultivated in local gardens. Gives a green color, quite infrequently used.

5 *Gul'khairi* – black mallow flower, cultivated in gardens for its attractive appearance. Used, albeit rarely, to dye silk black.

6 *Narpus* – pomegranate skin, brought in large quantities from Namangan. Used to produce a black dye.

7 *Kyzyl-Bakam* – sandalwood, imported from Russia and used to dye silk and suede red. Since the introduction of fuchsin, use of sandalwood and cochineal has fallen off significantly.

8 *Kara-Bakam* – [possibly] brazilwood, imported from Russia, produces a dark violet color.

9 *Buzgunch* – galls from pistachio tree leaves – used for tanning.

10 *Kermyak* – rhubarb root, grows abundantly in local mountains. Used for tanning leather.

11 *Nil* – indigo, various qualities available for purchase, all imported from India. Used to dye all shades of blue and green (by soaking yellow cloth in an indigo solution).

12 *Asil ren* – cochineal, brought from Bukhara and used to dye silk red. Sold for 3 rubles per funt.[5] Cochineal insects were found in great abundance in spring on the young leaves of ash and other trees in Tashkent, but the local people did not make use of them at the time of writing [1872].

SILK DYEING RECIPES

1 for black, *kara*: for 3lb [1.36kg] silk, take 2lb [900g] *narpus* (pomegranate skin) and ½lb [227g] *agaisaf* (iron filings). Mix and boil almost the whole day in water, stirring constantly. Strain and dye the silk, which has been previously washed in lye.
2 for gold, *milya-saryk*, take 6lb [2.72kg] *isparak* (yellow delphinium), 1½lb [680g] *ruyan* (madder) and 3 ounces [85g] *achik-tash* (alum). Boil together in water "for quite a long time". Dip silk in the resulting liquid.
3 for cherry color, *yugungli*: for 5lb [2.27kg] silk, take 1lb [454g] *buzgunch* (pistachio tree galls), 1lb [454g] *kyzyl-bokam* [sic] (sandalwood) and ½lb [227g] *asilren* [sic] (cochineal) and boil together in a kettle, then strain.
4 for light green, *zainabe'*, take silk previously dyed yellow in a decoction of *isparak* (yellow delphinium) and dip it in a weak *nil* (indigo) solution.
5 for pink, *pshti*, use a weak solution of *fereng-ren* (fuchsin).
6 for blue, *tokok*, use a solution of *nil* (indigo) with *agak* (lime).
7 for red, *kyzyl*, previously sandalwood and madder were used; more recently fuchsin has been used increasingly, dissolved directly in hot water. The silk is dipped in this solution. This is not a stable dye; it fades.
8 for dark green, *barikaram*, silk previously dyed yellow using *isparak* is dipped in a medium-strength indigo solution.
9 for violet, *koi-indy*, take 1½lb [680g] *kara-bakam* [brazilwood?] and 1lb [454g] *achik-tash* (alum), dissolve in water and boil in a kettle. Strain and use.
10 for yellow, *saryk*, *isparak* (yellow delphinium).
11 for a steely color, *saus*, take silk previously dyed yellow and dip it in a black dye solution. Silk is bleached by soaking in a solution of *ishkar* (potash) and *agak* (lime).

Krauze concludes his recipes with a disparaging assessment of the skills of the Central Asian dyer. "The dyers' art among the indigenous inhabitants of Central Asia is at the lowest possible level of development and offers nothing that is edifying or worthy of imitation."[6] Two decades later, a very different attitude is taken by an unknown author, who writes, "It is particularly sad to observe that in Central Asia they have recently begun to dye the more valuable locally-produced items – woolen and silk carpets, fabrics and yarns – with synthetic organic dyestuffs, disregarding the vegetable dyes, despite the fact that only thanks to the latter has this entire category of Central Asian products gained its superior reputation."

The recipes that follow appeared in an undated pre-revolutionary article, "Dyeing Crafts in the Central Asian Russian Protectorates".[7] Within the article there is reference to data collected in 1897–98, which might give the article a date around the turn of the century.

1 In Bukhara, per vat (1 *arshin* deep and ¾ *arshin*[8] wide), the dyers take 2⅓ *funt* of indigo (*nil*), and, depending on its quality, an appropriate quantity of lime (*achaka*), potash (*ishkar*) and dried mulberries (*gyt'-mais*). Before placing the indigo in the vats, they grind it with a stone or an iron pestle. In cold weather, the vats are warmed to hand-hot; in summer when the temperature reaches 50–55 Réaumur [on which scale water freezes at 0 and boils at 80], they are not heated at all. In Bukhara, the strength of the dye is such that yarn immersed for a total of 10 minutes will turn light blue, darker blue after 15 minutes, dark blue after half an hour. Bukharan indigo dyers assert that it takes 5 *funts* of indigo to color 10–12 *puds*[9] of cotton yarn.
2 It is less common in Central Asia at this time to find items dyed using madder (*ruyan*), which is cultivated in Kokand, Samarkand region, etc. Four years after sowing, the seed produces a root which is dried and ground, and in this form used as a dyestuff. Before dyeing, cotton items are dipped in an alum (*achik-tasha*) solution, wrung out and dyed with the madder, which has been soaked in water and placed into a dye-bath along with the liquid. One *pud* worth of cotton items takes ¼ *funt* of alum and 3 *funt* of madder. One *funt* of madder costs 70 kopeks in the bazaar.
3 In addition to madder, in Central Asia, sandalwood (*mukhan*) is used for red and pink. The cotton items are dipped in an alum solution, wrung out and heated to a simmer in a water solution of red sandalwood, in the presence of zinc sulphate salt. Each *funt* of e.g., cotton yarn takes 6 *zolotniks* [approximately an ounce (28g)] of red sandalwood and 8 *zolotniks* [approximately 1¼ ounces] of zinc sulphate salt. In the Central Asian Russian protectorates red sandalwood and zinc sulphate salt come from India.
4 For yellow dyeing, the seeds of a plant of the pistachio family, known in Central Asia as *buzguik* or *buzguichak* [also *buzgunch*], are used. Cotton items are first soaked in a solution of *buzguik*, wrung out and processed is a cold potash solution. A *pud* of yarn takes 3 *funt* of *buzguik* and a *funt* of potash. The local potash comes from *buzguik* ash. Since no pre-mordanting is done in obtaining this yellow color, *buzguik* must be a substantive vegetal dyestuff.
5 In addition to the above, there are other methods of yellow dyeing in Central Asia, which involve mordants. In one of these, the cotton item is first soaked in an alum solution, wrung out and dyed in a decoction of *isparak* or *zaparan*.
6 The home-based dyers in Central Asia achieve green by re-dyeing in indigo an item previously dyed yellow in *isparak*.
7 The mordant used with pomegranate-skin extract is copper sulphate. Cotton thread is boiled/simmered in the dye after the double-mordanting with copper sulphate and potash.

1

1. A general map of the area traversed by the Silk Route showing relevant cities and archeological sites.
2. Central Asia and surrounding area in the 19th century.

2

NOTES

INTRODUCTION

1 Meer Izzut Oollah, *Travels in Central Asia in the Years 1812–13*, trans. Capt. P.D. Henderson, Foreign Department, Calcutta, 1872.

CHAPTER I

1 "The Journal of Friar William of Rubruck, 1253–1255 AD", Manuel Komroff, ed., *Contemporaries of Marco Polo*, Boni and Liveright, NY, 1928, p. 82.

2 Dr Irene Good, personal communication, 1996.

3 Curtius 8.1.35 in F.L. Holt, *Alexander the Great and Bactria*, E.J. Brill, Leiden, 1988, p. 82.

4 Guitty Azarpay, *Sogdian Painting*, University of California Press, Berkeley and Los Angeles, 1981; also Sylvia A. Matheson, *Persia: An Archaeological Guide*, Faber and Faber, 1979, p.151.

5 F. L. Holt, op. cit., pp. 54–70.

6 Guitty Azarpay, op. cit., p. 3.

7 Roman familiarity with Central Asia can be seen in works such as Isidore of Charax's *The Parthian Stations*, an early travel guide. *The Periplus of the Red Sea* was a companion edition for the competing sea trade. See D.S. Richards, ed., *Islam and the Trade of Asia*, Bruno Cassirer, Oxford, 1970, p. 1.

8 John Vollmer, *Silk Roads, China Ships*, Royal Ontario Museum, Toronto, 1983, pp. 29–30.

9 Luce Boulnois, *The Silk Road*, trans. Dennis Chamberlin, Allen and Unwin, London, 1966, p. 113-16; also David Whitehouse and Andrew Williamson, "Sasanian Maritime Trade", *Iran, Journal of the British Institute of Persian Studies*, Vol XI, 1973, pp. 29–49.

10 T'ang Shu, 221b, 4153d, in Edward H. Schafer, *The Golden Peaches of Samarkand, A Study of T'ang Exotics*, University of California Press, Berkeley and Los Angeles, 1963, p. 153.

11 John Vollmer, op. cit., p. 24. The medicinal root of rhubarb was prized for its purgative qualities, and control of the rhubarb trade would lead to major disputes between Bukharan traders and the Russian Tsar in the 17th and 18th centuries. See Audrey Burton, *Bukharan Trade*, Papers on Inner Asia, Indiana University, Bloomington, 1993.

12 G.F. Hudson, "The Medieval Trade of China", D.S. Richards, op. cit., p. 164. The Empress Hu (AD 521) and her ladies in waiting were said to have dressed exclusively in Indian cotton. See Boulnois, op. cit., p. 156. Edward Schafer dates the introduction of cotton to China in the third century AD and its cultivation to Later Han times. Schafer, op. cit., p. 209.

13 Recent discussions with archeologists working in the field of the Central Asian Bronze Age have led to the conclusion that the pieces of "silk dresses'" said to have been found at Sapalli Tepe and dated to about 1800 BC, (first cited in Philip L. Kohl, ed.,*The Bronze Age Civilization of Central Asia*, M.E. Sharpe, Armonk, New York, 1981, pp. xxi, 265) were neither silk, nor dresses, but merely fragmentary textile remains, as yet unidentified, from the head of an excavated skeleton. Frederick Hiebert, personal communication, 1996.

14 *The Art of Central Asia, The Stein Collection in the British Museum*, Kodansha International, 1985,Vol. 3 plate 66; also M. Aurel Stein, *Ancient Khotan*, Hacker Art Books, New York, 1975, pp. 134, 259–60.

15 Karl Jettmar, *Art of the Steppes*, Crown Publishers, New York, 1964, p. 120.

16 *The Art of Central Asia, The Stein Collection in the British Museum*, op. cit. Vol. 3; also *Cultural Relics Unearthed in Sinkiang*, Wenwu Press, Peking, 1975.

17 The fragment was identified by Dr Irene Good and Dr Elizabeth Barber, on a recent trip to Xinjiang. It was displayed at the local archeological museum in Turfan, without identification except for the site.

18 A.F.P. Hulsewe, *China in Central Asia*, E.J. Brill, Leiden, 1979, p. 148.

19 Carl Schuster, "Remarks on the Design of an Early Ikat Textile in Japan" in *Festschrift Alfred Buhler*, Pharos – Verlag Hansrudolf Schwabe AG, Basel, 1965, pp. 339–40, plate 87.

20 Alfred Buhler, *Ikat, Batik Plangi*, vol. 3, Pharos-Verlag Hansrudolf Schwabe AG, Basel, 1972, plates 158, 159, 160.

21 A.Ghosh, ed., *Ajanta Murals*, Archaeological Survey of India, New Delhi, 1967; plates XI, XIII, XIV.

22 Alisa Baginski and Orit Shamir, "Early Islamic Textiles, Basketry and Cordage from Nahal 'Omer", *Atiqot*, Vol. XXVI, Israel Antiquities Authority, Jerusalem, 1995, pp. 28–31.

23 Buhler, op. cit., Vol. 1–23, plate 36.

24 Phyllis Ackerman and Arthur Upham Pope, *Survey of Persian Art*, Souroush Press, Tehran, 1977, pp. 2043, 2196–97.

25 Carl Schuster, op.cit.. See also Buhler, op. cit., Vol. I, p. 125, and L. Pollet, S. Daems, et al, *Ikat, Internationale Textieltentoonstelling*, 19.1.91 – 28.4.91, Education Department of the Museums, Antwerp, 1991. p. 7.

26 Carol M. Bier, "Textiles", *The Royal Hunter*, Prudence O. Harper, Asia House Gallery, 1975, pp. 119–40, also Dorothy G. Shepherd, "Zandaniji Revisited", *Ars Islamica*, 1979.

27 Guitty Azarpay, op. cit.; also Mario Bussagli, *Painting of Central Asia*, Editions d'Art Albert Skira, Geneva, 1963; also Herbert Hartel and Marianne Yaldiz, *Along the Ancient Silk Routes*, The Metropolitan Museum of Art, New York, 1982.

28 Another name for this material may have been "parniyan". Melikian Chirvani cites Asadi Tusi's *Language of the Ancient Persians* (mid-11th cent.): "Parniyan is a silk from Eastern Turkestan which has patterns in roundels". "Parniyan and Parand Identified", *Bulletin of the Asia Institute*, New Series/Vol. 5, 1991.

29 Luc Kwanten, *Imperial Nomads*, University of Pennsylvania Press, 1979, p. 39; also David Whitehouse and Andrew Williamson, op. cit., 1973, pp. 44–45.

30 Thomas Barfield, *The Perilous Frontier*, Blackwell, Cambridge, Mass., and Oxford, 1989.

31 Luc Kwanten, op. cit., pp. 39–41.

32 Larry Moses, "T'ang Tribute Relations with the Inner Asian Barbarian", in John Curtis Perry and Bardwell L. Smith, eds, *Essays on T'ang Society*, E.J. Brill, Leiden, 1976.

33 See Dorothy G. Shepherd, "Zandaniji Revisited", p. 108. In regard to the European finds, see D.G. Shepherd and W. B. Henning, "Zandaniji Identified?", *Aus der Welt des Islamischen Kunst: Festschrift fur Ernst Kuhnel*, ed. R. Ettinghausen (Berlin, 1959), pp. 22–23.

34 K.N. Chaudhuri, *Trade and Civilization in the Indian Ocean*, Cambridge University Press, Cambridge, 1985, pp. 34–36.

35 S.D. Goitein, *Letters of Medieval Jewish Traders*, Princeton University Press, 1973, pp. 76–77.

36 Originally a Persian term meaning embroidery, *tiraz* came to refer to a textile workshop closely connected to a court that supplied the court with clothing for its own use and for gifts, with materials for furnishings and often with goods used as payment for taxes. In Central Asia, the relationship between factories and the court was often tenuous. A *tiraz* is also a weaving – a narrow band bearing the name of a ruler, and sometimes the date, place of manufacture and religious benedictions. R.B. Serjeant,"Materials for a History of Islamic Textiles up to the Mongol Conquest", *Ars Islamica*, Vol. 9–15/16, 1942-51, Chapter I, The Origin of the Tiraz System", also Chapter X, "Transoxiana"

37 Ibid., Chapter II, p. 76.

38 Idrisi, *Geographie*, trans. by P.A. Jaubert, Paris, 1836–40, II, #201, cited in Serjeant, op. cit., Chapter X. Widhari was a village about six miles from Samarkand.

39 D.G. Shepherd and W. B. Henning, op. cit.

40 Serjeant, op. cit., Chapter IX, "Khorasan".

41 Also transliterated as *karbas* and *karbaz*. This very long-lived fabric is probably the same material as the *kirpas* mentioned in the biblical Book of Esther, Chapter 1.

42 V.V. Barthold, *Turkestan Down to The Mongol Invasion*, The E.J.W. Gibb Memorial, 3rd edition, pp. 395–96.

43 Richard N. Frye, *The History of Bukhara, Translated from a Persian Abridgement of the Arabic Original by Narshakhi*, The Mediaeval Academy of America, Cambridge, 1954, p. 21.

44 Henry Sauvaire, trans., *Histoire de Jerusalem et D'Hebron, Fragment de la Chronique de Moudjir-ed-dyn*, Paris 1926, p. 53.

45 *Barchin* cannot be identified with certainty, but it may have been a type of brocaded trade cloth. Makhmud Kashgari, *Divanu Iugat at Turk* (Dictionary of Turkic Languages), 1072–74, quoted by S.A. Mahkamova, "K istorii tkachestva v Srednei Azii" (For a history of weaving in Central Asia), *Khudozhestvennaya Kul'tura Srednei Azii. IX – XII Veka* (Arts and artistry of Central Asia, 9-13th centuries), p. 82.

46 S.A. Mahkamova, op. cit., p. 76.

47 Richard N. Frye, personal communication, 1995.

48 Serjeant, op. cit., Chapter XV, p. 76, footnote 8 citing E.W. Lane, *Arabic English Lexicon*, London, 1863–93, Vol. I, p. 2058.

49 The first appears in Serjeant, op. cit., citing Azraki, *Die Croniken der Stadt Mekka*, F. Wusterfeld, ed.,Leipzig, 1857–61, I, 173–74. The second is from Serjeant, op. cit., citing Kitab al-Aghani, Cairo, 1927, XIX, 75.

50 Alfred Buhler, op. cit., Vol.3, plates 1–10, also N.P. Britton, *A Study of some Early Islamic Textiles in the Boston Museum of Fine Arts*, Boston, 1939.

51 Alfred Buhler, op. cit., plates 21–25.

52 The Yasa of Chengis Khan is a collection of verbal traditions that served as legal precedents – a code of ethics and behavior on which Mongol law was based. V.A. Riasonovsky, "The Yasa of Chengiz Khan", *The Fundamental Principles of Mongol Law*, Tientsin, 1937, p. 88, quoted by Ross E. Dunn, *The Adventures of Ibn Battuta*, University of California Press, Berkeley and Los Angeles, 1989, p. 81.

53 Thomas W. Lentz and Glenn D. Lowry, *Timur and the Princely Vision*, Los Angeles County Museum of Art, 1989, pp. 216-21, cat. nos. 116, 49, 117 and figs 80, 81.

54 Phyllis Ackerman and Arthur Upham Pope, op. cit., Vol. IV, pp. 2043, 2046. See also S.A. Mahkamova, 1983, pp. 70–85.

55 Ibid., Vol. V, Islamic Textiles, p. 2055. Our knowledge of weaving after the Mongol invasion is limited to a few extant pieces and the selective documentation of miniature painting. It is largely unknown how the weaving villages around Samarkand and Bukhara fared during the upheaval; whether they were recruited as suppliers to the court or left alone to produce their traditional wares. The carpets and felts of the nomads and traditional home-based crafts such as embroidery may have preserved styles which disappear from view in this period.

56 Gavin Hambly, "An Introduction to the Economic Organization of Early Qajar Iran", *Iran, Journal of the British Institute of Persian Studies*, Vol. II, 1964, p. 77, and Robert Mc Chesney, personal communication, 1996.

57 Linda S. Steinmann, "Sericulture and Silk, Production, Trade and Export under Shah Abbas", in Carol Bier, ed., *Woven From the Soul, Spun From the Heart*, The Textile Museum, Washington, DC, 1987, pp. 12–19, and Charles Issawi, "The Decline of Middle Eastern Trade 1100–1850" in D.S. Richards, ed., op. cit., p. 245.

58 Ahmed Ibn Arabshah, *Timur, the Great Amir*, transl. by J.H. Sanders, Progressive Books, Lahore, p. 216.

59 Jonas Hanway, "Attempts made to open a Trade to Khieva and Bokhara in 1740", *An Historical Account of the British Trade over the Caspian Sea*, London, Vol 1, 1753, p. 353.

60 Audrey Burton, op. cit., p. 1.

61 *Zenden* was made in three styles for the Russian trade; the thickest type was used for clothing, the thinnest for lining church vestments. A Russified version of the old trade name *zandaniji*, *'zenden'* continued to be used well into the eighteenth century, but the word *zandaniji* disappeared within Central Asia by the sixteenth century. Ibid., p. 41.

62 *Azyam'* robes are described as "knee-length damask or satin...with narrow sleeves ...gathered and buttoned at the back". Ibid., p. 17.

63 Ibid., p. 24.

64 V. Klein, "Inozemnye tkani, bytovavshie v Rossii do XVIII veka, i ikh terminologiya" (Foreign fabrics found in Russia before the 18th century, and their terminology), *Sbornik Oruzheinoi palaty* (Armory Anthology), Moscow, 1925, pp. 22–38. Mahkamova has speculated that the "hoofed velvets" may be of Central Asian

as well as Turkish origin. S.A. Mahkamova, personal communication, 1995.
65 V. Klein, op. cit., 1925, pp. 45–47.
66 Mahkamova has stated that the "sheepskin *obir*'" mentioned in the 1328 will of Ivan Danilovich Kalita, Grand Duke of Moscow, and the same sheepskin, listed in Kalita's second will as being made of "yellow *obir*'" may be evidence of an idiosyncratic local pronunciation of the word *abr*. V. Klein believed that this obir' is the ancient designation of *obyar'*, a luxurious silk fabric of both Western and Eastern provenance that was favored in the Russian royal court of the seventeenth century. S.A. Mahkamova, personal communication, 1996.
67 One *obyar'* moiré silk was made by combining thin warp threads with thicker weft threads. In another, a watered effect was achieved by pressing silk cloth through metal rollers engraved with wave-like designs. "Eastern" *obyar'*, imported from Turkey and Persia, was a silk cloth in a plain twill weave with very thin gold or silver weft stripes. V. Klein, 1925, op. cit., pp. 38–44.
68 Ibid., 1925, pp. 60–62. The descriptions of *alacha* and *dara'i* in the early sources are inconclusive. Both Persian *dorogi* and Bukharan *dorogi* are listed in Russian customs records, although it is not clear that the fabrics were entirely similar. Printed imitations of *dorogi* made in eighteenth-century Ivanovo, in Russia, utilized simple ikat-like patterns. The *alacha* striped fabrics with sections of ikat-dyed warp were made in Bukhara until the mid-nineteenth century. Phyllis Ackerman and V. Klein, op. cit., pp. 2163–74, and *Ivanovskie sitsy,* XVIII – *nachala* XX *veka*, Leningrad, Khudozhnik RSFSR, 1983, p. 17. See also Robert Chenciner and Magomedkhan Magomedkhanov, "Persian Exports to Russia From the Sixteenth to the Nineteenth Century", *Iran, Journal of the British Institute of Persian Studies*, Vol. XXX, pp. 123–30.
69 Carol Bier has suggested that *dorogi* refers to a two-faced cloth, whereas *dara'i* is a striped fabric, sometimes containing sections of ikat dyed warp. Carol Bier, op. cit., 1987, p. 161, and personal communication, 1996.
70 *Alacha* was called *pestred* in Russian. According to this seventeenth-century document, it was made of either cotton and hemp, or cotton and silk. Audrey Burton, op. cit., p. 17. The Indian name *alleja* is defined as "a stuff from Turkestan ...described as a silk cloth 5 yards long, which has a sort of wavy line pattern running in the length on either side". Yusuf Ali (monograph on Silk Fabrics) accepts the derivation from alcha or alacha, and says it was probably introduced by the Mongols. "This fabric differs from the Doriya [note similarity to *dara'i,* ed.] in having a substantial texture, whereas the Doriya is generally flimsy. The colors are generally red or blueish red, with white stripes." Col. Henry Yule and A.C. Burnell, *Hobson-Jobson*, Routledge and Kegan Paul, London and New York, 1903.
71 Other types of Persian ikat fabrics were *marmul*, plain *kutny* (a "multicolored unfigured shot satin with an 'all over ikat design'" – and *dara'i* (*dorogi* in Russian). Indian *aurangschtschagi* or *abrashaj* fabrics, described as made of silk, silk/cotton and grass fiber, may also have been ikat-dyed cloth. Phyllis Ackerman and V. Klein, op. cit., pp. 2163–74.
72 Cotton *zenden*, unpatterned calico *kindyak*, block-print cotton *chit*, and plain muslin *karbas*, were the most common textiles in trade. Audrey Burton, op. cit., pp. 11–12, 17.
73 Phyllis Ackerman and V. Klein, op. cit., pp. 2163–74.
74 Edward Allworth, ed., *Central Asia*, Duke University Press, 1994, Durham and London, pp. 3–4.
75 Audrey Burton, op. cit., p. 2.
76 Jonas Hanway, op. cit., Vol. 1, pp. 345–57.
77 Gavin Hambly, op. cit., pp. 69-82.

CHAPTER 2

1 Eugene Schuyler, *Turkestan*, 1877, Scribner, Armstrong & Co., New York, Vol. 2, pp. 81–82.
2 Dr Eversmann and P.L. Jakovlew, "Account of Bucharia", *Russian Missions into the Interior of Asia*, Sir Richard Phillips and Co., London, 1823, p. 45.
3 Mary Holdsworth, *Turkestan in the 19th Century*, Central Asian Research Centre, Oxford, 1959, p. 21. Riza Quli Khan, the Persian emissary to Khiva in 1851 estimated the number of slaves as equal to about one half of the settled population.
4 Nikolai Vladimirovich Khanykov, *Description of the Khanate of Bukhara*, St Petersburg, 1843.
5 O.A. Sukhareva, op. cit., 1976, pp. 173–74.
6 F.D. Liushkevich, "Etnograficheskaia gruppa Ironi" (The Irani ethnic group), *Zaniatia i bit narodov Srednei Azii*, Nauka, Leningrad, 1971, pp. 36–71.
7 O.A. Sukhareva, *Kvartal'naia obschina pozdnefeodalnovo goroda Bukhare* (Neighborhood communities of the late feudal town of Bukhara), Moscow, 1976.
8 Edmund O'Donovan, *In the Country of the Turkomans,* Oguz Press and the Royal Geographical Society, London, 1977, p. 200.
9 G. Whitney Azoy, *Buzkashi, Game and Power in Afghanistan*, University of Pennsylvania Press, 1982.
10 Arminius Vambery, *Travels in Central Asia*, Harper and Bros., New York, 1865, p. 227.
11 Rev. Joseph Wolff, *Narrative of a Mission to Bokhara in the Years 1843–45*, Harper and Brothers, New York, 1845, p. 285.
12 This embroidery work was called *gulduzi* and *zamanduzi*. Gold and silver threads were made by drawing and rolling the metal into a flat, very thin wire, which was then spun around a silk core, to gain the maximum effect from the least amount of gold. According to tradition, the tarnishing of the threads by women's hands resulted from contact with menstrua. P.A. Goncharova, *Bukharo zarduzlik sanbati, Zolotoshvennoi iskusstvo Bukhare* (Bukharan gold embroidery), Gafur Guliama, Tashkent, 1986.
13 The Pit was a hole in the ground into which prisoners were lowered, often never to see the sun again. It was kept full of particularly unpleasant bloodsucking vermin.

CHAPTER 3

1 Viktor M. Beliaev, *Central Asian Music*, trans. Mark Slobin, Wesleyan University Press, Middletown, Conn., 1975, p. 131.
2 O.A. Sukhareva, op. cit., 1976.
3 *Waqf* property was sometimes agricultural land, sometimes a building leased for residence or business, but the income derived from *waqf* property was dedicated to an institution, usually a mosque, *medresse* or *khanaqah*. See Robert D. McChesney, *Waqf in Central Asia: Four Hundred Years in the History of a Muslim Shrine, 1480-1889*, Princeton University Press, 1991.
4 Eugene Schuyler, op. cit., Vol. 1, pp. 191–94.
5 N.O. Tursunov, *Iz istorii gorodskovo remesla severnovo Tadjikistana* (History of urban trades in northern Tadjikistan), Dushanbe, 1974, pp. 154–57.
6 In a document dated 1824–25, there is mention of a large weaving artel in the Gaukushan neighborhood in which individual craftsmen owned their own looms, and a wheel was available to prepare the warps for the guild members' use. A workshop of similar size and identical function was located in the Zanguliasazi neighborhood at the end of the nineteenth century. O.A. Sukhareva, op. cit., 1976, p. 190.
7 Three late eighteenth-century *risolas* of the *chit* woodblock print makers have been studied. R.G. Mukminova, personal communication, 1995.
8 B.A. Farmanova collected a *risola* of the weavers guild in the 1980s in Marghilan; it was mimeographed. B.A. Farmanova, personal communication, 1995.
9 N.O. Tursunov, op. cit., p.167.
10 The payment to the devil was called the *khakkash khar*. O.A. Sukhareva, *O tkatskikh remeslakh v Samarkande* (Weaving Trades of Samarkand), Dushanbe, 1981, p. 34.
11 N. Kiziliakov, "Burkh – gorney kozel" (Burkh – the mountain goat), *Sovetskaya Etnografiya*, 1934, no. 2, pp. 181–89.
12 N.O. Tursunov, op. cit., pp. 163–64.
13 Mary Holdsworth, op. cit., 1959, p. 26.
14 B.A. Farmanova, "Remeslennoe proivodstvo v Ferganskoi doline vo vtoroi polovine XIX – nachale XX vv" (Handicraft production in the Ferghana Valley in the second half of the 19th century – early 20th century), dissertation, Tashkent, 1994.
15 See ibid., for twentieth-century employment. Women commonly acted as spinners, and wove a rough, tabby-weave cotton cloth, *karbas*, both for home use and commercial sale. Women weavers had their own guild-like organization, holy patroness and special rituals and festivals. N.O. Tursunov, op. cit.
16 O.A. Sukhareva, op. cit., 1981, pp. 27–29.
17 N.O. Tursunov, op. cit., pp. 119–51.
18 The *Mazhuma-i-vasaick*, compiled in the office of the Samarkand *Kazi*, or head judge, in the years 1588–91, consisted of 700 legal documents, of which 25 were agreements between a master craftsman and an apprentice. The professions for which the agreements were made included the weaving of *alacha*, striped cottons and silks, and *futa*, scarf-like belt fabrics, pattern weaving, felting, and dyeing, among others. See R.G. Mukminova, "Training of specialists-handicraftsmen in Samarkand in the sixteenth century", *Social Science in Uzbekistan*, no. 10, 1972.
19 N.O. Tursunov, op. cit., pp. 119–51.
20 O.A. Sukhareva, op. cit., 1981, pp. 27–29.
21 O.A. Sukhareva, op. cit., 1976, p. 92.
22 Ibid., 1976, pp. 101–23.
23 It is noteworthy that within the sixteenth-century legal documents studied by R.G. Mukminova there are no Jewish names in the lists of dyers. The absence of Jewish names might also indicate that separate records were kept by Jewish administrators. R.G. Mukminova, personal communication, 1996.
24 O.A. Sukhareva, op. cit., 1976, p. 218.
25 Mir Izzatullah, an Indian Muslim agent for the British, stated that in 1813 the most substantial trade was with Russia, that there were 4,000–5,000 camels in every caravan, mostly carrying *chit-i-luk*, colored calico, white cotton fabrics, shawls muslin and yarn. Y.A. Sokolov, "Bukhara, Samarkand, Kelif v 1813 godu" (Bukhara, Samarkand and Kelif in 1813), *Proceedings of the Central Asian State University* (SAGU), No. 90, Historical Sciences, Vol. 14, Tashkent, 1957, pp. 198–207.
26 *Asiatskaya Russia, zemlia i khoziaistvo*, Vol. 2, St Petersburg, 1914.
27 Attempts by Muslim Central Asians to counter a Bolshevik takeover resulted in the establishment of the Kokand Autonomous Government in the Ferghana Valley in 1917. The Bolshevik response was to destroy the city of Kokand, and to institute a series of food blockades. Helene Carrere d'Encausse, "Civil War and New Governments", Edward Allworth, ed., op. cit., pp. 225–28.
28 Nationalist sources gave the number as 1,114,000. Ian Murray Matley, "Population and Land", Edward Allworth, ed., op. cit., pp. 97–98.
29 L.M. Kantor, *Tuzemnye Evrei v Uzbekistane* (Indigenous Jews in Uzbekistan), UZSSR State Publishing House, Samarkand/Tashkent, 1929, pp. 18–19.
30 S.A. Mahkamova, personal communication, 1995.
31 Bernard Dupaigne, "Un Artisan d'Afghanistan", *Objets et Modes*, Vol. 14, 1974, p.143–68.
32 Bernard Dupaigne, "Les Ikats d'Uzbekistan et d'Afghanistan", *Texilhandwerk in Afghanistan*, Bibliotheca Afghanica, Liestal, 1983, pp. 81–92.
33 Harriet Sandys, "Dyeing Under Fire, Part 1: The Ikat Project", *Hali Annual*, 1994, pp. 62–68.

CHAPTER 4

1 The *Tresor* was written around 1260, at a time when the silk industry was well established in the Levant, Sicily and Spain, and demonstrates the contrast between didactic and practical knowledge available at the time. Leonardo Olshiki, *Marco Polo's Asia*, University of California Press, 1960, p. 44.
2 *Asiatskaya Russia,* op. cit., Vol. 2, pp. 392–96; also N.O. Tursunov, op. cit., p. 35.
3 This coarse thread, *kaliava,* is unsuitable for weaving, but is still extensively produced in northern Afghanistan for home use in embroidery.

4 85% of total Turkestan production came from the Ferghana Valley by 1910. *Asiatskaya Russia,* op. cit., Vol. 2, pp. 392–96.
5 The finest silk thread was called *chillia*, *homiak* was export quality, *guliya* was also mid range, and *sarnak* the worst.
6 N.O. Tursunov, op. cit., p. 38.
7 Ibid., p. 54.
8 These processes were all described in a single name. In Bukhara it was *korchubi kardan*, and in Khodjent *akhiazi*. Ibid., pp. 56–57.
9 In the Ferghana workshops the *gullavardar* stretched the warp, the *chizmokchi* applied the patterns to the warp and the *annurband* wrapped the bundles. B.A. Farmanova, op. cit.
10 N.O. Tursunov, op. cit., pp. 56–57.
11 A.S. Melikian Chirvani, op. cit., cites Asadi Tusi, op. cit., in which *haft rang* refers to polychrome fabrics. On propitious numbers; seven is a lucky number associated with family festivals, as in the preparation of *haft mewa*, "seven fruits", a holiday dish.
12 A Colorational Appendix, *Technical Anthology and Industrial Bulletin*, V.A. Oglobin, ed., c. 1898–1900.
13 O.A. Sukhareva, op. cit., 1976, p. 69.
14 I. Krauze, op. cit.,1872, pp. 209–12.
15 O.A. Sukhareva, op. cit., 1976, p. 115.
16 Hans E. Wulff, *The Traditional Crafts of Persia*, MIT Press, Cambridge, Mass. and London, 1966.
17 Viktor M. Beliaev,op. cit., p. 179.
18 A.I. Shakhnazarov, *Sel'skoe khozyaistvo v Turkestanskom krae*, (Agriculture in Turkestan), St Petersburg, 1908, pp. 388–89, identifies the inventor as a German weaver, brought from Berlin to enhance production. Tursunov writes that the people of Khodjent claimed it was invented by a Mir Vali Mirsadikov. N.O. Tursunov, op. cit., p. 72.
19 S.A. Mahkamova, personal communication, 1995.
20 The hammer was called a *kudung*. It was made of wood from a *ziran* tree that grew locally. S.A. Mahkamova, personal communication, 1995. Grebyenkin, "Remeslennaia deiatel'nost' tadzhikov Zaravshanskogo okruga" (Crafts of the Tadjiks around Zerafshan), *Statistical Yearbook*, N.A. Mayev, ed., Turkestan Statistical Committee, Vol. 2, 1873.
21 The Bukharan neighborhoods in which late nineteenth-century fabric glazers worked were Khoja Gunjori (name of holy place) or Pardozgaron (fabric glazers) and Turki Djangi. O.A. Sukhareva, op. cit., 1976, pp. 92, 125.
22 S.A. Makhamova, personal communication, 1995.
23 L. Pollet, S. Daems, et al., op. cit., p. 16.
24 N.O. Tursunov, op. cit., pp. 86–87.
25 This process would relate to the well known Central Asian cotton *chit* fabrics, in which mordants are applied with wood block to the woven fabric, and the final dyeing produces the pattern. L. Pollet, S. Daems, et al., op. cit., p. 30.
26 In the second half of the nineteenth century, *alacha* begins to refer only to striped cotton fabrics. From the medieval period, *alacha* had meant a striped, warp-faced fabric in either cotton, silk, or mixed threads.
27 For Persian velvet making, see Hans E. Wulff, op. cit.; also Carol Bier, *The Persian Velvets at Rosenborg.* Copenhagen, 1995; Dorothy K. Burnham, *A Textile Terminology: Warp and Weft*, Routledge and Kegan Paul, London, 1981; Irene Emery, *The Primary Structure of Fabrics*, The Textile Museum, Washington, DC, 1966.
28 This complete bolt has the following surface appearance: finished end to first white tie lines:15", 1st – 2nd: 23.75", 2nd – 3rd: 35", 3rd – 4th: 39.75, 4th – 5th: 39.75, 5th – 6th: 38.75, 6th – 7th: 40.5", 7th tie line to finished end: 26.75". The distance between the pattern repeats changes slightly throughout the length of velvet, indicating a slight inconsistency in the hand weaving.
29 For the most part, the velvet ikat fabrics in the State History Museum and the State Museum of Art in Tashkent came to the Uzbek museums from Russian collections, which acquired them as gifts from the later Uzbek Khans to the Russian Tsar. The consensus of many Uzbek scholars, including Dr S.A. Mahkamova and Dr Umarbekova Daliafruz, was that the velvet ikats were made only during the last third of the nineteenth and the first decade of the twentieth century. Personal communication, 1995.

CHAPTER 5

1 Quoted by Abu'l-Qasim Muhammad al-Junayd in response to Nuri, "who objected to his sitting quietly while the Sufis performed their whirling dance". Junayd (died in 910), was the leader of the Iraqi school of mysticism. Annemarie Schimmel, *Mystical Dimensions of Islam*, University of North Carolina Press, Chapel Hill, 1975, p. 181.
2 Frederik T. Hiebert, "Pazyryk Chronology and Early Horse Nomads Reconsidered", pp. 117–29, *Bulletin of the Asia Institute*, No. 6, Bloomfield Hills, 1993. Recent excavations in the Altai point to a local origin for most of the material remains, and the development of a regional style that was largely influenced by Central Asian rather than Greek, Persian, or Chinese fashion.
3 A.M. Belenitsky and B.I. Marshak, "The Paintings of Sogdiana", in Guitty Azarpay, op. cit., p. 27.
4 Thomas W. Lentz and Glenn D. Lowry, op. cit., p. 214.
5 The term *abr/abri* describes both the marbling of paper, and the brush application of cloud-like designs to paper for calligraphy or painting. "Calligraphers and Painters, a Treatise by Qadi Ahmad, son of Mir Munshi, C AD 1606", trans. from the Persian by V. Minorsky, *Freer Gallery of Art Occasional Papers*, Washington, 1959, p. 178, footnote 621; also Richard J. Wolfe, *Marbled Paper, Its History, Techniques and Pattern*, University of Pennsylvania Press, Philadelphia, 1990, p. 8. M. Ugur Derman has suggested that *ebru/'abr* came from *ab-ru* (water-surface) in *Turk Sanatinda Ebru*, Nisani:Ak Yayinlari, 1977.
6 S.A. Mahkamova, op. cit., 1983, p. 81.
7 Lisa Golombek, "The Paysage as Funerary Imagery in the Timurid Period", *Muqarnas*, Vol. 10, Leiden, 1993, p. 248.
8 A popular and well distributed series of newspaper articles in the early Soviet years effectively introduced a number of new designs into *suzani* and other articles made for household decoration, often to the chagrin of the older generation. Personal communication, S.A. Mahkamova, 1995.
9 V.K. Rozvadovsky, *Tkani, predmeti domashnego obikhoda* (Fabrics, domestic articles), album, archive of the Khamza Scientific Research Institute of Art Studies, Uzbekistan Ministry of Culture, No. 151, 1941.
10 The poetry of Mir, trans. by Dr Syed Abdullah, *Naqd-i Mir*, Lahore, 1958, p. 117, cited in Annemarie Schimmel, op. cit., p. 289.
11 *Turkestanskii al'bom, po rasporiazheniu Turkestanskago General-Gubernatora K.P. fon Kaufman*, Tashkent, 1871–72. Kaufman was the first Governor General of Turkestan in 1867–81, and is known as the creator of Russia's Central Asian empire. The Kaufman albums were published in a very limited edition of approximately seven copies. They vary slightly in size and composition in their present condition. The Library of Congress has four of the six volumes in the complete set, while there is a somewhat larger collection in the Navoi Library in Tashkent.
12 Robert Shaw, *Visits to High Tartary, Yarkand and Kashgar*, Vanguard Books, Lahore, 1996, first published 1871, pp. 356–61.
13 Before coming to Kashgar, Yacub Beg and his troops had fought fiercely alongside the Kokand Khanate, which was centered in the Ferghana Valley, to repulse the Russian advance into western Central Asia. The Kokand Khanate was essentially Yacub Beg's home base. See Marwat, Fazal Ur Rahim Khan,*The Basmachi Movement in Soviet Central Asia*, Peshawar, 1985.
14 Specialized striped fabrics produced in the Surkhandarya area were dyed with pomegranate-based natural dyestuffs that gave tones of burgundy, red, brown, and orange. Surkhandarya fabrics similar to the Shaw robe were shown to the authors in Tashkent by Dr S.A. Mahkamova, in 1995.
15 Dr Barnes permitted the authors to examine the Shaw materials in 1995. Much of the Shaw ikat collection was subsequently published in Maria Zerrnickel's article "Textile Kultur in Usbekistan", in the catalog *Usbekistan, Erben der Seidenstrasse*, eds. Johannes Kalter and Margareta Pavaloi, Stuttgart, 1995, pp. 211–62.
16 Y.A. Sokolov, op. cit., pp. 198–207.
17 Audrey Burton, personal communication, 1995.
18 *Shahi* was made in the neighborhoods of Pukhtabofon, Khalif Khoda id, Valida Khani shaheed, Mekhtar Orif, TupKhana, and Goziion. O.A. Sukhareva, op. cit., 1976.
19 Shahmurad Ruzimaradov, personal communication, 1995.

CHAPTER 6

1 N.O. Tursunov, op. cit., p. 165.
2 Lisa Golombek's apt phrasing in her article, "The Draped Universe of Islam", in *Content and Context of Visual Arts in the Islamic World*, University Park and London, 1988, pertains to nineteenth-century Central Asia as well.
3 The Persian word *firdaws* means a walled garden, and is related to the English *paradise*. For the place of the garden in Islamic social life, see E.B. Moynihan, *Paradise as a Garden*, George Braziller, New York, 1979.
4 Ahmed Ibn Arabshah, op. cit.
5 The *mihrab* is an arched niche or decoration within a mosque that shows the direction for prayer. The use of the arch as a decorative or secular architectural element may carry a resonance of Islam, but it is not explicitly Islamic in character.
6 The verb *caroq*, to patchwork, is also used as a noun to denote any material, from silk to felt, in which pieces of different colored fabric are joined together with sewn seams.
7 R.G. Mukminova, personal communication, 1995.
8 Jennifer Mary Wearden, *Persian Printed Cottons*, Victoria and Albert Museum, London, 1989.
9 *Ivanovskie sitsy*, op. cit., pp. 21–22.
10 Ibid., p. 17.
11 Ibid., plate 73, made by the P. Zubkov factory.
12 Among many other instances of similar use, numerous Lakai and Kungrat Uzbek *ilgitsch* tent hangings have ikat backings. A pair of knee high sock-slippers of ikat were collected by Robert Shaw in Kashgar in the late 1860's and now form part of the Ashmolean Museum collection.

CHAPTER 7

1 Robert Shaw, op. cit., p. 361.
2 As quoted by Georgina Thompson, "Iranian Dress in the Achaemenian Period", *Iran, Journal of the British Institute of Persian Studies*, Vol. III, 1965, p. 123. See also Herodotus, *The Histories*, trans. Aubrey de Selincourt, Penguin Books, London, 1972, p. 68.
3 Ibid., p. 122.
4 Xenophon, *Cyropaedia*, VIII, iii,10.
5 These stone tombs were filled with the articles used by the nomad kings buried within. They were plundered soon after, and water seeped in and froze, preserving silks, felts, carpets and even the mummified body of a tattooed nobleman. S.I. Rudenko, *Frozen Tombs of Siberia*, 1970. The dates for Pazyryk may lie somewhat later than the fifth century BC date Rudenko gives. See also Frederik T. Hiebert and C.C. Lamberg-Karlovsky, "Central Asia and the Indo-Iranian Borderlands", *Iran, Journal of the British Institute of Persian Studies*, Vol. XXX, 1992.
6 Clavijo, *Embassy to Tamerlane*, Guy Le Strange, trans., London, 1928, p. 219.
7 The undershirt was made of *karbas*, coarse cotton, or from *katan*, probably an Egyptian linen. The over-shirt was called a *kaba*, the *faragi* is an outer robe (also noted in Sergeant as a long-sleeved scholar's coat), and the robe worn outermost was a *chekmien*. R.G. Mukminova, "Kostium narodov Srednei Azii po pis'mennym istochnikam XVI V" (Central Asian folk costume from sixteenth-century written sources), in O.A. Sukhareva, ed., *Kostium narodov srednei azii*, (Central Asian Folk Costume), Izdatelstvo "Nauk", Moscow and Leningrad, 1979.
8 Richard N. Frye, op. cit., p. 9.
9 Lisa Golombek, op. cit., p. 28.
10 Henri Moser, *A Travers L'Asie Centrale*, Plon, Nourrit et Cie, Paris, 1885, p. 155.

11 Arminius Vambery, op. cit., pp. 170–72.
12 Edmond O'Donovan, *The Merv Oasis*, New York, 1883, Vol. 2, p. 283.
13 Many sayings of the Prophet Muhammad, collected as traditions called *hadith*, make reference to habits of excessive luxury. Excess on the part of a few was felt to be damaging to the community at large, and many *hadith* express a desire for sobriety and restraint. While they are not generally considered as a source for Islamic law, *hadith* do often form a justification for customary law, *adat*.
14 Arminius Vambery, op. cit., p. 208.
15 The words *khalat* or *khelat* come from the the Arabic *khil'at,* meaning an open robe, and often, through history, the type of robe suitable at that time to be given as a robe of honor. *Chapan* is used most frequently in Afghanistan, whereas *khalat* is used in the former Soviet republics.
16 Annemarie Schimmel, op. cit., p. 103.
17 This *zhiak* braid was made primarily by Tadjiks in Bukhara, O.A. Sukhareva, op. cit. 1976, pp. 177–78. Peter Collingwood has identified the majority of Central Asian trims as loop-manipulation rather than card-weaving. Peter Collingwood, *The Technique of Tablet Weaving*, 1982, pp. 396–98.
18 The *Hidaya fi fura 'al hanafiyya* of Shaykh Burhanuddin Ali Qilich al-Marginani (c. 1135–97) was a major work of Hanafi jurisprudence. The Hanafi school of Islamic law is one of four, and was the dominant school of law within Central Asia.
19 The part silk *alacha* was sometimes called *alacha ifeklik*. Adult males used about 3–4 pounds (1.4–1.8kg) of *alacha* a year, women wore it very little. Grebyenkin, op. cit.
20 For continuous use of sixteenth-century terms, see R.G. Mukminova, op. cit., pp. 70–77.
21 Complete seclusion of women within the home, and the donning of the veil was not possible for families who had to labor in the fields. Rural women would have worn only a head scarf that could be pulled before the face if a stranger was encountered. The veil was, in a sense, a luxury that only the well-off could afford, and meant that a woman did not have to work at hard labor. Women who sold foodstuffs or handicrafts in the bazaars did wear the traditional horsehair veil, as did city shoppers.
22 According to Shahmurad Ruzimuradov of the Samarkand Museum, a suzani embroidery from the woman's dowry might be used as a covering instead. Personal communication, 1995.
23 The fifteenth-century use of dark blue and black mourning robes is cited in V. V. Bart'old, "O Pogrebenii Timura" (The Burial of Timur), trans. J. M. Rogers, *Iran, Journal of the British Institute of Persian Studies*, Vol. XII, 1974, pp. 75–76.
24 Grebyenkin, op. cit.
25 For example, *bir cuyam*, the distance between the thumb and index finger, *bir en*, the distance from the thumb to the joint, *turt en*, the distance to the fourth finger, and *bir karich*, the distance between the thumb and little finger.

CHAPTER 8

1 Itzhak Ben Zvi, *The Exiled and the Redeemed*, The Jewish Publication Society of America, Philadelphia, 1961, p. 59.
2 Mikhail Zand, "Bokharan Jews", *Encyclopedia of Islam*, details p. 532.
3 Benjamin of Tudela, the twelfth-century traveler, reported large Jewish populations in Khiva and Samarkand, but may never actually have reached those cities. See Manuel Komroff, ed., op. cit., p. 304. The discovery of Jewish inscriptions on tombstones of the eleventh to thirteenth centuries, in the area of Ghor, in Afghanistan, is further evidence for the existence of continuous Jewish settlements.
4 R.B. Serjeant, op. cit. Appendix IV: Early Trade Routes, p. 84.
5 Robert S. Lopez, and Irving W. Raymond, *Medieval Trade in the Mediterranean World*, Columbia University Press, New York, 1955, p. 31, citing *The Book of the Routes and the Kingdoms of Abu al-Qasim 'Ubayd Allah ibn Khurradadhbah.*
6 Edward H. Schafer, op. cit., p. 11.
7 The Khorasani, Persian, rite was replaced by the *nosah sefarad*, the "Spanish rite". Mikhail Zand, op. cit., p. 535.
8 In Samarkand, the original Jewish community had fallen into decline, but was formally re-established in 1843, when a neighborhood was allocated to it.
9 An embassy sent from Russia in 1820–21 included two members who reported radically different estimates of the Jewish population. One gave the number of Bukharan Jewish males as 1,200 persons. The other wrote that in Samarkand (a city with a relatively small Jewish population at that time) and Bukhara combined there were 8,000 Jewish households, and a population of about 40,000. See Eversmann and Jakovlew, op. cit. In 1845 the missionary Joseph Wolff estimated that there were 10,000 Jews in Bukhara, of a total population of 180,000. See Rev. Joseph Wolff, op. cit., p. 209.
10 Walter J. Fischel, "The Leaders of the Jews of Bokhara", *Jewish Leaders*, Leo Jung, ed., New York, 1953.
11 Bernard Lewis, *The Jews of Islam*, Princeton University Press, Princeton, 1984, pp. 25–26, 35–36.
12 Mikhail Zand, op. cit., p. 535.
13 Goitein mentions medieval sources that refer to the Jews as scarf makers and silk-weavers of *hariri*, as well as dyers of indigo. S. D. Goitein, op. cit., p. 81.
14 For neighborhoods in which Chala lived and worked, see Sukhareva, op. cit., 1976, pp. 74, 79–80, 81, 82, 92.
15 Personal communications from S.A. Mahkamova and I. Boguslovskaya, 1995. There is a pattern called *djugut kuli*, "Jew's delight", in a collection of ikat designs made in 1942 in Marghilan with a color scheme of yellow, black and red. See V.K. Rozvadovsky, *Khudozhestvennaia narodnaya textilnaya proivishgenoct Uzbekistana*, Scientific Research Institute of Study of the Arts of Uzbek SSR, Tashkent, 1941.
16 The association of the color yellow with the Jewish community goes back to the introduction of the yellow badge in the 9th century. See Bernard Lewis, op. cit., p. 25.
17 C.J. Charpentier, *Bazaar-e Tashkurgan*, Uppsala, 1972, pp. 176–86.
18 Mikhail Zand, personal communication, 1995.
19 Eversmann and Jakovlew, op. cit., p. 54.
20 Zand, op. cit., p. 536, citing G. Spasskii, "Novieshee opisanie Velkoi Buharii [part 4]", *Aziyatskii vestnik*, May 1925, pp. 304–311.
21 Mikhail Zand, op. cit., p. 536.
22 Ibid., p. 537.
23 Ibid., p. 537.
24 Tursunov, op. cit., p. 59.
25 Farmanova, op. cit., p. 18.
26 "News on the House of Israel", in *Hahavatzelet,* No. 32, p. 249, 5 Sept. 1902; ed. Israel Dov Frumkin, cited in *Bukhara*, Israel Museum, Jerusalem, catalog No. 39, Winter 1967–68.
27 S. D. Goitein, op. cit., 1973, pp. 76-77 and footnote 23. The writer, who required the garments for his own family, had been pressured to sell them to a Muslim instead, under "the veiled (or open) threat that the old discriminatory laws on clothing for non-Muslims would be invoked".
28 No modern Central Asian bridegroom will omit the practice of stepping on his bride-to-be's foot as she exits her car at the wedding reception, and no bride fails to hop about trying to prevent him. This little exercise will determine who rules the roost in the new household. Kamil Khodjaev, personal communication, 1995.
29 A girl of twenty was too old to be considered marriageable. In the late nineteenth century most brides were 12–13 years old, grooms 14–16. The fictitious bride price contrasted strongly with nomadic practice, in which the bride price was often many times the value of the dowry, and marriage could bankrupt the prospective groom. Z.L. Amitin-Shapiro, *Ocherk pravovogo byta sr.-aziatskikh evreev* (An essay on the legal mores of Jews in Central Asia), Tel Aviv, Aticot, 1973, p. 58.
30 Ibid., p. 59.
31 According to Amitin-Shapiro, these actions were limited to light romancing. It was very important that the bride remain a virgin until her wedding night. When Amitin-Shapiro questioned the chief rabbi of Bukhara about this custom, the rabbi said that such immoral goings on only took place in the other Jewish quarter, where he had no authority, and that the practice had been introduced by Jewish Komsomol members. Amitin-Shapiro's informants told him that the practice was of long standing, and was intended to create *dil garm*, a warm heart, in the couple's relationship. Ibid., pp. 64–66.
32 Ibid., pp. 70–76.
33 O.A. Sukhareva, *Istoria Sredeaziatskovo Kostiuma* (History of Central Asian costume), Akademia Nauk SSSR, Moscow, 1982, pp. 15–18.
34 N.P. Lobacheva, "Marriage Ritual as an Ethnographic Source for Historical Research", *Soviet Anthropology* and Archeology, Winter 81–82, p. 39.
35 Reasons given for taking another wife were lengthy illness of the first wife, her failure to provide sons, the early death of her children, and finally, the insistence of the husband's mother. Amitin-Shapiro, op. cit., pp. 85–88. Neighboring Jewish communities occasionally practiced polygamy, but it was not common. See Reuben Kashani, *The Jews of Afghanistan*, Haifa Ethnological Museum, 1975, p. iv.
36 The Jewish festival of Sukkhot is one of the three main feasts of the Jewish year, commemorating the way that Jews lived in tents or 'booths' in the wilderness as well as the final harvest of the year.
37 Now in the collection of the State History Museum of Uzbekistan, Tashkent.
38 A comparative study undertaken in Tunisia is discussed in Lucette Valensi, "Religious Orthodoxy or Local Tradition: Marriage Celebration in Southern Tunisia", in *Jews Among Arabs, Contacts and Boundaries*, ed. Mark R. Cohen and Abraham L. Udovitch, Darwin Press, Inc, Princeton, pp. 65–84.
39 Mikhail Zand, op. cit., p. 538.
40 Ibid., p. 538.
41 In Tashkent there were one Ashkenazi and three Central Asian Jewish synagogues. Other towns had only a single synagogue. Zand, op. cit., p. 540. Writing in 1929, Kantor observes that at a certain date, unnamed, there were 32 synagogues in Samarkand for the Jewish population of 12,000. Kantor cites a local joke that there was one synagogue for each communist, so they would not be able to spot each other at temple. L.M. Kantor, op. cit.

CONCLUSION

1 Fakhri, *Geschichte Der Islamischen Reiche...*, in W. Ahlwardt, ed., Gotha 1860, cited in R.B. Sergeant, op. cit., p. 73.
2 Victor M. Beliaev, op. cit., p. 259.

APPENDIX

1 P'ei Yen, Preface to "Hsing-hsing ming", Ch'uan T'ang wen, 168, 1a–2b. Edward H. Schafer, op. cit., 1963, p. 209.
2 "Dyeing Crafts in the Central Asian Russian Protectorates", in V.A. Oglobin, ed., op. cit.
3 In the 1970s, in Tashkurgan, Afghanistan, the only man who still worked with natural dyestuffs was a craftsman who dyed silk thread for local embroiderers. It was the authors' experience that although plant materials for making dyes were available in the bazaars of Kabul, many village dyers had only vague notions of the quantities of natural dyestuffs needed, or the methods for obtaining the desired colors.
4 Ivan Krauze, op. cit.
5 *Funt* is usually translated as "pound", though it is equal to 14¼ oz (409.5g) according to one twentieth-century dictionary, 16oz (453.59g) according to another. According to Dal's nineteenth-century dictionary it is equivalent to 966 zolotniks, which equals 14¼oz (408.96g) [(@ 1 zolotnik = 1/100 oz (4.26g)].
6 I. Krauze, op. cit., pp. 206–07.
7 V.A. Oglobin, op. cit.
8 1 *arshin* = 28 ins (71 cm).
9 A *pud* = 36 lb (16.38 kg).

BIBLIOGRAPHY

Abdullaev, T.A. and C.A. Hasanova — *Odezhda Uzbekov XIX – nachalo XX v* (Uzbek costume, 19th to beginning of 20th century), Akademia Nauk Uzbekskoi SSR, Tashkent. 1978

Allworth, Edward, ed. — *Central Asia*, Duke University Press, Durham and London, 1994

Amitin-Shapiro, Z.L. — *Ocherk pravovogo byta sr.-aziatskikh evreev* (An essay on the legal mores of Jews in Central Asia), Tel Aviv, Aticot, 1973

Arseneva, E.V. — *Ivanovskie sitsi xviii – nachala xx veka* (Ivanovo textiles, eighteenth to beginning of the twentieth centuries), Khudozhnik RSFSR, Leningrad, 1983

Azarpay, Guitty — *Sogdian Painting*, University of California Press, Berkeley, Los Angeles and London, 1981

Barfield, Thomas — *The Perilous Frontier*, Blackwell, Cambridge, Mass., and Oxford, 1989

Barthold, V.V. — *Turkestan Down to The Mongol Invasion*, The E.J.W. Gibb Memorial, 1928

Boulnois, Luce — *The Silk Road*, translated by Dennis Chamberlin, Allen and Unwin, London, 1966

Browne, Claire Woodthorpe — *Ikats*, The Victoria and Albert Color Books, Victoria and Albert Museum, London, 1989

Buhler, Alfred — *Ikat, Batik, Plangi*, Pharos-Verlag Hansrudolf Schwabe AG, Basel, 1972

Burton, Audrey J. — *Bukharan Trade*, Papers on Inner Asia, Indiana University, Bloomington, 1993

Chaudhuri, K.N. — *Trade and Civilization in the Indian Ocean*, Cambridge University Press, Cambridge, 1985

Chevallier, Dominique — *Villes et Travail en Syrie*, G.P. Maisonneuve & Larose, Paris, 1982

Dupaigne, Bernard — "Les Ikats d'Uzbekistan et d'Afghanistan", *Texilhandwerk in Afghanistan*, Bibliotheca Afghanica, Liestal, 1983

Dupaigne, Bernard — "Un artisan d'Afghanistan", *Objets et Mondes*, Vol. 14, 1974

Eversmann and Jakovlew — "Account of Bucharia", *Russian Missions into the Interior of Asia*, Sir Richard Phillips and Co., London, 1823

Frye, Richard N. — *The History of Bukhara, Translated from a Persian Abridgement of the Arabic Original by Narshakhi*, The Mediaeval Academy of America, Cambridge, Mass., 1954

Goncharova, P.A. — *Bukharo zarduzlik sanbati, Zolotoshvennoi iskusstvo Bukhare* (Bukharan gold embroidery), Gafur Guliama, Tashkent, 1986

Grebyenkin — "Remeslennaia deiatel'nost' tadzhikov Zaravshanskogo okruga" (Crafts of the Tadjiks around Zerafshan), in *Statistical Yearbook, ed.*, N.A. Mayev, Turkestan Statistical Committee, Vol.2, 1873

Hakluyt, Richard — *The principle navigations, voyages, traffiques and discoveries of the English nation*, D.M. Dent and Sons Ltd, London; E. P. Dutton and Co., New York, 1926–31

Hayashi, Ryoichi — *The Silk Road and the Shoso-in*, Weatherhill, New York, 1975

Henning, W.B. and D.G. Shepherd — "Zandaniji Identified?" *Aus der Welt des Islamischen Kunst: Festschrift fur Ernst Kuhnel*, ed., R. Ettinghausen Berlin, 1959

Hiebert, Frederik T. — "Pazyryk Chronology and Early Horse Nomads Reconsidered", *Bulletin of the Asia Institute*, No. 6, Bloomfield Hills, 1993

Hiebert, Frederik T. and C.C. Lamberg-Karlovsky — "Central Asia and the Indo-Iranian Borderlands", *Iran, Journal of the British Institute of Persian Studies*, Volume XXX, 1992

Holdsworth, Mary — *Turkestan in the 19th Century*, Central Asian Research Centre, Oxford, 1959

Holt, F. L. — *Alexander the Great and Bactria*, E. J. Brill, Leiden, 1988

"Ikats", *Ciba Review*, Vol. 44, Basel, 1942

"Indigo" *Ciba Review*, Vol. 85, Basel, April 1951

Janata, Alfred — "Ikat in Afganistan", *Afghanistan Journal*, Vol. 5, No. 4, 1978

Jettmar, Karl — *Art of the Steppes*, Crown Publishers, New York, 1964

Kalter, Johannes and Margareta Pavaloi — *Usbekistan, Erben der Seidenstrasse*, Staib and Mayer, Stuttgart, 1995

Kantor, L.M. — *Tuzemnye Evrei v Uzbekistane* (Indigenous Jews in Uzbekistan), UZSSR State Publishing House, Samarkand/Tashkent, 1929

von Kaufman, K.P. — *Turkestanskii al'bom, po rasporiazheniu Turkestans-kago General-Gubernatora K.P. von Kaufman*, Tashkent, 1871–72

Klein, V. — "Inozemnye tkani, bytovavshie v Rossii do XVIII veka, i ikh terminologiya" (Foreign fabrics found in Russia before the 18th century, and their terminology), *Sbornik Oruzheinoi palaty* (Armory Anthology), Moscow, 1925

Klimburg, Max — *Ikat*, Galerie Kirdök, Wien, 1993

Krauze, Ivan — "Zametki o krasil'nom iskusstve tuzemtsev" (Notes on the painter's and dyer's art among the indigenous inhabitants), *Russki Turk-estan. Sbornik izdannyi po povodu politekhnicheskoi vystavki. Vypusk vtoroi. Stat'i po etnografii, tekh-nike, sel'skomu khozyaistvu i estestbennoi istorii* (Russian Turkestan. An anthology published for the Polytechnical Exhibition. No. 2. Essays on ethnography, manufacture, agriculture and natural history), Moscow, 1872

Kwanten, Luc — *Imperial Nomads*, University of Pennsylvania Press, Philadelphia, 1979

Lancet-Muller, Aviva, ed. — *Bukhara*, Israel Museum, Jerusalem, Catalog No. 39, Winter 1967–68

Landshut, S. — *Jewish Communities in the Muslim Countries of the Middle East*, The Jewish Chronicle Ltd., London

Le Strange, Guy, trans. — *Clavijo, Embassy to Tamerlane 1403–1406*, George Routledge and Sons, London, 1928

Lentz, Thomas W. and Glenn D. Lowry — *Timur and the Princely Vision*, Los Angeles County Museum of Art, Los Angeles, 1989

Lewis, Bernard — *The Jews of Islam*, Princeton University Press, Princeton, 1984

Liushkevich, F.D. "Etnograficheskaia gruppa Ironi" (The Irani ethnic group), *Zaniatiya i bit narodov Srednei Azii*, Akademia Nauk SSR, Leningrad, 1971

Liushkevich, F.D. "Odezhda tadjikskovo nacelennia Bukharskovo oazisa v pervoi polovine XXv." (Tadjik costume of the Bukhara oasis in the first half of the 20th century), *Materialnaya kultura i khoziaistvo narodov Kavkaza, Srednei Azii i Kazakhhstana*, Leningrad, 1978

Lobacheva, N.P. and M.B. Sazonova *Traditsionnaya Odezhda narodov Srednei Azii i Kazakhstana* (Traditional folk costume of Central Asia and Kazakhstan), Akademia Nauk SSR, Moscow, 1989

Mahkamova, S.A. "K istorii tkachestva v Srednei Azii" (For a history of weaving in Central Asia), *Khudozhestvennaya Kul'tura Srednei Azii, ix–xii Veka* (Arts and artistry of Central Asia, 9th to 13th centuries), Gafura Gulyama, Tashkent, 1983

Mahkamova, S.A. *Uzbekskie abrovie tkan* (Uzbek ikat fabric), *Gosudarstvennoi izdatelstvo khudozhestvennoi*, UZSSR, Tashkent, 1963

Moser, Henri *A Travers L'Asie Centrale*, Plon, Nourrit et Cie, Paris, 1885

Moynihan, E.B. *Paradise as a Garden*, George Braziller, New York, 1979

Mukminova, R.G. *Ocherki po istorii remesla v Samarkande i Bukhare v XVI bek*, Tashkent, 1976

Mukminova, R.G. "Training of specialist-handicraftsmen in Samarkand in the 16th century", *Social Science in Uzbekistan*, No. 10, special edition, 1972

O'Donovan, Edmond *The Merv Oasis*, New York, 1883

Oglobin, V.A., ed. "Dyeing Crafts in the Central Asian Russian Protectorates", A Colorational Appendix, *Technical Anthology and Industrial Bulletin*, c.1899

Pollet, L., S. Daems, et al. *Ikat, Internationale Textieltentoonstelling*, 19.1.91 – 28.4.91, Education Department of the Museums, Antwerp, 1991

Pope, Arthur Upham and Phyllis Ackerman, eds. *Survey of Persian Art*, Souroush Press, Tehran, 1977

D.S. Richards, ed. *Islam and the Trade of Asia*, Bruno Cassirer, Oxford, 1970

Rozvadovsky, V.K. *Tkani, predmeti domashnego obikhoda* (Fabrics, domestic articles), album, archive of the Khamza Scientific Research Institute of Art Studies, Uzbekistan Ministry of Culture, No. 151, 1941

Rudenko, Sergei I. *Frozen Tombs of Siberia*, University of California Press, Berkeley and Los Angeles, 1970

Schafer, Edward H. *The Golden Peaches of Samarkand, A Study of T'ang Exotics*, University of California Press, Berkeley and Los Angeles, 1963

Schmitz, Carl A. and Robert Wildhabereds *Festschrift Alfred Buhler* Pharos–Verlag Hansrudolf Schwabe AG, Basel, 1965

Schuyler, Eugene *Turkistan*, Scribner, Armstrong & Co., New York, 1877

Serjeant, R.B. "Materials for a History of Islamic Textiles up to the Mongol Conquest", *Ars Islamica*, Vol. 9–15/16, 1942–51

Shakhnazarov, A.I. *Sel'skoe khozyaistvo v Turkestanskom krae* (Agriculture in Turkestan), St Petersburg, 1908

Shaw, Robert *Visits to High Tartary, Yarkand and Kashgar*, Vanguard Books, Lahore, 1996

Shepherd, Dorothy G. "Zandaniji Revisited", *Ars Islamica*, 1979

Snesarev, G.P. "Remnants of pre-Islamic beliefs and rituals among the Khorezm Uzbeks", *Soviet Anthropology and Archeology*, Winter 1970–71, Spring 1971, Summer 1971, Winter 1971–72, Winter 1972–73, Spring 1973, Spring 1974, Summer 1974, Fall 1974, Spring 1977, Fall 1977

Sobolev, N.N. *Ocherki po istorii ukrashenii tkanei* (Essays on the history of fabric decoration), Academia, Moscow and Leningrad, 1934

Sokolov, Y.A. *Bukhara, Samarkand, Kelif v 1813 godu* (Bukhara, Samarkand and Kelif in 1813), *Proceedings of the Central Asian State University* (SAGU), No. 90, History of Science, Vol. 14, Tashkent, 1957

Soucek, Priscilla P. *Content and Context of Visual Arts in the Islamic World*, Pennsylvania State University Press, University Park and London, 1988

Sukhareva, O.A., Pisarchik Moshkova, et al. *Narodnoe Dekorativnoe Iskusstvo Sovetskogo Uzbekistana Tekstil'*, (The popular decorative arts of Soviet Uzbekistan textiles) Izdatel'stvo Akademii Nauk Uzbekskoi SSR, Tashkent, 1954

Sukhareva, O.A. *Bukhara, xix – nachalo xx v., pozdnefeudalnii gorod i evo nacelenie* (Bukhara from the 19th to the beginning of the 20th century, a late feudal town), Moscow, 1966

Sukhareva, O.A. *Istoria Sredeaziatskovo Kostiuma* (History of Central Asian costume), Akademia Nauk SSSR, Moscow, 1982

Sukhareva, O.A., ed. *Kostium narodov srednei azii* (Folk Costume of Central Asia), Akademia Nauk SSSR, Moscow/Leningrad, 1979

Sukhareva, O.A. *Kvartal'naia obschina pozdnefeodalnovo goroda Bukhare* (Neighborhood communities of the late feudal town of Bukhara), Moscow, 1976

Sukhareva, O.A. *O tkatskikh remeslakh v Samarkande* (Weaving trades of Samarkand), Dushanbe, 1981

Tursunov, N.O. *Iz istorii gorodskovo remesla sebernovo Tadjikistana* (History of urban trades in northern Tadjikistan), Dushanbe, 1974

Vambery, Arminius *Travels in Central Asia*, Harper and Bros., New York, 1865

Vollmer, John *Silk Roads, China Ships*, Royal Ontario Museum, Toronto, 1983

Wearden, Jennifer Mary *Persian Printed Cottons*, Victoria and Albert Museum, London, 1989

Wilber, Donald N. "The Timurid Court: Life in Gardens and Tents", *Iran, Journal of the British Institute of Persian Studies*, Vol. XVII, 1979

Wolff, Rev. Joseph *Narrative of a Mission to Bokhara, in the years 1843–1845*, Harper and Bros., New York, 1845

Zand, Mikhail "Bokharan Jews", *Encyclopedia of Islam*, E.J. Brill, Leiden, 1960

INDEX

Figures in italics refer to page numbers of illustration captions